World War 1

The Open University Press

Cover illustrations: Front cover: 'Bradford's Young VC gets an ovation', from the Manchester Guardian, *Autumn 1915.*
Back cover: Dead German Soldier outside his dug-out (Imperial War Museum).

69187
940.3 OPE

The Open University Press
Walton Hall Bletchley Bucks

First published 1973.

Designed by the Media Development Group of the Open University.

Printed in Great Britain by
MARTIN CADBURY PRINTING GROUP.

ISBN 0 335 00734 1

This text forms part of the correspondence element of an Open University Third Level Course. The complete list of units in the course is given at the end of this text.

For general availability of supporting material referred to in this text, please write to the Director of Marketing, The Open University, Walton Hall, Bletchley, Bucks.

Further information on Open University courses may be obtained from the Admissions Office, The Open University, P.O. Box 48, Bletchley, Bucks.

1.1

CONTENTS

Unit 14

Origins and Outline of World War 1

Prepared by Arthur Marwick for the Course Team

AIMS AND OBJECTIVES

General Aims

This unit fits into the general aims of the course as a whole in the following manner. It aims:

1   To relate the causes of this particular war to the question of whether it is fruitful to discuss the causes of war in general.

2   To relate an outline history of this war to the general question of the relationship between particular types of war and existing technological and social conditions.

3   To provide basic information, and analysis of this information, on an important period of modern world history.

Objectives

[1] J. M. Roberts, *Europe 1880–1945*, Longman (SET BOOK).

Note on Reading

Before embarking on this unit, read Roberts, Chapters IV, VII and VIII. Roberts provides the only compulsory reading for the main part of this unit, but if you wish to go beyond a bare sketch of the origins of the war you should also consult L. C. F. Turner, *Origins of the First World War*.[1] At the very end of the unit you will be asked to read *Fuller*, Chapter IX.[2] There are also references to I. F. Clarke.[3]

Since this unit was written (June 1971) there has appeared (September 1972) a book which reprints many of the articles referred to in my text: A. W. Koch (ed.). *The Origins of the First World War* (Macmillan paperback). You are strongly urged to acquire this book if you possibly can.

[1] L. C. F. Turner, *Origins of the First World War*, Edward Arnold, 1970.

[2] J. F. C. Fuller, *The Conduct of War, 1789–1961*, Methuen (SET BOOK).

[3] I. F. Clark, *Voices Prophesying War*, Oxford University Press, 1966.

4.1   THE IMPORTANCE OF THE SUBJECT

In reviewing my book, *The Deluge: British Society in the First World War*,[1] Mr A. J. P. Taylor in the *Observer* in April 1965, drew a comparison between the fascination asserted by the study of the First World War and the fascination of alcohol: however much we try to get away from it, he remarked, we keep coming back to the First World War. I imagine many of you have felt this fascination (for the war, I mean, not alcohol). It will be helpful for our overall study of war, and of this war in particular, if we examine some of the reasons for the fascination which this war (perhaps more than any other) has continued to assert.

There is, I think, a certain horrible immediacy about the First World War, even for those who were not born till long after the end of the Second World War. We are all susceptible to the myth of the tranquil older Europe still in existence before 1914 which tore itself to pieces in the most bloodthirsty encounter nations had yet seen. We are influenced by the poetry of Rupert Brooke, and by the impassioned, horrific, poetry of Wilfred Owen. If we know anything of the dreadful campaigns of that war, of the thousands of lives lost for the gain, often, of but a few yards of mud, it is very hard not to feel intense indignation against politicians and generals, and a very deep pity for the men who had to endure this war.

We may well feel that the whole world of violence, totalitarianism, enormous armaments, and deep national hatreds in which we live today was in a very real sense brought into being by the First World War. Or, if we have a deeper historical knowledge and appreciate that the world of 1914 was a world of deep inequality and sharp social contrasts, we may recognize in the First World War the great agency of change which ushered in the more democratic world of today. Whatever way we look at it, we can scarcely neglect the significance of the First World War, both in the actual reality of what happened, and in what, ever since, people have *believed* happened, something which is often just as important in historical study.

The scale of the horror and bloodshed is not in dispute. It is therefore natural that the question of the causes of the First World War, the reasons for this unprecedented holocaust, should be a continuing subject of interest and controversy. For those, Marxists and others, with a special interest in the material forces in history, the First World War has for long stood out as the most impressive evidence of the inevitable interrelationship between imperialism and war, and for Marxists it has seemed to provide solid evidence for theories about the inevitable self-destructiveness of modern capitalism. For those interested in international politics today, the First World War has seemed to offer the dreadful warning of how an arms race, and a series of alliances, theoretically designed to preserve peace, can in fact issue in world war. Both of these theories relate to the general causes of wars and have relevance today: they do not pin responsibility for this particular war on any one particular country or countries (all the major countries showed the characteristics of capitalist-imperialism, though many also combined with these the characteristics of feudal autocracy; all participated in the 'arms race').

However, discussion of the origins of World War I is inevitably bound up too with the question of 'war guilt'. At the end of the First World War the victorious allies pinned blame for the war firmly and definitely on Germany. From the late 1920s onwards this view went rather out of fashion, and there was a tendency to stress that no power was blameless in the miscalculations which produced war. With a second world war which seemed, more obviously, to have been caused by the

---

[1] A. Marwick, *The Deluge: British Society in the First World War*, Penguin Books (SET BOOK).

German Nazi government, there was renewed interest in the question of whether Germany was not in fact a natural trouble-maker and disturber of the peace. A. J. P. Taylor was one historian who, from the time of the Second World War onwards, seemed to take this view of the German nation as a whole. More recently, the German historian Professor Fritz Fischer gave the whole debate a new turn, with the publication of his outstandingly important book, *Griff Nach Der Weltmacht* (Düsseldorf, 1961), published in Britain as *Germany's Aims in the First World War* (though a literal translation would be *Grasp after World Power*).[1] Looking at the totality of political, social and economic forces before and, more critically, during the First World War, Fischer argued that among German politicians as well as German military leaders there was a conscious movement towards world domination both before and during the war. In what is, in part, an extension of the Fischer thesis, A. J. P. Taylor has endeavoured to link together Germany's policies before and after 1914 with her policies in the 1930s: in other words he has suggested that the two world wars are both part of the same drive on the part of Germany towards world domination.

Thus, by being linked with the even more horrific war policies of Hitler's Germany, German responsibilities in regard to the origins of the First World War have been thrown right back into the centre of the arena. Fischer, of course, was severely attacked in Germany and also elsewhere. Among other issues in this unit, I want you to consider carefully this whole question of the possibility of a special responsibility attaching to Germany for the causing of the First World War.

Naturally, ever since the war itself, attempts to lay a special burden of blame on each of the other powers have not been lacking. The actual outbreak of war in 1914 sprang directly from the conflicts between the Austro-Hungarian Empire and the racial minorities within its boundaries. It was easy in the 1920s to build up a case that this ramshackle autocratic empire had been the true villain of the piece: the case was made all the easier by virtue of the fact that the Austro-Hungarian Empire itself disappeared during the war, so that this argument had the particular convenience of placing the blame on a power which no longer existed. French desire for revenge against Germany could also be singled out as a special factor. Nor was it difficult to develop the theme that the internally repressive policies of the Tsarist autocracy in Russia went hand in hand with evilly aggressive intentions outside. It could be argued, too, that Britain had deliberately sought a means of halting Germany's challenge to her industrial and naval supremacy. Taking these three points together, it could be argued, as many Germans had always argued, that the real cause of the war was the 'encirclement' of Germany by these three hostile powers, aimed directly at her reduction as a great power; by this argument, Germany was justified in almost anything she did in her attempt to break out of the stranglehold of this encirclement. Britain here, then, is blamed for being too openly aggressive towards Germany. Certainly, one line of attack on the policies of Britain's Foreign Secretary, Sir Edward Grey, was that he too readily allowed himself to become entangled in a European alliance system aimed against Germany. But, equally, the opposite criticism was made of him that he did not announce sufficiently publicly or frequently that if Germany became involved in a war against France, Britain also would join in on the side of France. By this argument, war might have been averted if Sir Edward Grey had acted more positively to 'deter' Germany from becoming involved in war with France. It is not difficult to see the relevance of this 'deterrent' argument to much more recent controversies over international politics.

However, apart from the continuing debate over the question of Germany's war responsibility, it would on the whole be true to say that few historians today attempt

[1] F. Fischer, *Germany's Aims in the First World War*, Chatto and Windus, 1967.

to lay sole blame on any of the other powers along the lines just discussed. By and large the argument lies between those who lay a special blame on Germany, and those who see the war as arising from wider forces over which individuals had little or no control, or from misconceptions and miscalculations to which all statesmen contributed. And it is here that we return to another of the reasons for the eternal fascination asserted by a discussion of the causes of the war. Referring to the European statesmen of 1914, the distinguished Italian historian Luigi Albertini spoke of 'the disproportion between their intellectual and moral endowments and the gravity of the problems which faced them, between their acts and the results thereof'.[1] Professor James Joll has pointed this up by suggesting that

Historians argument today

Joll

Figure 1   Viscount Grey of Fallodon (*Mansell Collection*)

at least one of the reasons for the fascination asserted by the causes of the war lies 'in the discrepancy between the importance of the events themselves and of their consequences and of the ordinariness of most of the politicians and generals making the key decisions'.[2] In other words, in studying the origins of the war we may get a sense of the terrible power of an impending fate which mere mortals are helpless to avert. Without, perhaps, wishing to take quite such a hopeless view as this, we should certainly agree that one of the recurrent and most profound issues in historical study is the question of how far men really do control events.

The real point in the end is the vast scale of the war and the immensity of its destructiveness. This was because, for the first time in history, this war became a war of nations, a total war, a war of modern technologies. There is the real key to

[1] Luigi Albertini, *Origins of the War of 1914*, Oxford University Press, 1967.

[2] James Joll, *The Unspoken Assumptions* (L.S.E. Inaugural Lecture, April 1968) Weidenfeld and Nicolson, 1968.

its impact; and the tragedy was that however much they expected some sort of war, the statesmen of pre-1914 days had no vision at all of what twentieth-century war would really be like.

Exercise 1

In the light of the foregoing say what sort of views about the significance of the First World War and its origins underlie the following passages.

A

The disaster which had befallen Europe had its roots since 1870 in the giant expansion and uncontrolled ambition of the new Germany. Bismarck had sown the seed, through his memorable triumphs for militarism and unscrupulous efficiency; but between 1871 and 1890 he was very careful not to water it. After his fall it grew apace, unchecked by the statesmen and encouraged by the Emperor. In the many-sided quick-changing displays of the brilliant William II two features alone never failed—arrogant megalomania and an instinctive preference for methods of violence. These, it is not unfair to say, became the national vices of pre-war Germany; and they made her an object of alarm to every leading nation save her Austrian ally.

B

The war of 1914 was due to the unbearable national tensions within Austria-Hungary and the attempts of that power to escape from them by action dangerous to peace. The continued existence of the Habsburg monarchy as a great power was the thing at stake in the war, at least to start with. To this extent the war was a European rather than a world conflict, and it was 'imperialist' only in the sense that Austria-Hungary had always been a multiracial state and the subject races were now rebelling against it. But the Austrian crisis could not have grown into a general war among the powers had there not been tensions among them which prevented effective co-operation in the preservation of peace. These tensions were the result of imperial rivalries, and often concerned regions far beyond Europe and hardly touched by the ensuing war.

C

The Great War of 1914–18 lies like a band of scorched earth dividing that time from ours. In wiping out so many lives which would have been operative on the years that followed, in destroying beliefs, changing ideas, and leaving incurable wounds of disillusion, it created a physical as well as psychological gulf between two epochs.

D

Each side was defending its imperialist interests by preventing the balance of power from being tipped in favour of its opponents. These imperialist interests were in the last analysis the private interests of finance and monopoly capital, which, through the influence of the plutocracy on governments and public opinion, were identified in the minds of the rulers with 'national honour and vital interests'. There were, of course, other factors in the situation, and the psychological process by which promoting vested interests in imperialism and war preparations is transmuted in men's minds into loyalty to religious, philanthropic, and patriotic ideals is complex and largely unconscious.

E

Economic expansion was the basis of Germany's political world diplomacy, which vacillated in its methods between rapprochement and conciliation at one moment, aggressive insistence on Germany's claims the next, but never wavered in its ultimate objective, the expansion of Germany's power.

F

The search for historical watersheds is a notoriously unrewarding one. If not exactly a watershed, the First World War was certainly a steep and sharp waterfall in the course of British history. All the economic, social, cultural, and political forces which have moulded twentieth-century Britain were already in flow before 1914, but the war accelerated them with such suddenness and turbulence that they were transformed on a gigantic scale.

Discussion

A   This passage, concerned with the origins of the war, takes a very definite anti-German line. It is in fact from Sir Robert Ensor's *England 1870–1914* (Oxford University Press, 1936).

B   This passage, also concerned with the origins of the war, takes a rather broader view. If any one power is being blamed, it is Austria-Hungary; though there is the implication that the situation in which Austria-Hungary found herself in 1914 was beyond the control of any of her statesmen. However, imperialism is also pointed to as a wider cause which ensured that war, when it came, should be a general war. The passage is from an excellent general textbook *The End of European Primacy* by J. R. Western (Blandford, 1965) and it sums up quite well what was the general orthodoxy among historians until the matter was subjected to specialist re-examination in the 1950s and 1960s.

C   This extract concentrates on the consequences rather than the origins of the war, and puts forward the view of the Great War as one of the great dividing-lines in history. It is from a work of 'pop history', Barbara Tuchman's *The Proud Tower* (Bantam, 1971).

D   This is a sophisticated statement of the Marxist approach, seeing the war as, in the last analysis, a product of imperialism. It is from *The Mirror of the Past* by K. Zilliacus (Ambassador Books, 1944).

E   This is again a strongly anti-German view of the origins of the war. In fact it is from Fischer, *Germany's Aims in the First World War* (Chatto and Windus, 1967) and makes quite a good brief summary of Fischer's views.

F   This extract again concentrates on what are claimed to be the immense consequences of the war (this time for Britain alone). It comes, actually, from the opening of an early work of my own, *The Explosion of British Society* (Macmillan, Papermac, 1971).

Last Comment

It could, then, perhaps be said that interest in the First World War takes two forms: some writers concentrate on the origins of the war, others prefer to stress the consequences of the war.

4.2   AREAS OF POTENTIAL CONFLICT PRIOR TO 1914

The origins of the war can be analysed in many different ways. Although in looking at any problem of historical causation it is always worth bearing in mind the distinction between 'situational' or 'background' causes, and 'direct' causes, I believe that a phenomenon as wide and complex as the First World War is not fully amenable to any such rigid categorization. Here, as a basis for further analysis and discussion, I want to set out a list of eight sets of interrelated circumstances which cover most of the points different historians would raise in discussing at least the 'background' causes of the war. I say 'sets of circumstances' because I find it very hard to make distinctions between individual 'causes' and practically impossible to distinguish between, say, 'political causes' and 'economic causes'—political power, inevitably, is closely related to economic strength.

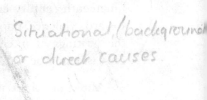

Situational (background or direct causes)

1   The existing *international morality* and *basic assumptions* of statesmen in the period before 1914, which accepted the inevitability of competition ·between

states for territory and trade, and which postulated that, in the last analysis, great power status depended upon a willingness, and ability, to wage successful war. In defining this state of affairs some historians have adopted the illuminating phrase coined in 1926 by the Liberal scholar, G. Lowes Dickinson, *international anarchy*.

2 The *scramble for overseas possessions*, which is a noteworthy and characteristic feature from the 1880s onwards. Without necessarily analysing the reasons for this 'imperialism', it is quite easy to demonstrate that this scramble undoubtedly took place, and that it frequently created incidents which sometimes seemed likely to touch off general war.

3 As rapid industrialization took place, *trade rivalry* intensified between the European powers, seen in the resort by many of them to protectionist tariffs against their neighbours' goods.

[These first three sets of circumstances have, in the case of all the powers, been summed up by some historians as 'imperialism'; other historians, concerned with the form in which these sets of circumstances manifested themselves in Germany, have spoken of 'Germany's drive to power'.]

4 The manner in which, in these circumstances, the various nations sought to maintain their own *security* by entering upon alliances and by building up military and naval power, resulting in the *arms race* and in the creation of two interrelated chains of alliances, usually referred to as *the two armed camps*. This unfortunate outcome was sometimes blamed on the diplomatists' belief in 'the balance of power'. But for most of the nineteenth century this theory had implied little more than joint resistance to any one potential aggressor. The theory itself would not explain this particular development of two rival alliances, though it might help to explain why Britain intervened in face of the threat of a German domination of Europe. From the German point of view the Entente between France, Russia and Britain, seemed to create a potentially disastrous 'encirclement'.

5 The growth of intense *national* and *racial hatreds*. This is most obvious in the Balkans where the various nationalities were often in rivalry amongst themselves, but where above all there was an intense hatred on the part of Slavs for both the Turks and the Austrians and Hungarians. But this force can also be seen in the French hatred of Germany over the loss of Alsace-Lorraine in 1871, and in the mutual hostility between Germany and Britain.

6 It may be that beneath this there was also the whole complex of what might be called *sociological factors* making for the likelihood of conflict. Rapid industrialization at the beginning of the century, population growth, and overcrowding in the cities can well be seen as a factor predisposing Europe towards large-scale violence. It has even been suggested that the repressive family structures of the nineteenth century created a predisposition among the offspring of these families towards violence. Popular literature and popular song, as well as painting, music and the writings of intellectuals, all suggest that there was something that can not unreasonably be termed a 'will to war' in the years before 1914.

7 Above all, there is the whole question of *military strategy*. It was (and is) the duty of the general staffs to prepare for the possibility of war. Their strategic plans, and the almost universal fear that the *new technologies* of war had made it vital for each power to get its blow in as quickly as possible if it was to survive at all, meant that once the first fumbling moves had been made towards war, military necessities made it almost impossible to put the process in reverse.

From out of this list of seven broad sets of circumstances, three particular points seem to me worthy of special attention, and one to a separate heading in its own right (thus completing my list of eight). These are: the precise manner in, and

Figure 2   London slum, pre-1914 (Mansell Collection)

series of stages by, which the relatively fluid international situation at the end of the nineteenth century steadily hardened into two counterpoised alliances; the actual areas in which dangerous imperial rivalry arose and:

8   The particular situation in *the Balkans* which, in a specially dangerous way, linked together many of the circumstances already discussed. The steady decline of the once-powerful Turkish empire provided scope for the ambitions both of the separate Balkan nationalities, and of the rival powers, Austria-Hungary and Russia. The situation is best understood if we see the Balkans as dividing politically into three (see map, Figure 3). First, the territories still ruled directly by Turkey; second, those areas where the Balkan peoples had succeeded in establishing independent or semi-independent states of their own: Greece, Romania, Bulgaria, Serbia and Montenegro; third, the areas ruled over by the Austro-Hungarian Empire: Transylvania, where the Romanian populace looked forward to joining independent Romania, and Croatia, Dalmatia and Bosnia-Hertzegovina, where the Slavs looked forward to uniting with Serbia. To preserve her multi-national empire, Austria-Hungary felt bound to resist any growth in the strength of the independent Balkan nations; Serbia, in particular, she regarded as posing a grave threat to her position as a great power. On the other hand, the Slavs looked to Russia as their champion. A final complication in the last years of peace was the growth of German influence in Turkey. (I recall, some years ago, visiting the ruins of the ancient Greek city of Troy which is situated in the north-west corner of Asian Turkey: commenting on the ruler-straight road, I asked, 'Who built this, the Romans?' 'No', replied my Turkish guide, 'the Germans'.)

[For those of you who are not familiar with nineteenth-century European history, it is probably worth while having a few more words about the Austro-Hungarian Empire (often referred to as Austria-Hungary). This great empire, covering central Europe and much of Italy, had its origins in the Middle Ages. The Empire suffered a series of defeats in the nineteenth century: first the Italian possessions were lost to the new unified state of Italy, and then the contest for the main body of the German nation was lost to Prussia which, in turn, became the nucleus of the new German Empire (or Germany) established in 1870. Among the other disaffected peoples within the Empire, the Hungarians had fought particularly tenaciously.

Figure 3   Map of the Balkans, 1900–1914

Thus, in 1867, in an attempt to stem the rot, the new system known as the *Ausgleich* (compromise) was settled upon, whereby in effect the Hungarians were taken in as equal partners in the ruling of the Empire, hence the new double-barrelled name. Many historians have seen this as the beginning of the long road to eventual disaster, since, in many ways, the Hungarians proved more ruthless in their treatment of racial minorities than the Austrians. It is sometimes said that the worst aspects of Austro-Hungarian foreign policy were determined by Hungarian politicians.]

Now let us look at each of these eight topics more closely, to see if any carry more weight, and any less weight, than the others. Perhaps, even though you may feel

16

that you do not yet have any decent knowledge of the subject, you would care to note down your own comments on each of my topics. You can then compare your comments with mine.

My Comments

1 *International morality*, etc. This may not seem very impressive. Perhaps international morality has always been like this; perhaps it is not much different today. I don't quite accept this latter point. I think there was a greater readiness before 1914 among all powers, to accept war as an immediate and legitimate instrument of national policy. I think, too, that there was a more naked and obvious expansionism before 1914 (this should emerge from what you have read in Roberts). It is probably truer that there has been very little difference in the position with regard to 'international anarchy', though again perhaps one can today detect a rather greater willingness to co-operate among nations. Today, among the super-powers, there is a relatively stable 'balance of terror', whereas in the early twentieth century there was an endemic condition of international disequilibrium. Certainly, to stress 'prevailing morality' would be to follow the emphasis Ken Thompson (Unit 2) placed on 'shared values'.

Exercise

To bring out the implications of what I call the prevailing international morality, it would be a good idea for you to quickly note down what, based on your reading in Roberts, you think were the basic overriding objectives in foreign policy of each of the great powers, the sort of objectives for which they might be expected to go to war. In your notebooks, then, put down the names of Germany, Austria-Hungary, Russia, France and Great Britain, and beside each note in a sentence or two the basic foreign policy objectives and assumptions of these countries.

Specimen Answer

1 *Germany*. The general impression given by Roberts and held to by many other historians is that Germany in fact revealed no basic objectives, but that her foreign policy kept changing and vacillating. But one clear aim (whether justified or not) was to avoid encirclement by a ring of hostile powers. To this end Germany also sought to preserve her alliance with Austria-Hungary, and to preserve Austria-Hungary as a strong ally. (I leave aside, as you may quite reasonably not have done, the question of a German 'grasp for world power').

2 *Austria-Hungary*. Fairly obviously: to stop Serbia from becoming any more powerful and therefore any more attractive to Slav minorities within the Empire. Austria-Hungary also had a definite interest in preventing expansion of Russian influence in this area, in particular at the straits and Constantinople.

3 *Russia*. Conversely, Russia wished to preserve access to the Mediterranean, and to resist any expansion of Austro-Hungarian influence which might make this difficult.

4 *France*. The overriding aim here was the creation of alliances which would help France to overcome the unavoidable fact that Germany was a much more populous and powerful nation than she was. France also opposed any change in the delicate balance of power in the Balkans.

5 *Great Britain*. In Europe: to prevent any one power from becoming overwhelmingly dominant in the West. Overseas: to prevent any threat to her lines of
communication with India.

Discussion

These are rather rough and ready points, but they are worth bearing in mind
when considering the attitudes of the powers at the various moments of crisis in
European history before 1914.

Now, to continue the main discussion of my eight 'sets of circumstances'.

2 There were certainly times when imperial rivalry did look like precipitating a
war crisis, though it is important to note that incidents were as frequent in the early
stages between France and Britain, or Russia and Britain, as between the powers
which finally lined up on opposite sides in the war. It also seems to be the fact that
much of the heat had gone out of the imperial situation by 1908 when attention,

*Figure 4 Miss Ogston, a
militant suffragette, using
her whip at the Albert
Hall during a speech by
Lloyd George, December
1908 (Mansell Collection)*

increasingly, was focused on the Balkans. Yet it could be argued that the Balkan
problem was in itself essentially one of Austro-Hungarian imperialism. However,
as Roberts, among others, points out, if we extend the meaning of the term
imperialism too far it begins to lose any precise relevance at all.

3 There can be no doubt that German economic power was growing, relatively,
at the expense of that of Britain, and there is evidence that certain circles in Britain
would like to have seen an end to German competition. But it was the German
naval programme, taking us into the realm of 'security', which really sharpened
tensions. The differences between the interests of industrialists, and those of traders
and bankers, is worth keeping in mind: many British traders and bankers believed
that war would be a universal disaster. Britain suffered from the competition of
other countries (e.g. the U.S.A.) but did not become involved in war with them.
None the less, I do believe that the fear of German industrial competition felt by
some Britishers merged with the more general hostility to the challenge Germany
seemed to offer to British supremacy, which is an important 'background' cause
of the war.

4 The deep craving for security, and the existence of the two 'armed camps'
does seem to offer an explanation of why once war broke out at all, it so quickly
became a *general* war, but they do not in themselves explain why tensions and
insecurity existed in the first place. In my view it is best, also, to take these two
points in close conjunction with the first general point about the prevailing
international morality.

5 Evidence of national and racial hatred (even apart from the Balkans) there is
in plenty. But when analysing historical causation at this level, it is important
always to remember that it is governments, not peoples, which finally declare war.
Undoubtedly governments and their representatives were in some degree influenced
by popular sentiments, and undoubtedly, for example, many French politicians
were dedicated to the notion of the recovery of Alsace-Lorraine. It would seem to
me impossible to discount this set of circumstances as a conditioning factor to the
outbreak of war, but it can scarcely be accounted an immediate cause. Within the
special case of the Balkans, we might, of course, regard national feeling, or the
frustration of national feeling, as the crucial factor. But again it is, in the last
analysis, the actual actions of the major governments which must concern us.

*Figure 5 Havelock
Wilson addressing seamen
strikers, June 1911
(Mansell Collection)*

6   Many of the points made above apply equally to the question of the sociological origins of the war. Again there is evidence of the 'will to war' which I postulated, and of actual violence among workers, nationalist agitators, and suffragettes, but practically none to show that this actually influenced the decisions of politicians and diplomats. But in the end perhaps all this is of greater relevance in explaining the almost universal support given by all peoples to the war once it had broken out, than in explaining why the war broke out in the first place.

Violence among workers etc.

7   As an immediate cause this question of military strategy is a crucial one (Roberts mentions the Kaiser's shock at discovering that it was impossible to stop his troops marching towards France, since that was what the German military plan demanded). Again, however, it has to be remembered that political initiatives towards war had to be taken before military plans became the determinate influences.

See above

8   If what we seek is the particular occasion of the war, rather than 'background causes' then undoubtedly it arose in the Balkans.

14.3.1   THE MAIN LINES OF INTERNATIONAL HISTORY UP TO THE OUTBREAK OF WAR IN 1914

If we are particularly interested in the question of why Britain became involved in war in 1914, we really have to answer two questions. First of all (the one with which we will be mainly preoccupied) why did a European war break out at all? And then, secondly, given that that war broke out, why did Britain become involved in it? In looking for answers to the second question one might examine the formation of the 'armed camps', with special reference to Britain's growing entanglement with France, and also the question of trade and naval rivalry between Britain and Germany.

Before looking at the narrative of actual events in the period 1901–14, discussed by Roberts in Chapter VIII of his book, I want you again to read Chapter IV, in order to note down answers to these two questions.

1   Set out my eight topics in the form of a table, and allocate the various points made by Roberts in the course of Chapter IV to the appropriate topic.

2   In my own discussion of topics 6 and 7 I mentioned that, regarded as causes of war, these were weakened by the fact that the final decisions had to be taken by individual statesmen. What arguments advanced by Roberts would tend after all to give greater significance to these wider popular trends?

Specimen Answers

Question 1

1   *International morality—basic assumptions—international anarchy*. The concept of Europe was coming to an end (p. 78). The essentially competitive nature of the European system (p. 79, top).

2   *The scramble for overseas possessions*. Franco-British conflict in Egypt (p. 95). Expansion by all major powers (p. 101). Franco-British conflict of interests in south-east Asia and the Pacific (p. 104). Germany and Great Britain come into

conflict over three African and two Pacific questions in the 1880s (p. 106). Anglo-Russian rivalry in central Asia (p. 110). Anglo-French crisis over Siam (p. 118 top). More Anglo-Russian rivalry in Asia (p. 121, middle). The Fashoda incident, 1898 (p. 122).

3 *Trade rivalry.* Economic rivalry between Germany and Britain (p. 120, top).

4 *Security, arms race, and armed camps.* The slow elaboration of alliances (p. 93, foot). Bismarck's elaborate commitments which increased likelihood of Russo-German conflict (p. 94, foot). Hardening of lines of alliance again (p. 99, foot). By 1890s the safeguards against the division into two camps had gone (p. 113, middle to foot). Growing Russian association with France (p. 114, middle to top). Russo-French agreement (p. 115, middle).

5 *National and racial hatreds.* The ideal of *revanche* in France that is to say *revenge* for the loss of Alsace-Lorraine (p. 88, foot). National irritations in Balkans (p. 90, foot). *Revanche* in France again (p. 98, middle).

6 *Sociological factors.* Industrialization (p. 89, middle). Jingoistic hysteria (p. 102, top).

7 *Military strategy.* The overriding aim, if war threatened, must be an early victory obtained by good initial deployment (p. 81, top). The German general staff assumed that it must defeat France first in any future war (p. 115, foot).

8 *The Balkans.* Conflict of Russian and Austria-Hungarian interests in Balkans where Turkish power was crumbling (p. 85, foot and p. 86, top). No equilibrium of forces existed in the Balkans (p. 87, top). The Balkan situation involved the interests of great powers and the claims of Balkan nationalists (p. 88, foot and p. 89). Desire of Bulgarians in Eastern Roumelia to unite with Bulgaria (p. 92, middle). Instability of Turkish Empire (p. 92, foot). The basic clash of interest between Austria-Hungary and Russia (p. 96, middle to top). War between Serbia and Bulgaria, 1885 (p. 97, middle to top). Austro-Russian rivalry again, determined by the attitude of the Hungarians (p. 99 middle to top).

Discussion

I am pretty certain you will not have listed all the points I have listed and in the way I have listed them. You may have thought some points not worth noting at all, or you may even have found others which I have not mentioned. In places, since my topics tend to merge into each other, you may have allocated certain points to different headings. I don't think this matters very much. It is quite likely that Roberts himself would not feel that his chapter was very suitable for organizing into the eight headings I have chosen. The main purpose of this exercise is to try to show you the value, from the point of view of understanding and remembering material of this sort, of organizing what is essentially a narrative presentation into organization by topic. I hope, at any rate, that working on this exercise has helped to add some flesh and blood to the bare bones of the argument and discussion I have been presenting so far.

Question 2

The growth of parliamentary democracy, the growth of newspapers, and the growing influence of 'public opinion'.

In a mainly narrative approach it is not in fact possible to spend much time on the broader economic, sociological or strategic topics. In fact the three topics which seem to me necessarily to dominate any narrative account of international relations between 1901 and 1914 are (from my list): 2, the scramble for extra-European possessions; 3, the emergence of the two rival sets of alliances; and 8, the intensifying crisis in the Balkans. Now read both *Roberts*, Chapter 8, and Section C in your Documents unit, with these three topics well in mind (in regard to 3, note especially how Britain is steadily drawn into the European alliance system).

Exercise 2

1 In what areas are there signs of potentially dangerous imperial rivalry, and which European countries are involved?

2 By what stages does Britain become more and more closely meshed in an association with France, and in what way do these stages relate to the imperial rivalries discussed in question 1?

3 Outline the main stages by which the Balkan crisis developed towards the immediate occasion for the outbreak of war.

4 What pieces of evidence does Roberts put forward which would seem to contradict the general view that this was a period of 'international anarchy'?

5 What does Roberts say is the crucial set of circumstances giving rise to the war?

6 On what country does he put most blame?

7 Set down the timetable of major events between the murder at Sarajevo and 6 August 1914 (Roberts gives a rather summary account. If you want to do this in detail you will need to refer to Turner).

Specimen Answers and Discussion

1 (i)   China. Conflict apparently most likely between Russia and Britain.
   (ii) Persia. To begin with, conflict most likely between Britain and Russia, but subsequent project for a German-dominated Baghdad railway created rivalry between Germany and Russia, and even between Germany and Britain.
   (iii) Afghanistan. Russia and Britain are the two powers involved here.
   (iv) Tibet. Also a bone of contention between Russia and Britain.
   (v)   Morocco. The countries directly involved here are France and Germany. The second Morocco crisis, Agadir 1911, also aroused British fears about German ambitions.

2 (i)   Anglo-French agreement of 1904.
   (ii) British support for France at the Algeciras conference 1905, and the opening of military conversations between Britain and France.
   (iii) German naval building plans, designed in the first instance simply to strengthen her bargaining position against Britain, alarmed that country and created an intensified naval building race.
   (iv) The Agadir crisis led to redisposition of British naval forces which in effect implied naval co-operation with France against Germany (*Roberts*, p. 256).

In all of these cases, save possibly that of the naval race, there is a connection between imperial events and growing British involvement with France. The first agreement, though perhaps Roberts does not bring this out very clearly, essentially rose from the desire to prevent Russo-Japanese conflict in China developing into a general war. The Entente (as Document C2 makes clear) and first military conversations are related to Britain's willingness to support France's claims in Morocco in return for support for her own imperial claims in Egypt. Even if, thereafter, Britain becomes more preoccupied with the potential threat of Germany to the balance of power in Europe itself, and the need to support France in order

GB moving closer to F.

Entente.

22

Figure 6   Kaiser Wilhelm II and Enver Pasha aboard The Goeben *(Radio Times Hulton Picture Library)*

to resist this threat, none the less the arrangements entered into after Agadir undoubtedly spring from German imperial ambitions in Morocco, and the fears these raised among some sections in Britain.

3   Roberts makes the following points in regard to the re-emergence of the Balkan crisis in a new acute phase:

(i)   growth of German influence in Turkey;

(ii)   continuing Turkish misgovernment of her Balkan subjects;

(iii)   return of Russia to an interest in the Balkans after her failures in the Far East;

(iv)   the young Turk revolution, which threatened both the Balkan nationalities and the interested great powers with the possibility of a rejuvenated Turkish rule;

(v)   October 1908, Austria (after securing prior support from Germany— Documents C4 and C5) annexes Bosnia and Herzegovina. This not only antagonized the small Balkan powers of Serbia and Montenegro, it also antagonized Russia, who now replaced Serbia as the principal opponent of Austria in the Balkans;

(vi)   The first Balkan war, 1912, between Montenegro, Bulgaria, Serbia and Greece on one side, against Turkey on the other;

(vii)   The second Balkan war when the Balkan nationalities fell out amongst themselves. Austro-Serbian relations were further aggravated, since Serbia was annoyed that Austria had been instrumental in preventing her from making even more gains, while Austria was deeply worried by the very substantial gains that Serbia had made in the wars;

Figure 7 Archduke Ferdinand and Duchess leaving the town hall, Sarajevo, 28 June 1914— a few minutes before their assassination (Mansell Collection)

(viii)   The murder of the Archduke Franz Ferdinand, which provided Austria with the opportunity for a showdown with Serbia (Documents C14, C15, C16 and C17).

4   The growth of international agencies and conventions. The growing acceptance of arbitration. The setting up of the international court at the Hague in 1899. The Hague conferences to control methods of warfare. The growth of peace congresses and of subsidiary organizations of international co-operation, with, for example, the institution of the Nobel peace prizes in 1901. However, these all seem peripheral to the major international issues we have just been discussing.

5   'The incapacity of Austria-Hungary to solve its domestic problems'; that is to say, a particular aspect of the Balkan situation.

6   Roberts quite clearly allocates most blame to Germany.

7   28 June 1914: Archduke Franz Ferdinand and his wife murdered at Sarajevo.

5 July 1914: Emperor of Austria appeals to Kaiser for support (Document C14).
6 July 1914: Bethmann-Hollweg gives support (Document C15).
8 July 1914; Kaiser gives support.
23 July 1914: Austria-Hungary presents ultimatum to Serbia (Document C16).
25 July 1914: Serbia replies in a conciliatory fashion, apparently, as Roberts says, accepting most of the terms, though much of the document (C17) seems to be deliberately obscure.
Evening of 26 July: Sir Edward Grey telegraphs proposal of Conference of Ambassadors to discuss crisis in London.
1 p.m. 27 July: Bethmann-Hollweg rejects this suggestion, saying 'we cannot drag Austria in her conflict with Serbia before a European tribunal'.
28th July: Austria-Hungary declares war on Serbia (Turner and other historians have argued that this was done under pressure from Germany, where it was argued that speedy and resolute action would be the best way of deterring Russian intervention; the Austrian General Staff itself realized it would be impossible to carry through the invasion before 12 August).
29 July: Russia declares mobilization of those forces which would be used in a war with Austria-Hungary.
29 July: Bethmann-Hollweg receives news that Britain would be likely to intervene if France were involved. He now makes panicky and fruitless attempts to reverse the whole trend of German policy.

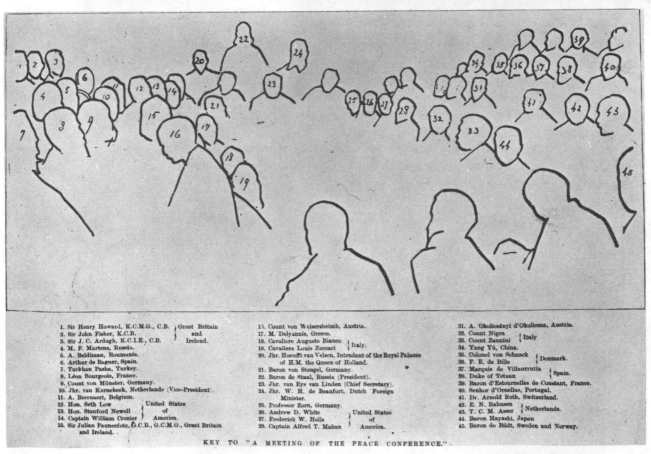

1. Sir Henry Howard, K.C.M.G., C.B. | Great Britain
2. Sir John Fisher, K.C.B. | and
3. Sir J. C. Ardagh, K.C.I.E., C.B. | Ireland.
4. M. F. Martens, Russia.
5. A. Beldiman, Roumania.
6. Arthur de Baguer, Spain.
7. Turkhan Pasha, Turkey.
8. Léon Bourgeois, France.
9. Count von Münster, Germany.
10. Jhr. van Karnebeek, Netherlands (Vice-President).
11. A. Beernaert, Belgium.
12. Hon. Seth Low | United States
13. Hon. Stanford Newell | of
14. Captain William Crozier | America.
15. Sir Julian Pauncefote, G.C.B., G.C.M.G., Great Britain and Ireland.

16. Count von Welsersheimb, Austria.
17. M. Delyannis, Greece.
18. Cavaliere Augusto Bianco | Italy.
19. Cavaliere Louis Zuccari |
20. Jhr. Hoeufft van Velsen, Intendant of the Royal Palaces of H.M. the Queen of Holland.
21. Baron von Stengel, Germany.
22. Baron de Staal, Russia (President).
23. Jhr. van Eys van Linden (Chief Secretary).
24. Jhr. W. H. de Beaufort, Dutch Foreign Minister.
25. Professor Zorn, Germany.
26. Andrew D. White | United States
27. Frederick W. Holls | of
28. Captain Alfred T. Mahan | America.

31. A. Okolicsányi d'Okolicsna, Austria.
32. Count Nigra.
33. Count Zannini | Italy
34. Yang Yü, China.
35. Colonel von Schnack | Denmark.
36. F. E. de Bille |
37. Marquis de Villaurrutia | Spain.
38. Duke of Tetuan |
39. Baron d'Estournelles de Constant, France.
40. Senhor d'Ornellas, Portugal.
41. Dr. Arnold Roth, Switzerland.
42. E. N. Rahusen | Netherlands.
43. T. C. M. Asser |
44. Baron Hayashi, Japan.
45. Baron de Bildt, Sweden and Norway.

KEY TO "A MEETING OF THE PEACE CONFERENCE."

30 July: Russia declares a general mobilization.
31 July: Austria declares general mobilization (i.e. against Russia as well as Serbia).
1 August: Germany and France both declare general mobilization.
1 August: Germany declares war on Russia at 6 p.m.

Figure 8 Peace Conference at the Hague, 1899 and key to the delegates (Radio Times Hulton Picture Library)

*Figure 9   Bethmann–
Hollweg (Radio Times
Hulton Picture Library)*

2 August: ultimatum requesting passage of German troops through Belgium delivered in Brussels.

3 August: ultimatum rejected.

3 August: Germany invents French frontier violations and bombing attack on Nuremberg and declares war on France at 6.45 p.m.

4 August: German troops cross the Belgian frontier.

11 p.m., 4 August: British ultimatum requesting their withdrawal disregarded and Britain's declaration of war against Germany takes effect.

6 August: Austria-Hungary declares war on Russia.

*Figure 10   Crowd outside
Buckingham Palace on the
declaration of war, 3
August 1914 (Mansell
Collection)*

3.2 EXERCISES ON DOCUMENTS

1   Write a commentary on Document C1, in the form of (1) a brief paragraph explaining the background to the document (2) comments and explanations as necessary on the individual clauses of the document, and (3) a summing-up of the general historical significance of the document.

Specimen Answer

1   As relations between Germany and Russia cooled, France and Russia drew closer together in the 1890s, partly because of their common hostility to Britain and partly because of their fear that the triple alliance of Germany, Austria-Hungary and Italy might be used against their interests. First of all there were French loans to Russia, followed up by military exchanges. Worried by her isolation in Europe, France in particular wanted to guarantee that Russia would go to war if Germany attacked her. Thus in August 1892 this military convention was signed between Russia and France.

[margin note: 1840's – Beginning of alliances.]

In the preamble it is stated that the convention is designed purely for the waging of a 'defensive war'. It is true that the French really did fear a German attack, but in a sense all the alliances and military conventions of the period were 'defensive'. In the end, this did not prevent a major war breaking out. Italy is mentioned in the first part of Clause 1: when it came to the test, of course, Italy actually dropped out of the Triple Alliance, and eventually in 1915 entered the war on the side of France and Russia. The second part of Clause 1 is more significant. It was really because of this provision that if Germany became involved in a war with Russia in the east, France would automatically be brought in, that the German General Staff devised the strategic plan which called for an immediate attack on France. So there is a direct line between this clause and the events of August 1914. Clause 2 expresses well the general principle of strategic thinking that once war threatened no time could be lost. If Germany mobilized, then Russia and France must also mobilize. As the event proved, once mobilization had been declared it was practically impossible to stop the steady roll towards war. Clause 3 brings out clearly that Germany is seen as the main potential enemy; Russia would have to preserve some troops for a potential war against Austria-Hungary. The clause also brings out clearly that Germany could expect to be involved in a two-front war: the nightmare of 'encirclement' which helps to explain some of the more neurotic German actions. Clause 4 mentions the co-operation between the respective general staffs, which was to have the inevitable effect of hardening the trend towards war. Despite Clause 5, it is perhaps worth noting that in the event Russia did conclude a separate peace during the First World War. Clause 6 shows clearly the way in which rival alliances came into being in response to each other. As Clause 7 states, the convention was to remain secret, and after the First World War there was a great outcry against 'secret diplomacy', which liberals and left-wingers indicted as one of the root causes of the war. In fact the general terms of the convention were well known in Europe: it would otherwise have been ineffectual as an intended deterrent to Germany.

[margin note: Defensive?]

[margin note: Preventive. No time to lose]

[margin note: Expectation of a '2 front war']

This coming together of Russia and France was one of the major events of the 1890s, and marked an important stage in the process whereby Europe divided itself into two armed camps. This system of alliances, backed by military arrangements, was an important factor in ensuring that once war came it should very rapidly become a general war.

Discussion

If you did not quite set out your answer like this, I hope you can now see the value as a historical exercise of a careful analysis of a document along these lines. Although many of the other exercises on documents will be much briefer, simply asking you to pick out the most important points, I would like you to keep this three-paragraph essay form in your mind as a kind of model for discussing documents. I will from time to time set essays of this sort for assessment, and part of the final examination will involve full-length commentaries like this on passages selected from your Documents unit. This sort of work, I believe, brings you as close to the actual thinking and working of the professional historian, as any exercise in an undergraduate course can do.

2   Comment briefly (one paragraph) on what seem to you the most significant points in Document C3.

3   Which is the most significant paragraph in Document C15? Explain its significance (one paragraph).

Specimen Answers

2   The first significant point is that Sir Edward Grey believes that if there is war between France and Germany it will be very hard for Britain to keep out. This shows clearly the way in which the lines of the Entente have hardened. But, secondly, Grey still hopes to put pressure on France to avoid war. It is for this kind of apparent vacillation that Grey has been blamed by many of his critics. Finally Grey foresees the prospect of the Triple Entente, including Russia. This did in fact come about; but, in terms of averting war, it was very far from being 'absolutely secure'.

3   The most significant paragraph is the last one, referring directly to the current Austro-Hungarian–Serbian crisis. This paragraph makes clear that the German Kaiser will 'faithfully stand by Austria-Hungary, as is required by the obligations of his alliance and of his ancient friendship'. In other words, Germany is giving Austria-Hungary a 'blank cheque' of support in her quarrel with Serbia. Many historians have argued that without this support from Germany, Austria-Hungary would not have launched her ultimatum which started a European war.

14.3.3   OTHER TOPICS

Naturally, in a brief narrative account such as is given in Chapter 8, Roberts has less room to deal with some of the broader topics which some historians have seen as contributing to the causation of the war. He does make some important points about the nature of military strategy which you should note.

Exercise 3

What point in particular with regard to German strategy does Roberts emphasize?

The answer to that should be pretty obvious, and I won't give an answer till I have said something about the military policies of other countries; it may be that Roberts places too much stress on Germany and too little on the equivalent military policies of other countries.

The general situation for all the major European powers is beautifully summed up by Professor Michael Howard in his essay 'Reflections on the First World War'. Stressing that an important factor in causing the war is 'the nature of the military machines on which the powers of Europe had for the past 40 years been lavishing so much loving care', he goes on to say:[1]

the first characteristic to notice about these machines is not the obvious one of their size, but that, no less important, of their inflexibility. Millions of men had to be recalled to the colours, organised into fighting units, equipped with a vast apparatus of arms and services and sent by railway to their points of concentration, all within a few days. The lesson of 1870 was burnt into the mind of every staff officer in Europe: the nation which loses the mobilisation race is likely to lose the war.

Mr. Taylor [i.e. A. J. P. Taylor in *War by Timetable*] rightly points out that it was only in the German army that mobilisation inevitably meant war, that general plans involved not only the concentration of the armies but, as a necessary consequence of that concentration, their *Aufmarsch* into the territory of their neighbours. But in no country could the elaborate plans of the military be substantially modified to meet political requirements. For the Austrian government a declaration of war was a political manoeuvre, for the Russian government a mobilisation order was a counter-manoeuvre; but such orders set in motion administrative processes which could be neither halted or reversed without causing a chaos which would place the nation at the mercy of its adversaries. Even the British government blithely assumed, on 5th August, that it retained complete freedom of choice where to send the BEF in Europe, if they sent it at all; when every ship, every train, and every wayside halt had in fact been designated years in advance, as they *had* to be, if British troops were to arrive in time, and in condition, to fight.

Full attention to strategic matters is accorded by Professor L. C. F. Turner in his brief study of *Origins of the First World War*. This book is recommended to you as supplementary reading for this unit, and if you are writing an essay on this subject or otherwise making a special study of it, you should certainly make sure of reading Turner. Here I just want to single out two points he makes in regard to German mobilization, slightly more subtle ones than that made by Roberts. The Roberts point, of course, is that expressed on page 261:

the German general mobilisation plans were based on the decision that France was to be the object of the major German effort. When William II asked his generals for redeployment to the east instead of the west on 1 August, he was told that such an operation was impossible. No machinery existed for such a change. Tied to one strategic plan, Germany's support for her ally meant that she had now to attack France. The soldiers were in command.

Turner places some emphasis on the significance of the fact that Austria's military plans were divided between two alternatives for mobilization, plan B whereby total mobilization was to take place in the Balkans against Serbia, or plan R, whereby total mobilization was to take place against Russia. He argues that on the night of 29–30 July the German Chancellor, Bethmann-Hollweg, on hearing that Grey had warned the German Ambassador Lichnowsky that Britain would almost certainly intervene in the war if Germany became involved against France, was trying desperately to reverse the whole trend of German policy since early July and *restrain* Austria. In this Bethmann-Hollweg had the support of the German

[1] M. Howard, 'Reflections on the First World War' in *Studies in War and Peace*, Maurice Temple Smith, 1970.

Chief of Staff, von Moltke. But suddenly, by the afternoon of 30 July, von Moltke had completely changed his mind on this, because, Turner argues, he had heard that Austria was preparing to adhere rigidly to plan B:

Unless Austria fully committed herself to plan R and launched a great offensive in Poland, the German eighth army in East Prussia would be overwhelmed by the Russian masses and the prospects for the success of the Schlieffen plan would be hopelessly compromised.

So now von Moltke urgently pressed Austria for immediate mobilization against Russia, promising unqualified German support in a European war. In such a way, according to Turner, was Germany hustled forward towards making war inevitable, because of the exigencies of Austrian strategic planning, and their repercussions for Germany herself.

The other point stressed by Turner concerns the great haste with which Germany proceeded to declare war on Russia at 6 p.m. on 1 August, followed by an ultimatum to Belgium requesting passage for the German armies, followed in turn by a declaration of war on France at 6.45 p.m. on 3 August, justified by fabricated allegations of French frontier violations and bomb attacks. The fact was that Moltke's modifications of the Schlieffen plan meant that it was vital for the German army to take Liège with great speed. Until Liège was taken no advance through Belgium would be possible (see map, Figure 11). As Turner explains: 'more than 600,000 men must pass through this bottleneck and everything hinged on its capture in the first days of the war.' Turner further quotes Professor Gerhart Ritter (the distinguished German author of *The Schlieffen Plan*, 1964 and of a great variety of other important historical works):

In other words: the gamble of the Schlieffen plan was so great that it could only succeed as the result of a rapid surprise advance by the Germans or by a sudden onslaught on Belgium. In the opinion of the general staff, Germany was obliged therefore by purely technical necessities to adopt before the whole world, the role of a brutal aggressor—an evil moral burden, which, as is well known, we have not got rid of even today.

Writing almost forty years before, Winston Churchill had made much the same point:

Nearly three weeks before the main shock of the armies could begin . . . six German brigades must storm Liège. It was this factor that destroyed all chance that armies might mobilise and remain guarding their frontiers while under their shield conferences sought a path to peace. The German plan was of such a character that the most irrevocable steps of actual war, including the violation of mutual territory, must be taken at the first moment of mobilisation. Mobilisation therefore spelt war.

(*The World Crisis: The Eastern Front*, Butterworth, 1931, p. 33.)

Now from the question of the influence of strategic planning, I want to return to the whole question of the 'sociological' causes of war, and in particular the question of whether there was a 'will to war' in the years before 1914, and how far this is directly relevant to the outbreak of war. In last week's unit you saw something of the nature of the literature of imperialism and you may have read Dr I. F. Clarke's fascinating study of the popular literature in the various European countries before the First World War. Referring to some of the writers who gained immense popularity from their novels about future war, Dr Clarke has written:

In the hands of writers like Lewis Tracy, Capitain Danrit, and August Niemann the tale of future warfare developed into an attractive and spectacular demonstration of how a nation could satisfy its every desire. Victory, is therefore, always absolute,

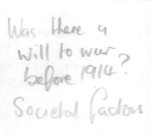

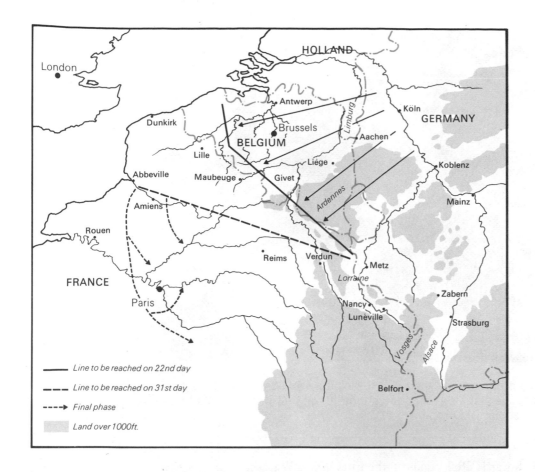

Figure 11 The Schlieffen Plan

Legend on map:
— Line to be reached on 22nd day
— — Line to be reached on 31st day
--→ Final phase
Land over 1000ft.

even to the detailed and exultant description of the entry into the enemy capital and the final symbolic act of surrender before the massed battalion of the invader. Danrit closes *La Guerre fatale* with the reading of the peace terms in the shattered ruins of the House of Commons. Similarly, in Niemann's story published in 1904, *Der Weltkrieg*, the Germans land at Leith and rapidly overrun the United Kingdom. The German author ends on the happy thought that 'His Majesty the Emperor will enter London at the head of the allied armies. Peace is assured. God grant that it may be the last war which we shall have to wage for the future happiness of the German nation.'

(*Voices Prophesying War*, Oxford University Press, 1966, pp. 126–7.)

As Clarke sums it up (p. 127) 'these writers were trying to create a Beowulf myth for an industrial civilisation of iron-clads and high-speed turbines, a new and violent *chanson de geste* for an age of imperialism, told in the inflammatory language of the mass Press'. One of the most significant things is that these novels treat of war as both 'normal' and 'romantic'. Thus (p. 131), 'until 1914 most Europeans believed that they could have their wars and enjoy them'. Clarke discusses the most famous of all the imaginary war novels. This was a serialized story, first appearing in the *Daily Mail* in March 1906, written by Queen Alexandra's favourite novelist, William Le Queux. When published as a book, his account of the *Invasion of 1910* (a German invasion of Britain) sold over a million copies throughout the world. It was even given a different ending and translated into German. Undoubtedly the enormous popularity of such works tells us a good deal about the attitude prevalent among the lower middle-class and upper working-class reading public of pre-1914 Europe. It is harder to know whether one can agree fully with Clarke when he writes that

there can be no doubt that the authors of the many tales of future warfare shared in the responsibility for the catastrophe that overtook Europe. Men like Danrit, Le Queux, and August Niemann helped to raise the temperature of international

31

*Figure 12   Boy's Brigade
at Burgess Hill, Sussex
(Mansell Collection)*

disputes. And many others played their part in helping to sustain and foment the self-deception, misunderstanding, and downright ill-will that often infected relations between the peoples of Europe.

(Clarke, p. 135.)

Professor Michael Howard ('Reflections on the First World War', in *Studies in War and Peace*) has stressed the way in which many leading intellectuals of the period glorified and prophesied war. He mentions Bernhardi, Von der Golz, Treitschke, Frederic Harrison, Seale, Péguy, Psichari, Mahan and D'Annunzio. And he remarks that if one reads such writers,

or if one explores further and reads the pre-war editorials and the speeches at prize givings and the pamphlets ; or soaks oneself in the military literature of the period ; one learns far more about the causes of the First World War than in a life-time of reading diplomatic documents.

The question is whether this spirit was taught from above or rose up naturally from below. Professor Howard argues that if young people howled for war, 'it was because for a generation or more they had been taught to howl'. The Edwardian period is the period of the founding of the Boy Scout movement, quite openly at that time designed to provide the soldiers of the future; the Boys' Brigade and the Territorials were also founded at this time. The patriotic and militaristic tone is certainly apparent in speechifying everywhere (for an example see *The Deluge*, pp. 26–7). To quote Howard again, 'the children of Europe were being trained for war, and war was regarded as something natural and inevitable'.

Exercise 4

And this brings us back to an important theory put forward in one of the essays in Bramson and Goethals. What was it?

Discussion

I am thinking of Alport's idea of 'Expectancy'. It may be that these various books, speeches, etc., trained people to *expect* war, and thus made war more likely. Again, in fact, we come back to the idea of 'shared values' making for war.

Violence was pretty evident in other aspects of social life before 1914, too. If you have any general knowledge of the period at all, or if you managed to see the television programme on the origins of World War I, you will probably be able to think of some examples of this for yourself.

Exercise 5

Note down some of the areas in which violence was apparent in the European countries in the years immediately before 1914. (If you are completely stuck, try *Roberts*, Chapter VII).

Figure 13   General Baden Powell talking to a group of Boy Scouts, autumn 1908 (Mansell Collection)

Figure 14   Women of Ulster prepare to take their part in 'civil commotion', volunteer nurses on the march, 1914 (Mansell Collection)

Specimen Answers

1   In working-class and trade-union agitation.
2   In nationalist agitation, for example in the Balkans as we have seen, but also in Ireland.
3   Among the suffragettes.
4   In the painting of the Futurists, and in the new music of Stravinsky and others.

33

If we do take it as established that there is evidence that violence was widespread and accepted in Europe before 1914, what further two questions would one want to ask before taking this seriously into account as a cause of the First World War?

Figure 15   Ulster volunteers in retreat, 1914 (Mansell Collection)

Specimen Answer

I would want to know why there was this violence, and then, as I have said before, I would want to try and have it shown that there is an actual connection between this violence and the decisions of statesmen and soldiers which brought the war about as a real event.

Why violence before 1914

Exercise 6

Look at (1) the first four columns in the table in *Roberts*, Appendix II; (2) the table below; (3) the graph in Figure 16. Do they suggest any reasons why violence should be endemic at this time?

	Population (in Thousands)		
	1880	**1900**	**1910**
London (excluding suburbs)	3,830	4,537	4,522
Birmingham	437	522	842
Manchester	462	544	719
Sheffield	285	381	479
Berlin	1,122	1,889	3,730
Munich	230	500	596
Essen	119	295	443
Paris	2,269	2,714	2,936
Marseilles	360	491	551
Milan	322	539	702
Lodz (Poland)	34	315	404
Vienna	726	1,675	2,031
Budapest	371	732	881
Bucharest	—	276	338
Moscow	612	989	1,506

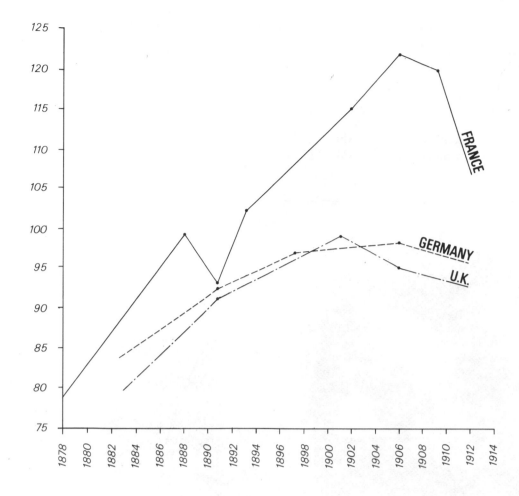

Figure 16 Real wages of the working classes in the U.K., Germany and France, treating each country individually with 1900= 100 for the U.K. and Germany, and 1895= 100 for France. (In other words, there is no suggestion that actual wages were higher in France.)

Exercise 7

In what ways might there be actual connections between the violence and the actions of political and military leaders?

Specimen Answers and Discussion

The tables do bring out I think, that the late nineteenth and early twentieth century was a time of rapid increase in population and urbanization. In the light of some of the things we said in Unit 2, this might be held to be one of the causes of a trend towards violence. The graphs suggest that while real wages had been rising steadily from the late nineteenth century, they suddenly levelled off, or even fell, around 1906 or after: this could well be a cause of working-class militance in the decade before the First World War.

Exercise 7

The second question I raised was the connection between these trends, if we accept that they existed, and actual political events. Roberts suggested some answers in referring to the growth of parliamentary democracy and of the newspaper press, which meant that statesmen were more likely to be influenced by wider popular feelings. Probably this influence was most critical as statesmen made their final hasty decisions in July 1914. 'It is reasonable to assume', writes Professor L. C. F. Turner, 'that the actions and judgement of statesmen and soldiers were profoundly modified by the tremendous surge of public opinion and the flaming headlines and comments of the daily press.' In other words, once the beginnings of a crisis had begun to take shape, these wider popular feelings, just as much as the needs of military strategy, had the effect of pushing matters on towards final crisis, instead of encouraging statesmen to be cautious.

Exercise 8

Comment briefly (one paragraph on each) on the significance of Documents C6 and C10 with regard to the origins of the First World War.

Figure 17   Field-Marshal Von Moltke (Radio Times Hulton Picture Library)

Specimen Answers

C6   The author's preface to this popular German novel reveals his immense hatred for, and jealousy of, Britain. He clearly looks forward to, and expects, a 'great war' against Britain which will result in 'a new division of the possessions of the earth'. It is interesting to note that he expects the war to be fought by Germany, France and Russia as allies (though in fact France and Russia eventually fought against Germany); but the main point is the expectation and enthusiasm for war.

Such novels as this were very popular in the decade before the outbreak of the First World War, and form a significant part of the evidence which suggests that there was a 'will to war' in the period before 1914.

C10 Von Moltke, chief of the German General Staff, accepts the basic principle of the Schlieffen plan, that France should be knocked out of the war first, before the German forces turn against Russia. This basic decision in itself meant that it was inevitable that when a war crisis broke out in East Europe involving Germany, France should also be involved in war: even when the Kaiser wished to turn the German forces against Russia, he found this to be impossible. Von Moltke also accepts Schlieffen's premiss that this plan would necessarily involve the violation of Belgian neutrality. Violation of Belgian neutrality, though not really the cause of British involvement in the war, certainly made it easier for Britain to declare war on Germany. Von Moltke does, however, reject Schlieffen's plan to proceed through Holland as well. As Moltke himself recognizes, this modification meant that Liège must be speedily taken; and this in itself meant that once the war crisis developed Germany had to get into the war as quickly as possible in order to take Liège with the speed which Moltke's modification of the Schlieffen plan demanded. This document brings out very clearly the importance of military strategy in making war inevitable once the first fumbling political moves had been made.

Speed & Milit. strat.

Figure 18 Von Schlieffen, Chief of Staff 1891–1905 (Radio Times Hulton Picture Library)

37

14.3.4   THE FISCHER THESIS AND ITS CRITICS

It is unlikely that you will have the time to read Fritz Fischer's very long book, *Germany's Aims in the First World War*, though you may perhaps be able to dip into it in your local library or reading room. There is always the problem in the study of history that one seems to be encouraging students to talk about so-and-so's thesis without students actually ever reading the original works by the historian concerned. However, I think this an inevitable and necessary risk; it is important that in studying the origins of the First World War you should be aware of the significance of some of the main points put forward by Fritz Fischer. And the whole controversy is in itself illuminating of some of the basic methods and principles of the historian and brings out very well a point I stressed in Units 5–8 the *Introduction to History* block of the Arts Foundation Course[1] and have been repeating ever since, the very imperfections of primary source material.

The vast part of Fischer's immense study concentrates, as the title suggests, on the period of the war itself. Fischer examines in great detail the various plans and programmes being put forward inside Germany to meet the eventuality of a German victory. One of the most important documents he quotes is Bethmann-Hollweg's September programme of 1914 (Document C19): notes made by Bethmann-Hollweg during the earlier stages of the Battle of the Marne when it still seemed likely that the original aims of the Schlieffen Plan would be fulfilled, and that the speedy defeat of France would follow. The aims expressed in the document are, to say the least, aggressively expansionist, and seem, above all, to be motivated by desire for economic expansion. According to Fischer these ideas remained 'the essential basis of Germany's war aims right up to the end of the war, though modified from time to time to meet changing situations'.

But, more crucially, Fischer argued that these notes were no isolated inspiration of the moment, but that they represented the ideas of leading economic, political and military thinkers, not just in September 1914, but in the entire period before the First World War. Thus, a document actually dating from the period of the war itself, could be used to throw light on German aims and policies before the war, and therefore, by implication, to show German responsibility for creating a warlike situation. The bulk of the introductory part of Fischer's book, then, is devoted to a broad study of all the forces operating in Germany from the late nineteenth century onwards. We have already noted his statement that 'economic expansion was the basis of Germany's political world diplomacy' whose 'ultimate objective' was 'the expansion of Germany's power'. In the preface to the first edition of the book Fischer spoke of how 'consciousness of strength, an urge for expansion and a need for security combined to mould the policy of Wilhelm II's Germany'. Less attention is devoted to the diplomatic manoeuvres which followed the Sarajevo assassination, but Fischer is in agreement with traditional diplomatic historians in blaming Bethmann-Hollweg for giving full and unconditional backing to Austria-Hungary.

The main criticism of the Fischer thesis has taken the form of objecting to the way in which he uses material from the war period itself to bolster an argument about German policies before the war, but his brief discussion of the final diplomatic moves has also been criticized, and Turner and others have accused him of failing to understand the military necessities under which Germany laboured. In an article in the journal *Past and Present* Dr P. M. H. Hatton made the point that

---

[1] The Open University, A100 *Humanities: A Foundation Course*, Units 5–8 *Introduction to History*, The Open University Press, 1971.

quotations from the British records during the war could also be made to look like evidence for a drive towards war in the pre-war years. He also quotes from a minute of the British Imperial Defence Committee of January 1913 which directed that 'in order to bring the greatest possible economic pressure on Germany it is essential that the Netherlands and Belgium should be compelled to declare at the outset to which side in the struggle they will adhere'. Such quotations as this could equally be used to cast an unfavourable light on British policies before the war. Hatton points out that, once embarked upon war 'states in both alliance groups thought in terms of what they might gain if the war was won'. He adds that 'care should be taken not to assume too readily—as it seems to this writer that Fischer has done—that specific national objectives expressed during the war presuppose more than vague aspirations before August 1914'. On the question of diplomacy after Sarajevo Hatton argues that it 'looks as if' Bethmann-Hollweg thought that Britain would accept Austro-Hungarian absorption of Serbia, so that the backing given to Austria-Hungary does not equal deliberate seeking of war. Hatton argues that Bethmann-Hollweg put too much faith in governments which wanted peace putting pressure on their own allies.

In 1914 the German Chancellor's calculation proved wrong because Poincaré was determined not to desert Russia, and Grey was determined not to desert France, regarding the suggestion that Britain and Germany should secretly collaborate to solve the crisis as unthinkable disloyalty to Britain's ally. Thus Russia was emboldened to stand firm and the pattern of the crises of 1908–9 and 1912–13 was not repeated. Neither Germany nor the western powers dared to fail allies about whose internal strength they had misgivings.

('Britain and Germany in 1914: The July Crisis and War Aims', *Past and Present*, No. 36, April 1967, reprinted in H. W. Koch (ed.) *The Origins of the First World War*, Macmillan, 1972, pp. 33–4.)

Professor James Joll, who writes sympathetically of Fischer's achievements as a historian, arguing that what is now needed is for other historians to follow Fischer's lead in examining the war aims of the other powers, points out that in the end our reading of the documents really depends on our understanding of the basic assumptions which underlay what the statesmen actually put down in writing.

When political leaders are faced with the necessity for taking decisions the outcome of which they cannot foresee, in crises which they do not wholly understand, they fall back on their own instinctive reactions, traditions and modes of behaviour. Each of them has certain beliefs, rules or objectives which are taken for granted; and one of the limitations of documentary evidence is that few people bother to write down, especially in moments of crisis, things which they take for granted. Yet if we are to understand their motives, we must somehow try to find out what, as we say 'goes without saying'.

(J. Joll, *The Unspoken Assumptions*, L.S.E. inaugural lecture, April 1968, reprinted in Koch (ed.) op. cit.)

What this really boils down to in discussing the Fischer thesis is the question of whether we accept that the September programme was, as Fischer argues, a natural part of discussions and attitudes which had already been taking place between German political, economic and military leaders in the years before the war, or whether we take it as a hasty jotting to meet an immediate situation. Fischer insists that far from being exceptional and eccentric, as many historians have argued, Bernhardi's views (Document C8) are extremely representative of influential sections of German opinion in the years before the war: if you read the document you will see clearly the emphasis on colonial and economic expansion, and the insistence that 'what we now wish to attain must be *fought for*' and the expectation that 'we shall be called upon to draw the sword'.

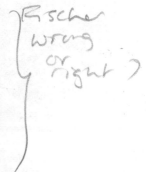

In the preface to the second edition of *Germany's Aims in the First World War*, Fischer replied to some of his critics in the following terms:

Essentially, German war aims were not merely an answer to the enemy's war aims, as made known in the course of the war, nor the problem of the war situation created by the 'beleaguered fortress' and the blockade; they are explicable only in the light of factors operating since 1890 or even earlier—naval policy, the 'policy of bases' [i.e. the policy of trying to establish naval bases throughout the world, as at Tangier], colonial, eastern, Balkan and European economic policies, and a general political situation which—primarily as an effect of Germany's own policy—produced after 1904 and 1907 the attempt to overthrow Germany by 'encircling' her.

On behalf of the Fischer thesis, it can be said that, though there has been no systematic and detailed examination of allied war aims, it does seem fairly clear that they were in a sense much more 'defensive' than were Germany's: what France was really aiming at was the liberation of her territory, and what Britain was aiming at was the ending of the German threat to the European balance.[1]

Figure 19   British troops in the trenches in Northern France, October 1914 (Mansell Collection)

[1] This view is not seriously challenged by V. A. Rothwell's *British War Aims and Peace Diplomacy* (Oxford University Press, 1971), which does, very properly, stress the concern of British politicians with British Imperial interests.

Figure 20   Winter campaigning on the Western front: the mud of Flanders, c. 1915 (Mansell Collection)

However, as you may have seen in my 'Origins of World War I' television programme, there are bits and pieces of film evidence which suggest strong economic aims on the part of certain people in Britain. My own view of the whole controversy is that what it has done is to illuminate still more the prevailing assumptions of international morality in the era of the First World War, that is to say the first of my general sets of circumstances. And I would myself come back to the point that one of the keys to the First World War does lie in this willingness of all powers to resort to force, if circumstances seemed right, to carry through expansionist political and economic objectives.

Exercise 9

What conclusions about German responsibility for the war could you draw from (a) Document C13; (b) Document C18; (c) Document C19? Confine yourself to a brief paragraph on each.

*Figure 21 'Happy
Memories of the Zoo',
from Bairnsfather,* More
Fragments from France,
1916, *p. 17*

Specimen Answers

(a)   This document shows the military arrangements entered into by France and
Russia in expectation of a war against Germany. Clearly then it would not be
possible to put all the blame on Germany and see France and Russia as innocent
of any military intentions.

(b)   This seems on the one hand to suggest that Bethmann-Hollweg was horrified
by the prospect of general war, and, above all, that he had no wish at all to be
involved in a war against Britain. On the other hand, the reference to the 'scrap of
paper' shows a kind of contempt for international agreements which could be held
to be one aspect of German responsibility for the war.

(c)   There can be no doubt that as it stands this document reveals extreme
expansionist objectives as far as Bethmann-Hollweg is concerned. In regard to
determining German responsibility for the war, one has to decide whether this
document represents a consistent attitude in Germany followed in the years
preceding the war, or whether it is simply an immediate reaction to a particular

wartime situation. Whatever the rights and wrongs of that, the aims expressed here go far beyond any expressed by the allied powers, so that this document can scarcely be ignored in an assessment leading to a conclusion that Germany was in a sense the most expansionist of all the powers, and that therefore a degree of responsibility attaches to her which perhaps does not attach to the other powers.

4.1 THE CHARACTER AND COURSE OF THE WAR

Your main work for these two brief final sections of this unit consists of reading *Roberts*, Chapter 9 and *Fuller*, Chapter 9. To help clarify the accounts given there, here is the briefest possible outline.

When the war broke out the two main theatres of operations were the Western Front, where the Germans faced the French and the small British Expeditionary Force, and the Eastern Front, where the Germans and Austrians faced the Russians. Operations also took place in colonial Africa where on the whole the Germans did badly, and in the Far East, where the Japanese took over the German possession of Shantung.

Italy came into the war in 1915 on the side of the Allies, and thus opened up a new theatre of war on the Italian–Austrian frontier. Because of the stalemate on the Western Front, certain politicans in Britain, known as the 'Easterners', were keen to see new fronts opened up elsewhere: thus in 1915 the unsuccessful Gallipoli operation took place; it was followed by troop landings at Salonica in an attempt (also unsuccessful) to open up a new theatre of war in Macedonia. Turkish involvement in the war on the side of the central powers involved Britain in two further theatres of war, Mesopotamia and Palestine.

There were no great naval battles. The German high seas fleet ventured out only once, returning again after the inconclusive Battle of Jutland. The two most significant operations on high seas were the British economic blockade of Germany, and the German submarine campaign.

Figure 22 H.M.S. Dreadnought, launched 1906 (Imperial War Museum)

Exercise 10

Using Roberts and Fuller, answer the following questions.

1   The First World War can be characterized as a 'total war'.
   (a)   What does this mean?
   (b)   Why was it a 'total war'?

2   The First World War was a static, 'stalemate' war, with very high loss of life proportional to very small gains of territory. Why was this?

3   What were the main technological innovations used in the war?

4   What defences can be made for the fact that the British and French generals insisted on fighting in the West?

14.4.2   DOMESTIC IMPLICATIONS OF THE WAR

This is a subject for detailed study in the next few units. To form the bridge, as it were, answer this one question:

5   In what main ways, mentioned in the two chapters by Roberts and Fuller, does the war impinge on the social and domestic political and economic history of Europe?

Discussion

1   (a) A war involving whole populations; a war in which organization of the domestic front became as important as organization of the military front; a war into which was thrown every resource of science and technology and every resource of propaganda: an 'all-out' and an 'all-embracing' war.

(b)   Because the strength of nationalist and patriotic feeling combined with the expectation of, or will to, war meant that whole peoples *wanted* to be involved in the war. Representative institutions and a mass press made it more possible for peoples to be involved. Industrialization was in any case creating a mass society, and the existing level of military technology depended for necessary supplies upon mass organization and mass participation upon the domestic front.

I think that these are the main points, though you may well have found others.

2   The basic reason lies in the existing stage of military technology, where the existence of rapid-firing weapons gave a pronounced advantage to the defence; Fuller prosaically speaks of 'the combination of bullet, spade and barbed wire'. Within this state of affairs, the military leaders on both sides seemed incapable of developing new tactics to overcome the stalemate. Where it might have been overcome by superior power of artillery, this did not come about because of supply and transport problems which prevented provision of the unprecedented quantities of guns and shells required to break the stalemate. When finally artillery fire was stepped up, this simply had the result of turning the landscape of war into a completely impassable terrain, intensifying the stalemate. Such technological innovations as might have broken the stalemate were used wrongly or too sparingly: the classic instance here is the tank, but perhaps also, as Fuller maintains, gas.

3   Machine guns, quick-firing field guns, howitzers, poison gas, tanks, dreadnoughts, airships and aeroplanes, submarines, food-processing and new medicines.

4   Fuller argues that war had to be fought in the West because that was where the 'allied main bases' were. Possibly an even more simple reason which may have occurred to you is that after all France was where the Germans were. Certainly the French would be bound to concentrate their main effort there purely to liberate their homeland, and the British were bound to fight alongside their main allies.

5   Through the domestic organization needed to meet the demands of war; through the blockade which affected civilian populations in central Europe; through the revolutionary situation created by the war, and the 'chaos' which followed it; through the colossal loss of life.

We shall amplify some of these points in the next units.

Acknowledgements

Acknowledgement is made to the following for illustrations used in this unit:
Imperial War Museum; Mansell Collection; Radio Times Hulton Picture Library.

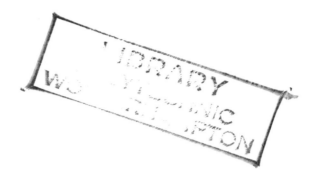

Unit 15

Russia and Germany in World War 1

*Prepared for the Course Team by Harry Hanak, Lecturer in History at the
School of Slavonic and East European Studies, University of London*

CONTENTS

5.1 PRELIMINARIES

With this unit we again have the opportunity to invite a distinguished authority to contribute to the *War and Society* course. Quite understandably, Harry Hanak has not followed the carefully structured approach, with its attempt to involve you directly, which is favoured by the 'home' members of the War and Society team. In some ways, perhaps, this unit is more analogous to the 'straight' lecture in a traditional university. You may well find it interesting to compare the two approaches, particularly since we shall ourselves probably be following the more austere approach in the fourth-level history course, A401 *Great Britain 1750–1950: Sources and Historiography*.

Historically, it seems right to start our study of the consequences of the First World War with Russia and Germany, since the most dramatic events of all took place in Russia, and since there are very interesting parallels and contrasts to be drawn between the experiences of the two countries. If you are following the series of archive film compilations broadcast on television, you will need to do 'minimum coverage', at least, of this unit in order to make the accompanying television programme fully comprehensible. Otherwise, because of the undoubted difficulties involved in this unit, you may, if you like, regard it as OPTIONAL. It may be that after working through Unit 16, you will find that you can with profit return to Unit 15.

If you are proposing to make a full study of the very important subject-matter of this unit, you should, since the unit takes a certain amount of knowledge for granted, be sure to do the prescribed reading before embarking on the main part of the correspondence material. You should in fact have already read Chapter 9 of Roberts' *Europe 1880–1945*,[1] while working on last week's unit; for the moment therefore, the main thing is to read Michael Florinsky's, *The End of the Russian Empire*.[2] At the end of the unit I shall suggest some further reading from Roberts to round off this week's work.

In all those parts of the course which deal with the consequences of the war it is worth bearing in mind, as a kind of frame of reference, the four points about the relationship between war and social change which have been made from time to time during the course, namely war as *destruction*, war as *test*, war as involving *participation*, and war as a great *psychological* experience. Bear these points particularly in mind as you work your way through Florinsky. It is also always important, as the first exercise, which is to be done in conjunction with your reading of the book, stresses, to be clear about the nature of any secondary book one is reading, what type of book it is, how authoritative it is, and so on.

Exercise 1

Question 1

Who is Florinsky; how did he come to write this book; what special qualifications, and what disqualifications, does he have for writing it?

Question 2

In what other respects does this seem to be either an authoritative, or not an authoritative book?

[1] J. M. Roberts, *Europe 1880–1945*, Longman (SET BOOK.)

[2] M. T. Florinsky, *The End of the Russian Empire*, Collier–Macmillan (SET BOOK).

Question 3

Of the four points reiterated above about the relationship between war and social change, which one is overtly stressed by Florinsky?

Question 4

Is there any implicit reference to any of the other points?

Question 5

What answer does Florinsky suggest to the question, 'What would have happened to Russia, had there been no war?'

Now take up your reading of Florinsky, and don't read any further till you have attempted answers to these questions. My suggested answers come at the end of this opening section.

Here and there throughout the correspondence unit I have inserted a few more exercises of my own, not all of them necessarily directly related to Harry Hanak's correspondence material. You should, perhaps, look upon the correspondence material rather as you would treat a distinguished guest lecturer at a conventional university. The lecture will not provide a complete introduction to the subject, but it will provide you with many useful, and indeed striking, points which you would not get elsewhere. In order to prepare yourself to get the best out of the lecture, as I have suggested, it is necessary to do some reading in advance. My exercises, and my 'further remarks' at the end, you should regard as serving the function of a short personal tutorial with me, in which we discuss some of the subject-matter of Harry Hanak's paper.

In all discussions of the consequences, or 'impact' of a war, it is very important to be clear about the existing state of the countries we are studying on the eve of the war—otherwise we will not be able to distinguish between what seems to be due to the war, and what was about to happen anyway. Thus this unit opens with studies of Germany and Russia as they were in 1914.

Specimen Answers to Exercise 1

Florinsky was himself a Russian citizen, who served in the Russian army during the First World War, and who later became Professor of Economics at Columbia University in New York. The book was originally written as a volume in the massive Carnegie Endowment for International Peace Social and Economic History of the World War, and as such was published in 1931. As a Russian who participated directly in some of the events described, Florinsky obviously has some unique qualifications for writing a book of this sort; but, at the same time, such participation could lead to obvious blindnesses and prejudices. Clearly, however, he has the qualification of considerable academic status, since he became Professor of Economics at Columbia.

2   The very style of the book is, in my view, well reasoned and persuasive, and it is very fully backed up by an elaborate system of convincing-looking references. The fact that the book was published as long ago as 1931 might suggest that it is outdated. On the other hand, this is contradicted by what Florinsky himself says in the preface and, perhaps more convincingly, by the fact that it was felt to be worth republishing in 1961. I should say that, on the whole, this is a pretty authoritative book; though of course you certainly need not accept the general interpretations put forward by Florinsky.

3 The *test* of war. This is repeated over and over again, e.g. on pages 31, 32, 246.

4 There are, I think, throughout the book, implied references to the importance of the *destructive* influences of the war. There is also at the beginning of Chapter 7 a suggestion of the importance from the point of view of Russian labour of the *participation* effect of war.

5 Florinsky in fact refuses to answer this question; in fact he says it is 'idle to speculate' on it (p. 31). But you should note, and this is very relevant to the way in which Harry Hanak's correspondence unit begins, that he stresses the important changes which were already taking place in Russia before 1914. He undoubtedly puts tremendous emphasis on the weaknesses and inadequacies of the Tzarist system, but there is perhaps some suggestion that without the war Russia might have been able to proceed more slowly towards democracy and industrialization. That is the sort of question you should be puzzling over for yourself while you are working on the unit, and after you have finished it.

15.2 GERMANY IN 1914

The monarchical systems under which both Germany and Russia lived in 1914 and the cordial relations of the two countries for more than a century hid the vast political, social and economic differences between them. In 1910 Russia had a population of 160 millions; Germany a population of 65 millions. The area of Russia was immensely vaster than that of Germany. Russia's industrialization had been very rapid but only of recent vintage. Her resources were immeasurably greater than those of Germany but they had been only imperfectly exploited. Germany was the largest producer of coal in Europe (with the exception of Great Britain). She produced 277 million tons, Russia only 36·2 million tons. The Industrial Revolution of the nineteenth century was based on coal; and coal remained the most important source of power. In 1914 Germany produced 14·7 million tons of pig iron and 14 million tons of steel. The figures for Russia were 3·6 and 4·1 million tons respectively. Even Britain produced less than Germany, though much more than Russia, France and Austria-Hungary. In the rate of industrial production Russia was catching up. In the years 1885 to 1913 Russian industrial production increased at the rate of 5·72 per cent per annum, which was higher than that of Germany (4·5 per cent), higher than that of Britain (2·11 per cent), and higher than that of the United States (5·2 per cent).

Germany was a constitutional monarchy. The centre of the constitutional system was the German Emperor, King of Prussia. He also had sixty-three other titles which bore witness to the extraordinary expansion of the house of Hohenzollern to the premier position in Germany. The traditions of the Kings of Prussia were those of enlightened absolutism. In 1871 Germany was united and the King of Prussia became German Emperor. As Emperor he symbolized the Reich, while the empire symbolized German national unity and evoked the greatness of the medieval emperors. The Emperor appointed the Imperial Chancellor and the State Secretaries. Together with the upper chamber of the German parliament he could declare war and make peace. As supreme war lord he commanded the army and navy. He appointed all the officers of the navy, of the Prussian (but not the German) army, and all State officials. Moreover, he held in the upper house seventeen of the forty-three votes and controlled at least five more, from small adjoining States of Prussia. This assured the Prussian delegates a working majority.

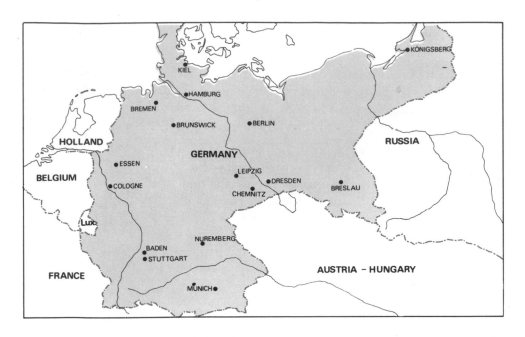

Figure 1   Germany in 1914.

The German empire was a federation. It was divided into twenty-two princely States and the three cities of Lübeck, Bremen and Hamburg. They were all represented in the upper house which was more a conference of ambassadors than an upper house of parliament. Decisions were made by majority votes, but were more frequently the result of delicate negotiations. It was thus a body that helped to preserve intact the princely States and was, of course, intensely conservative.

The hopes of German democrats were centred in the Reichstag elected by universal manhood suffrage. At the elections of 1912, of the 12,208,000 votes cast, the Social Democrats polled 4,250,000, the Catholic Centre 1,997,000. If to these votes are added the few hundred thousand votes cast by other dissident groups, it will be seen that there was a majority in Germany opposed to the Bismarckian system.

Next to the Reichstag stood the legislatures of the other States. Most important of these was the Prussian parliament. Its electoral system was one of the curiosities of Europe. The total taxable revenue of a constituency was divided into three equal parts and the taxpayers were correspondingly divided into three classes, with each class paying an equal total sum.

One of the bizarre results of this system was that the Imperial Chancellor and Prussian Prime Minister had to manage a Reichstag with a left-centre majority and at the same time a Prussian parliament which had a conservative majority. Experience had shown that the union of the two offices in the same person was necessary to avoid endless friction. In any case it was a useful weapon because it further increased the hold that Prussia had on the rest of the Reich. One of the results of this dual system was that the government of the Reich and the government of Prussia tended to avoid friction by avoiding controversial legislation.

This peculiar constitutional arrangement underlined the hegemony of certain political classes in Germany. Most important, next to the Emperor and the ruling dynasties, were the Junkers of Germany, east of the river Elbe. They were not ogres plotting future wars and grinding the poor into the dust. They were a class of medium-sized estate owners whose economic position had been much threatened by the influx of cheap American grain in the later nineteenth century. They used their position to protect their economic well-being. They controlled the Prussian parliament. This control enabled them to influence the Prussian government and ensure that the Prime Minister and Imperial Chancellor were well disposed to their cause. By the control of the Prussian government they controlled the majority of the upper house. Hence the constitutional position of the Prussian parliament was the main topic of German political controversy. In order to democratize Germany, to fulfil the dreams of 1848, the first essential step was the reform of the Prussian voting system.

The position of the Prussian Junkers was buttressed by the officer corps and the bureaucracy. Moreover, the general staff was directly responsible to the supreme war lord, that is, the Emperor. It was not under civilian control. Hence during the First World War the army made decisions of great political importance, like the violation of Belgian neutrality and the unrestricted submarine warfare, without the Chancellor being able to veto their decisions even if he had wanted to do so. It also meant that in war, when military matters were paramount and when the great prestige of the German officer class reached absurd proportions, the army achieved practical dictatorship over the State. Even the Kaiser became a shadowy ruler while Germany was ruled by General Ludendorff. It is interesting to note that the German edition of the war-time diaries of Admiral Müller, the chief of the Kaiser's naval chancery is entitled in German, 'Did the Kaiser rule?'

For a number of reasons the Empire was not democratized before 1918. English political history leads one to think of a process of gradual democratization and liberalization; a series of extensions of the franchise. In Germany this could not happen. The forces of reaction were strong and had no intention of surrendering their power.

1   In spite of the increase in socialist voting strength, few doubted that a German soldier would fire on a revolutionary mob.

2   The Reich possessed great prestige in an age of nationalism. It was the Prussian State and the Prussian army which had created the Reich.

3   Many of the German middle class were prepared to abandon their liberalism on the altar of German material success. They were, moreover, deeply disturbed by the rapid rise of socialism. In the last resort the Reich protected their property, even if it excluded them from political influence.

4   The federal structure of the Empire tended to be anti-democratic. A democratic reformation would result in a weakening or disappearance of Prussia but also of the other states. Especially in the south, in Bavaria, Würtemberg and Baden, anti-federalist ideas were strongly resisted by the kings but also by the people at large.

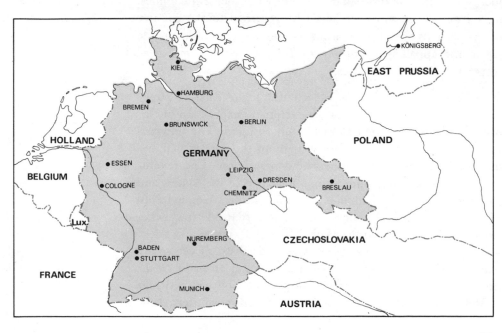

Figure 2   Germany post-1918.

5   The government of the Reich was, it is true, dependent on the Reichstag for military appropriations. Yet the result of the constitutional conflict between Bismarck and the Prussian parliament from 1862 to 1866 had weakened this power. In those years parliament had refused to vote taxes until its will prevailed in matters relating to the army. Bismarck, aware that he had donned the mantle of Strafford, collected the taxes without parliamentary sanction. The Prussians paid.

6   Many of the political parties in the Reichstag were opposed to the Bismarckian system—at least in theory. The Catholic Centre is a good example. Its right wing in northern Germany had allied itself with the Prussian conservatives in 1910 to defeat some very mild reforms of the Prussian franchise system. Why should they oppose the three-class franchise which gave them most Rhenish constituencies without opposition? Why should they work to bring atheist Marxists into parliament? The southern branch was more genuinely democratic but they were aware that such democratization would place in jeopardy the privileges enjoyed by the southern Catholic States, and especially Bavaria.

15.3   RUSSIA IN 1914

In the last decade of the nineteenth century the rate of industrialization in Russia was spectacular. It slowed down in the years 1900–9, only to redouble after 1910. The most characteristic feature of this late development was its degree of concentration. Russia was still primarily a peasant country with a *per capita* national income eight to ten times less than in the United States. In 1914, 76 per cent of Russian workers were employed in factories with more than 100 employees, 56 per cent in factories with more than 500 employees, and 40 per cent in factories with more than 1,000 employees—the last percentage had been 31 in 1901. In the United States giant enterprises employing over a 1,000 workers were 17·8 per cent of the working force. For the most important industrial districts of Russia this concentration of labour in large enterprises was even more marked: for the St Petersburg district, 44·4 per cent, for the Moscow district, 57·3 per cent.

A second feature of Russian industry was the relative youth of the workers, and a third the relatively close links that bound the proletariat to the countryside. An appreciable number of Russian workers had only recently left their rural homes, and there were some six million seasonal workers who returned to the country at harvest time. This was perhaps one of the reasons why so many found it easy to escape to the villages in the appalling conditions of 1918–20. Still, some three million workers lived permanently in the cities.

The political condition of these new workers, as indeed of much of Russia's population, was one of seething discontent. The most characteristic expression of this discontent was terrorism and dissemination of revolutionary ideas. The impossibility of changing the system by legal means forced many of the young men and women of the middle classes to conspiracy, terror and revolution. The revolutionaries were all socialist—that is if one understands socialism in its vaguest and widest sense. The Decembrists in 1825 had as one of their leaders Colonel Paul Pestel, who believed in totalitarian-state socialism. In the 1840s Petrashevsky attempted to popularize the ideas of Fourier. With Michael Bakunin and Alexander Herzen we come to the founders of Russian socialism. Even more influential was Chernyshevsky, who wrote a book called *What is to be Done?* It is no coincidence that one of Lenin's more important political writings bore the same name. It is a novel of the new men and women, absolutely dedicated to the task of revolution and terror, irrespective of human beings and irrespective of what the mass of the people want. After the emancipation of the serfs in 1861 the intellectuals turned to the peasants. But the 'going to the people' was a failure. The Russian peasant was not a natural socialist and he found no common language with the student from the town. The failure meant that the new revolutionaries, men like Peter Zaichnevsky, or Nechaev, a demented young fanatic, who denounced his rivals to the police, had contempt for the people. Such also was Peter Tkachev who believed that all those over the age of twenty-five should be liquidated. He died in a lunatic asylum. Tkachev expressed also the great fear of many revolutionaries. He feared that the growth of capitalism and industrialization would result in Russia following the West politically. Thus she would eventually receive parliamentary institutions and the people would be lulled into acquiescence. The terrorists' most spectacular success was the assassination of Alexander II in 1881.

In 1904 Russia and Japan went to war. No one doubted that the Russians would defeat the 'monkeys' as the Tsar referred to the Japanese. However, the Russian armies and navy were beaten. These defeats provoked unrest at home and this unrest soon turned to revolution when the authorities treated it with their usual brutality. When on 22 January 1905 a monster crowd led by Father Gapon, who was trying to form trade unions loyal to the government and who was subsidized by the police, tried to present a humble supplication to the Emperor, the crowd was dispersed by volleys of rifle fire. Several hundred were killed. This was the first shot of the revolution. There were many others, the best known being the mutiny on the battleship *Potemkin*, immortalized in Eisenstein's film. The autocracy had to give way and Russia for the first time in her history was given the kind of parliamentary institutions which all Western States had enjoyed for a long time, the State Duma. It is true that when the autocracy recovered control it soon clipped the wings of the Duma but it remained in being till the Bolsheviks took over—a reminder of what might have been.

The 1905 revolution produced one other institution of greater permanence. On 26 October, a historic date, thirty or forty delegates, many of them workers, met in St Petersburg in the first session of the *Soviet*. The word means council. Soon soviets were established in many other cities. They were not, in Lenin's words, 'a workers' parliament and not an organization of proletarian administration, but a fighting organization for the achievement of definite ends'. The most prominent member of the St Petersburg Soviet was Trotsky.

The revolution in the towns was soon followed by a peasant uprising. It was more of a jacquerie than a revolt. In any case the government regained control. Lenin described 1905 as a dress rehearsal for 1917.

5.4   RUSSIA 1914–17

Russia was badly prepared to fight a modern war. The Russian steam-roller was a myth. It is true that the Russians had the superiority in numbers but this superiority simply resulted in greater casualties. No belligerent nation lost more men killed and wounded than did the Russians. The Russian generals, Trotsky wrote, would 'comfort themselves and the allies with columns of figures when columns of fighters were wanted'. About five and a half million men were killed. The Russian armies needed about eighteen million rifles for a three-year period. They had nearly seven million for the same period. Only twelve per cent of the required 133,000 machine guns were available at the beginning of 1917.

Figure 3   Trotsky at Brest-Litovsk, 1918 (Mansell Collection).

The leadership was inferior. Trotsky records that the generals wasted hours in those days discussing whether to remove or not to remove the bones of the saints from Kiev in case the Germans took the city. The Tsar submitted that it was not necessary since, 'the Germans would not risk touching them, and if they did touch them, so much the worse for the Germans'. 'This', Trotsky comments, 'happened not in the epoch of the Crusaders, but in the twentieth century when the news of the Russian defeats came over the wireless.'[1]

In spite of all this the Russians had some initial successes. But after the spring of 1915 they were constantly on the retreat. 'I place my trust,' said the Minister of War, 'in the impenetrable spaces, impassable mud, and the mercy of St Nicholas, Protector of Holy Russia.'

War is the great test of society. In the case of both Germany and Russia power passed out of the hands of those who had hitherto held it. In the case of Germany it was the army which concentrated power in its hands, especially after Hindenburg's and Ludendorff's arrival at army headquarters in 1916. Similarly in Russia the Tsar no longer possessed the powers that he had had before the war.

[1] Leon Trotsky, *History of the Russian Revolution*, Sphere Books, 1967, Vol. I, p. 36.

The bureaucracy, too, could not cope with all the exigencies of war and other non-State bodies took over vital duties which in Germany and in other belligerents remained in the hands of the government. There were, for instance, what have sometimes been called the 'voluntary organizations': in 1864 provincial and district assemblies (*zemstvos*) were established and in 1870 elected municipal councils. Since then liberals had come to consider these institutions as the seed out of which an all-Russian parliament would grow. It was in the zemstvos that party political life began before the establishment of the Duma.

During the Russo-Japanese war the zemstvos and municipalities carried out some of the tasks of government. Thus they gave assistance in relief work for wounded soldiers. They took up this task again in 1914 and on a very much extended scale. They organized hospitals, distributed parcels to the troops, and housed and fed refugees who fled before the advancing Germans. Very soon they began to provide a great number of the commodities which they supplied to troops and refugees and by 1916 the number of factories and workshops controlled by the zemstvos and municipalities exceeded two thousand. In the spring of 1915 they turned to the production of armaments. Later in that year a number of industrialists created war industry committees and a central committee to co-ordinate their work. Indeed, without their work of armament production and distribution Russia would hardly have been able to continue the war for as long as she did.[1]

It was natural that these three organizations, the zemstvos, the municipalities and the central war industry committee, having taken over many of the tasks of the government, should demand internal reforms. Like the Duma deputies they argued that the war would be prosecuted successfully only if a government responsible to the Duma was established, and all the evil and supposedly pro-German elements removed from government and from the court.

The Tsar weakened his constitutional position by taking over command of the army in 1915. This removed him from the seat of power in Petrograd. In any case he did not do much good at army headquarters, being unversed in military affairs. The actual direction of operations was in the hands of General Alekseev, the chief of staff. Moreover, being at army headquarters, the Tsar became more directly responsible for the defeats that the army suffered. He left his wife, the empress Alexandra Feodorovna, behind him in the capital. Indeed, it was she who persuaded him to go to army headquarters, contrary to the advice of all his ministers. Nicholas was a weak man, obstinate and unyielding to everyone but his wife. She possessed the strength that he lacked. A princess from a rural corner of Germany, educated in London by her grandmother Victoria, she ascended the throne of Russia and adopted its Byzantine obscurantism and its religious orthodoxy. She was determined to pass on the heritage of absolutism unimpaired to her son who suffered from haemophilia. Alexandra Feodorovna was an even more stupid reactionary than her husband. Her court became the home of quacks. It seemed to many, after Nicholas had gone to the front, that Russia was ruled by this ignorant, neurotic woman and 'our Friend'—Rasputin. Eventually, even the nobility tired of her antics and Rasputin was murdered during a drinking bout. From Petrograd she poured a stream of letters to her 'lovey' and 'sweety'. She wrote in English. Without exception her advice was bad. It was very simple: never give way! Strike your fist on the table! Do not concede a responsible ministry! Don't give anything they want—meaning the Duma. Two and a half months before the revolution the Tsarina writes to the Tsar: 'Everything is getting quiet and better, but people want to feel your hand. . . Russia loves to feel the whip. That is their nature.' Trotsky comments: 'Thus writes the Russian Tsarina to the Russian Tsar about the Russian people two and a half months before the revolution.'[1]

[1] Trotsky, op. cit., Vol. I, p. 71.

Figure 4   Czar Nicholas II and family, 1917 (Mansell Collection).

Exercise 2

In this section, Harry Hanak has described the growing importance of the 'voluntary organizations', i.e. the zemstvos and the municipal councils. In agreement with Florinsky, he introduces this paragraph with the sentence: 'War is the great test of society.' Now read this declaration issued on 25 July 1914 by an assembly of representatives of the zemstvos:

Gone are now the barriers which have divided our citizens; all are united in one common effort . . . who, if not the members of 'a voluntary organisation' whose business it is to provide for the needs of the people, who have many years of practical experience in caring for the sick, and who have organised forces at their command, should undertake the task of uniting isolated efforts in their work, which demand so immense an organisation.

Quoted in T. J. Polner, *Russian Local Government during the War and the Union of the Zemstvos*, Carnegie Endowment for International Peace, Yale University Press, 1930, p. 55.

Question 1

Do you think the growth of, and the attitudes of, the 'voluntary organizations' illuminate any other aspect of war's effect on society apart from that of being a 'test'?

Question 2

Comment on the date of the declaration quoted above.

Question 3

Comment on the opening phrase of this declaration: 'Gone are now the barriers which have divided our citizens.'

Specimen Answers

1   I should think personally (and this is very much a personal interpretation) that there is a strong element of the *participation* effect of war in the manner in which middle-class organizations are able to play a national role hitherto largely denied to them. There are also shades of the *psychological* effects of war in the invocation of national unity, and so on.

2   The declaration was issued some time before the actual outbreak of war; obviously war was already regarded as pretty well inevitable in Russia by this time.

3   This, obviously, encapsulates the emotional aspect of war, or the threat of war, mentioned in the answer to Question 1. Clearly it does express a certain amount of truth; but from your reading, and from the very fact of the events which were to follow in Russia, you will be aware that such unity as there was rapidly broke down in Russia.

5.5   THE FEBRUARY REVOLUTION

The February 1917 revolution was unexpected. (It took place in March, just as the October revolution took place in November, the Julian calendar being thirteen days behind the Gregorian calender used in the West.) Shortly before it Lenin in Switzerland admitted that he did not think he would live to see it. Nor did anyone else. Sukhanov, a Menshevik, who produced an eye-witness account of the revolution, wrote: 'Tuesday, February 21st. I was sitting in my office. . . . Behind a partition two typists were gossiping about food difficulties, rows in the shopping queues, unrest among the women, and an attempt to smash into some warehouse. "D'you know," suddenly declared one of these young ladies. "if you ask me, it's the beginning of the revolution!" '[1]

The revolution was a spontaneous movement of war-weary workers. It began as a riot and became a revolution when the soldiers refused to disperse the crowds and joined them instead. It was a city revolution, indeed a Petrograd revolution.

The February revolution resulted in the establishment of a provisional government. Its Prime Minister was Prince Lvov and its most energetic and most flamboyant character was Kerensky, who later became premier. But the revolution left the problem of authority unsolved. The revolution also created the Soviet of Workers' and Soldiers' Deputies.

From the very first moment the Soviet began to exercise important government functions. It was, for instance, the intention of the provisional government to allow Nicholas and his family to go to England. The Soviet decided otherwise. The government bowed to its will. It was also decided that other members of the imperial family should be confined to their estates. 'All this', Sukhanov wrote, 'was to be dictated to the provisional government for appropriate action.'[2] Even more important was the extension of the power of the Soviet. Order Number One of the Soviet of 14 March 1917 insisted on the obedience of all soldiers to orders of their officers and NCOs, but it also ordered all companies, battalions, regiments, warships, etc., to elect committees of representatives. The committees should dispose of all weapons and armaments and these were not to be given out to officers, 'even upon their demand'. Finally it stated that 'the orders of the mili-

[1] N. N. Sukhanov, *The Russian Revolution*, 1917, ed. Joel Carmichael, Oxford University Press, 1955, pp. 3–4.

[2] Ibid, p. 200.

tary commission of the State Duma are to be fulfilled only in those cases which do not contradict the orders and decisions of the Soviet of Workers' and Soldiers' Deputies'. Order Number Two gave the military committees the right to confirm commissions in the army and navy.

The Soviet concerned itself with everything. The Soviet controlled the State bank, the treasury, the mint, the printing office and, of course, all the factories. War Minister Guchkov wrote to the commander-in-chief of the army Alekseev:

The provisional government possesses no real power and its orders are executed only in so far as this is permitted by the Soviet of Workers' and Soldiers' Deputies, which holds in its hands the most important elements of actual power, such as troops, railroads, postal and telegraph communications. One may say directly that the provisional government exists only so long as it is permitted by the Soviet.
(Quoted in the Appendix to W. H. Chamberlin, *The Russian Revolution*, 2 Vols., Macmillan, 1935, Vol. I, p. 435.)

The most important problem facing both the government and the Soviet was the continuation of the war. Here opinion was sharply divided. The government was determined to continue fighting. They could hardly do otherwise. As Western-style liberals they supported the democracies of the West (joined in April 1917 by the United States) in their determination to crush the military autocratic monarchies of central Europe. The Soviet, which had a majority of Mensheviks and Socialist Revolutionaries (SRs), demanded an end to the war on the basis of no annexations and no reparations. In fact a return to the *status quo ante*. It did not, however, demand a separate peace with Germany. Unfortunately, both for the Soviet and the provisional government, the disintegration of the army, which had already begun before March, continued at a quickened pace.

It is estimated that the Tsarist authorities put fifteen and a half million men into uniform between 1914 and 1917. In March 1917 there were still nine million men in the armed forces, but their numbers rapidly decreased. Between March and November 1917 nearly a million deserted. The process of disintegration progressed at a different pace. Troops nearest to Petrograd were affected more rapidly than those farther away. The infantry was also more prone to desert than the cavalry, artillery and motorized units. But then the average infantryman was a peasant who wanted to get back to his land or the land that he hoped to acquire as a result of the revolution. The Cossacks were always the most conservative. The navy, and especially the Baltic fleet with its headquarters at Kronstadt, was the most radical. The Russian navy did little fighting. The proximity of living together had the same effect on the sailors that working together had on workmen in factories. In any case the social distinctions between naval officers and sailors were greater than those in the army. The officer corps had had very heavy losses and had been replaced by middle-class officers. The naval officers were more aristocratic and more imbued with pre-war conceptions.

Following the instructions of Order Number One of the Petrograd Soviet, committees sprang up throughout the army like mushrooms. The Minister of War, Guchkov, ordered that the committees should control the supplies of the unit, take measures in the event of abuse and exceeding of authority by responsible persons in the unit, settle differences between soldiers and officers, help in the maintenance of order and discipline and prepare for elections to the constituent assembly. In practice the committees far exceeded these duties. At the same time, in the early days they were by no means extremist. Their membership was usually in the hands of junior officers, doctors, NCOs and the more educated privates. The number of Bolsheviks was very small and the SRs predominated. Indeed, the existence of the committees probably prevented excesses which were becoming normal immediately after March.

The situation deteriorated considerably after the Kornilov revolt. The committees were now driven to the left by soldiers who felt that officers who had served the Republic were seeking to re-establish the old order. Indeed, so strong was this feeling that when a handful of Bolsheviks seized power in Petrograd in November 1917 Kerensky could find no troops to chase them out and put him back into power. An eye-witness of the post-Kornilov army has this to say:

The authority of the commanders was destroyed once for all. The masses of soldiers, seeing how a General, Commander-in-Chief, had gone against the Revolution, felt themselves surrounded by treason on all sides and saw in every man who wore epaulettes a traitor. And whoever tried to argue against this feeling also seemed a traitor.
(Chamberlin, Vol. I, pp. 236–7.)

It was not only the officers who suffered. The committees could no longer prevent the dissolution of the army. The lynching of officers became a favourite sport.

Trade unions sprang up all over the country after March, and the figure of trade union members was about $2\frac{1}{4}$ millions by the end of 1917. More radical than the trade unions were the factory committees. It was a characteristic of the revolution that the most extreme bodies were the ones most closely in touch with the masses —workers, peasants or soldiers. The first conference of factory committees, held in Petrograd in June, adopted, by an enormous majority, the Bolshevik programme of workers control. It was to these bodies that Lenin turned after the Bolsheviks had failed to seize control of the soviets.

The factory committees resisted the closing of factories and took other measures of a syndicalist nature. The Bolsheviks profited by this. At the same time Lenin was as hostile to worker participation as he was to the peasant ownership of land. Neither the peasants nor the workers were to be the beneficiaries of the revolution.

The craze to form soviets and committees of various kinds was not confined to workers or soldiers. Peasant soviets sprang up over the country and the provisional government soon authorized this development. Very soon they began to run their localities. At the end of May and the beginning of June a congress of peasant soviets was held in Petrograd. The congress was dominated by the SRs and a resolution was passed which stated that the right of private property in land was abolished. On the other hand all citizens had the right to use land. Hired labour was not permitted. This was an extremist programme but on other matters the peasants were moderate and anti-Bolshevik.

Yet the peasants, like other sections of the Russian population, became more and more left wing. The refusal of the government to deal with the agrarian question, that is to sanction the seizure of land, was resented by the peasants. Equally infuriating to the peasants were the ineffectual attempts made by the government to check agrarian disorders.

The incidence of peasant radicalism varied. It was most intense in the provinces south-east of Moscow, where there had been a considerable amount of it in 1905 too. The reason is probably that the landlords in this area had leased their land to the peasants and the aim of the peasants was now to remove a class of absentee landlords. Conversely, in those areas where landlords farmed their own land, there was less rural disorder. In spite of communist propaganda, the richer peasants, the kulaks, were as keen as the poorer ones to seize land. The countryside was also radicalized by the return of soldiers who had learnt revolutionary phrases plus a lust for disorder in the army.

One of the first acts of the Bolshevik government was to give the land to the peasants. They were soon to take it away again. But for a time it seemed that the peasant was the great beneficiary of the revolution. The large and medium-sized estates vanished. On the other hand, the very small landowner or the landless peasants benefited greatly. In many countries peasants form a vital element of conservative politics. In Russia this was not so. The encouragement of the small farmer by the government was one of the more progressive developments of the decade before the revolution, but it was of too recent a vintage to make much difference to the rural scene. The Russian peasant exploded in 1905 and in 1917 with an elemental force. As such he became a valuable ally of the Bolsheviks.

Neither the government nor the soviets could do much to improve the appalling social conditions which had caused the February revolution. In fact they got very much worse. The raging inflation continued. Although between mid-1916 and mid-1917 nominal monthly wages rose from 36 rubles to 135, the real wages, calculated on a basis of the pre-war buying power of the ruble, declined in the same period from 21·7 to 13·8 rubles. There was a shortage of corn. The harvest of 1916 was very bad and that of 1917 only a little better. It amounted in European Russia to a little less than fifty million tons, as against an average pre-war yield of over sixty-two million tons. Moreover, with the very rapid disintegration of the railway system, it was in many cases impossible to get these foodstuffs to the towns.

Figure 5   Kerensky at the time of his fall (Mansell Collection).

Although it is no doubt true that the tide of revolution flowed rapidly towards the left from March 1917 onwards there was one serious check to it. In mid-July there was a disorganized demonstration which turned into a Bolshevik attempt to seize power. There was in fact little to prevent both the government and the Soviet being overthrown. But the movement which the Bolsheviks joined rather than led was too disorganized to do so. The Bolsheviks were dispersed. Some were arrested. Others, like Lenin and Zinoviev, went into hiding in Finland.

This was an opportunity to destroy the Bolsheviks, but the government did not do so. Kerensky now became premier but, though some thought of him as a future dictator, even as the Russian Bonaparte, Kerensky was notable for his poses, his passionate but meaningless speeches, rather than for tough government. To the socialists of the Soviet the thought of suppressing a political party which was socialist was repugnant. The Bolsheviks were to display no such scruples a few months later.

The July uprising was followed, as many feared, by a right-wing counter coup. As expected it was led by a general. His name was Kornilov and his humble origins—he came from a Cossack peasant family—made him acceptable to the moderate revolutionaries also. He was described as 'a man with the heart of a lion, brains of a sheep'. Early in September Kornilov moved on Petrograd. His revolt was an even greater fiasco than were the July days. He had totally misunderstood the unalterable hostility of most of the working class or peasants to anything that looked even remotely like a restoration of the *ancien régime*. And what else could a revolt led by ex-Tsarist generals be? Railway workers refused to allow trains with Kornilov troops to proceed. The troops were surrounded by crowds of agitators who soon undermined their resolve and weakened further the links of obedience between soldiers and officers. So without bloodshed—with the exeption of the drowning of ten officers in Viborg and the shooting of four naval officers aboard a battleship, suspected of being friendly to Kornilov—the revolt collapsed.

The result of the plot was again a lurch to the left. The Petrograd Soviet passed into the control of the Bolsheviks shortly after the revolt, and on 8 October Trotsky became—as he had been in 1905—its president. The Moscow Soviet also went Bolshevik and it was soon followed by the soviets of various other industrial cities. It is interesting to note that in municipal elections in Moscow in July the Bolsheviks received eleven per cent of the votes, but fifty-one per cent in October, while the SRs and Mensheviks declined from a combined total of sixty to eighteen per cent. In Petrograd the Mensheviks were in a state of paralysis. The SRs combined so many different tendencies, from Kerensky on the right to those on the extreme left, who were prepared and did co-operate with the Bolsheviks. Nor could Kerensky depend on the old bourgeois classes and parties. It is true that there was a certain rallying of moderate forces. In the Moscow elections mentioned above they increased their voting strength from seventeen to twenty-six per cent between July and October but they and the other right-wing groups were as discredited as the generals.

In October the Soviet created a Military Revolutionary Committee whose task it was to defend the enemy in case the government abandoned it. The Committee was practically purely under Bolshevik control—the Mensheviks and SRs refusing to have anything to do with it. It soon gained control over much of the army in Petrograd. Yet the amount of force that either side had at its disposal in Petrograd was minimal: a few hundred cadets and a women's battalion on the side of the government and a rabble of soldiers and workers on the Bolshevik side, plus the inevitable Kronstadt sailors, 'the pride and beauty of the revolution'.

15.6   THE OCTOBER REVOLUTION

Lenin arrived in Petrograd on 16 April 1917 and with his arrival a new era began in the history of the Russian revolution and indeed in world history. The forces released by the revolution were controlled by Lenin and the Bolsheviks and then diverted into different channels. Lenin's programme was worked out most precisely in a long brochure published in 1903 under the title of *What is to be done?* In this Lenin was at pains to point out that socialists must work for political power and that they must not be diverted into the side lines of trade-union activity and reformism. They must not follow the heresies of the 'Economists'. In a remarkable passage Lenin stated that 'socialist consciousness cannot exist among the workers. This can be introduced only from without. The history of all countries shows that by unaided efforts the working class can only develop a trade union consciousness. . .' And the result of this is the acceptance of bourgeois capitalist society. In order to avoid such dreadful evils a highly disciplined and conspiratorial party was needed. 'The organizations of revolutionaries', wrote Lenin, 'must consist first and foremost of people whose profession is that of a revolutionary.'

In 1903 the second congress of the Russian Social Democratic party met in Brussels, but the attentions of the police soon forced it to move to London. The congress was stormy. Most of the causes of disagreement seem too trivial to have caused such passion, especially if one remembers the minute following that the

Figure 6   Lenin at parade of Ysevobach troops, Moscow, 25 May 1919 (Mansell Collection).

RUSSIAN TERRITORY
LOST AFTER THE WAR

*Figure 7   Russia 1914
and 1922, showing
territorial losses.*

party had in Russia. On some of the issues Lenin's group had a majority, especially after the Jewish socialists walked out. On the final issue of the congress, the membership of the editorial board of the party paper *Iskra*, Lenin had his way. On the base of this slender majority his group were christened the Bolsheviks—the majoritarians—and his opponents the Mensheviks—the minoritarians. Within a year the name stuck, in spite of the fact that the Bolsheviks were and remained, even in 1917, a minority in Russia.

It is estimated that just before the February revolution the Bolsheviks numbered less than 24,000. In May the party had 79,000 members, and in November about 240,000. How is it then possible that this small number could seize power in Russia and hold it? Lenin answered that under Tsarism an equally small number of landlords and industrialists ruled the country. Yet this small number of men managed to seize power in Petrograd with hardly any bloodshed. The extension of Bolshevik power to Moscow and to the rest of the country, was, however, far from bloodless. How did it happen? In broad outline, the inability of the government either to pursue the war successfully or to bring it to an end by direct negotiation with the Germans was one of the reasons. In any case there was a kind of political vacuum which the government was too weak to fill and which the soviets did not want to fill.

The type of rule that the Bolsheviks instituted was seen very clearly when the constituent assembly met in January 1918. In these, the only free elections that Russia has ever had, the moderate socialist parties, that is the Mensheviks, the SRs, and other socialist groups polled sixty-two per cent of the votes. The Bolsheviks got a mere twenty-five per cent. But this vast anti-Bolshevik majority meant little. The Bolsheviks controlled most of the large towns like Petrograd and Moscow. The constituent assembly met in a hostile city and its one and only meeting was held with armed Bolshevik troops all round. The deputies were finally asked to go home in the early hours of the morning by the commander of the guard who told them that the soldiers were tired. They decided to meet again at noon. This session never took place. The constituent assembly was dissolved. The parliament building was surrounded by troops who barred all entry. As one of the supporters of the Assembly said: 'On our side were legality, great ideals and faith in the triumph of democracy. On their side were activity, machine-guns, weapons.'

The Bolsheviks succeeded where their predecessors had failed because they fulfilled some of the yearnings of the Russians. They took Russia out of the war in March 1918, even though they had to surrender a third of European Russia to the Germans to do so. They gave land to the peasants, though the peasants were not to know that their enjoyment of the land was to be brief. They humiliated and eventually destroyed the bourgeoisie and the landlords, amidst the universal approval of the workers and peasants. They also armed themselves.

Compulsory military service was out of the question in the first period because the country was sick and tired of war. Yet there were enough men about prepared to volunteer for the Red Army, especially as this assured them of pay at a time of considerable unemployment, and some privileges. Actually the army increased in numbers rapidly and a selective form of conscription was introduced. At the end of 1918 the Red Army numbered 800,000 men, at the end of 1919 3 millions and in 1920 it numbered $5\frac{1}{2}$ millions.

Of course the figures were not as impressive as they sounded. According to Soviet figures there were nearly 3 million deserters in the years 1919 and 1920. In any case the fighting value of many of these troops was extremely low and they were badly armed. They certainly could not stand up to organized forces like the German, Austrian or Turkish armies. Even the 70,000 Czechoslovak troops were superior to any Bolshevik force. The Bolshevik Red Army was reasonably effective in fighting the Whites but then the Whites had the same kind of problems of organization and armament as the Reds.

Trotsky, who was the architect of the Red Army, saw the need for officers. The training of officers began immediately but there was going to be a gap of some years during which the Red Army would have no militarily expert corps of officers. Trotsky, in spite of criticism, used old Tsarist officers. In the two years between the summer of 1918 and the summer of 1920 nearly 50,000 Tsarist officers were taken into the Red Army. Another 40,000 were produced in crash courses by the new military academies, and many more thousands had been NCOs in the old army.

Next to the army the most important weapon was the *Cheka*—the All-Russian Extraordinary Commission for Fighting Counter-Revolution and Espionage. It was founded in 1917 and headed by the Polish Communist Dzerzhinsky. It was the Cheka that inaugurated the Red Terror. Its aim was to destroy all opponents of the regime. It was also calculated that the mass killings of opponents would have a salutary effect on the bourgeoisie and would strike terror in the hearts of workers and peasants too, thus making them more subservient to the regime and more prepared to carry out its orders. It seems nearly that the Tsarina's advice to the Tsar that the Russian people like the whip was not all that wrong.

Thus, when the head of the Petrograd Cheka was killed and Lenin wounded, 500 persons were shot in reprisal. The numbers that were killed directly by the Cheka or by other Red units will never be known. It cannot be doubted that the Terror formed an important element in the Bolshevik success. It also had an unfortunate effect. The use of terror was never abandoned by the Soviet regime. It is sometimes believed, and Khrushchev gave credence to this myth at the twentieth party congress in February 1956, that terror began with Stalin, with the murder of Kirov at the end of 1934. Nothing could be further from the truth. The imprisonment and killing of real and imagined opponents began under Lenin. A further element was of course the importance of the Cheka itself and in particular of its head. It was a privileged group in the State, and its head eventually became, next to the party secretary, the most important and powerful State official.

5.7 'WAR COMMUNISM' 1917–20

The building of communism, combined with perpetual warfare from 1917 to 1920, resulted in a development of the system known as war communism. 'The essence of a war communism', Lenin admitted, 'was that we actually took from the peasant all his surpluses and sometimes not only his surpluses but part of the grain the peasant needed for food. We took this in order to meet the requirements of the army and to sustain the workers.'[1]

There is little doubt that the compulsory requisitioning of agricultural produce saved the Bolshevik regime from defeat. Yet the inevitable price was the estrangement of the peasantry. Forced at gunpoint to hand over their surpluses and denied the compensation of badly needed consumer goods, the villagers responded in predictable fashion. In 1920 it was estimated that more than a third of the total harvest was successfully hidden from the government's collection teams. The peasants, moreover, began to till only enough land to meet their own needs, so that by the end of 1920 the amount of sown acreage in European Russia was three-fifths of the 1913 figure. At the same time the requisitioning rekindled the struggle between Russia's peasants and the city-based government. There were serious risings against the government. In February 1921 the Cheka reported 118 separate peasant risings. Full-scale military campaigns had to be waged against them. One of the partisan movements numbered some 50,000 men. In one single district of western Siberia the guerrillas numbered 60,000.

The situation in the towns was even worse. By the end of 1920 total industrial output had shrunk to about a fifth of the 1913 level. The production of coal was only a quarter, and of oil a third, of the 1913 figure. Cast-iron production had dropped to less than three per cent and the production of copper had all but ceased. Hence many factories had to close down or greatly reduce their working time. The allied blockade, not lifted till 1920, prevented any foreign trade. The railroad system was nearly destroyed. At the end of 1919 there were only a quarter of a million freight cars, while there had been over half a million in January 1917. Before the revolution there had been 20,394 locomotives (of which 16·5 per cent were unfit for use). At the end of 1919 there were only 8,955 left (of which 47·8 per cent were unfit for use).

The shortage of food reached famine-like proportions in the towns and, if it had not been for the flourishing black market which the authorities attempted to suppress by the usual methods of terror, many in the towns would actually have died of starvation. There was a shortage of fuel and people literally froze to death in unheated flats. Anything that could burn was burnt, including abandoned wooden houses. Typhus and cholera swept the cities. Only by escaping to the country could many save themselves. Petrograd lost two-thirds of its population and Mos-

[1] V. I. Lenin, *Polnoe sobranie sochinenii*, 55 Vols., Moscow, 1958–65, Vol. 43, p. 219.

cow a half. There was no point staying in the towns without food, fuel or work. For the Soviet government, ruling as it did in the name of the industrial proletariat, the situation was fraught with dangerous implications. It diluted the social basis of Bolshevik authority and the renewed contacts between workers and peasants served to heighten existing popular tensions.

Another major grievance was the militarization of labour. Trotsky, flushed with the victories of the Red Army which he had created sought to use its example in the factories. All able-bodied adults had to work and women celebrated their new equality with men by sewing underwear for the Red Army. Whole detachments of the Red Army were used as labour armies and set such tasks as building roads, etc. An attempt was made to reinforce labour discipline by posting soldiers in factories. One of the Kronstadt revolutionaries said in 1921 that the factories of Petrograd looked more like the prisons of Tsarist days.

The syndicalist slogan of workers control was soon abandoned by the Bolsheviks. Beginning in June 1918 factories were taken out of workers' control and by the end of 1920 about eighty per cent of the large factories were State-owned and nationalization had been extended to small factories and shops. There was plenty of opposition even within the Communist party, but the Workers' Opposition, as it was known, could not get the party to change its policy. What did make it change its policy was the revolt of the Kronstadt sailors in March 1921— the very men who had helped the Bolsheviks to come to power in 1917. Policies were then put into reverse and the New Economic Policy was introduced.

15.8   GERMANY AUGUST 1914–JULY 1917

The suffering of the Russian people in the years 1917–20 is one of the tragedies of our time, now largely forgotten, at least outside Russia. No estimate can be made of the numbers that died. In spite of all adverse circumstances the Bolsheviks triumphed. They survived the blockade; they drove out the allied interventionist forces though the efforts of these forces were at best half-hearted; they defeated the White armies, which at one time converged on Moscow, the new capital, from all directions; they overcame the national governments which had sprung up in the non-Russian areas. They failed to reconquer the territories lost in the west but at one time the Red Armies reached the outskirts of Warsaw.

On 4 August 1914 the Reichstag voted for war credits. The socialists voted for them too. There were very good reasons for this. The original resistance to war vanished in the three or four days before the actual outbreak. The SPD deputies saw around them the enthusiasm of the masses for the war. They realized that the future of the party was at stake. If they opposed the war it was likely that they would be swept away as a political force—not to speak of the fact that many of them would land in prison. In such an eventuality the aims of German socialism, that is, the democratization of Germany, would be put off for many years.

Secondly, the German socialists saw the war primarily as a war against Russian imperialism. Ever since 1848 European socialists, liberals and radicals regarded Russia, with justification, as the most oppressive and obscurantist government in Europe. Engels, in an article in 1892, had argued that every German socialist should take up arms against Russia and its allies. A defeat of Germany would be a defeat of socialism. The part played by the Russian danger in influencing German left-wing opinion was as decisive as the part played by the violation of Belgian neutrality in influencing British opinion.

Figure 8   Hindenburg, Kaiser Wilhelm and Ludendorff at Army Headquarters, 1914 (Staatsbibliothek Berlin. Preussischer Kulturbesitz Bildarchiv).

On the face of it, such a changed attitude had much significance. The Kaiser announced that he no longer knew parties, only Germans. The SPD, which had previously been treated as a party opposed to the whole concept of the German Reich and which had been politically and socially ostracized, was now included in the nation. In fact the SPD gained very little. In France and Britain socialist ministers entered the governments. This did not happen in Germany until October 1918. By voting for war credits the SPD gave its support to the government and identified itself with its aims. The whole political situation in Germany was frozen for the duration of the war. This meant that the *status quo*, that is, a situation very inimical both to socialism and democracy, could not be changed until after the war. As time went on, it struck a number of observers that it would not be changed even afterwards, if Germany were victorious.

Among all the belligerents the army remained in a subordinate position to the political leadership. Germany was the only exception. An important stage in this process occurred on 29 August 1916. On that day the Emperor, bowing to the pressure of public opinion, dismissed General v. Falkenhayn from army command and replaced him by Field Marshal v. Hindenburg, who brought with him to headquarters General Ludendorff as First Quartermaster General. Hindenburg and Ludendorff were the heroes of the great victories on the eastern front and as such their popularity among Germans was immense. It was natural to believe that if victory were ever to be achieved the Hindenburg and Ludendorff team would achieve it and no one else. It was also well known that the abler of the two, and the real architect of victory, was Ludendorff. Yet the prestige of Hindenburg was greater and in any case the two generals worked harmoniously together.

The changeover from Falkenhayn to Hindenburg–Ludendorff brought about a complete change both in the military and political leadership of the Reich. The supreme command of the German army had been vested in the Emperor as War Lord. In theory the Emperor, in giving his commands, relied on the advice of the chief of staff, at first the younger Moltke and then Falkenhayn. The chief of the General Staff was responsible to the Emperor for the execution of the imperial commands and for the proper administration of the army. The Emperor could deprive the chief of staff of his office and replace him by someone else. Ludendorff, as chief Quartermaster General, shared with Hindenburg full responsibility for military operations. Thus the Kaiser now had two chiefs of staff. In fact he was pushed more and more into the background. Hindenburg became, in all but name, supreme commander and Ludendorff his chief of staff. Ludendorff, as he had done on the eastern front, drew up the plans to which Hindenburg lent his authority.

The basis of Ludendorff's authority was the implicit faith that the German citizen and soldier had in him. There was thus a popular element in his authority. He exploited the situation by an interpretation of the relationship between himself and the Kaiser and government. He spoke much of his 'responsibility'. Thus, for example, when the Chancellor pursued a policy which Ludendorff disliked or judged to be unwise, he declared that he could not assume the 'responsibility' for such a policy and proffered his resignation. If Ludendorff proffered his resignation Hindenburg did likewise. As neither the Kaiser nor the government could do without the two generals it was the Chancellor, and not they, who resigned.

Such an attitude was not confined to military affairs. Thus, when in January 1918 a German general expressed views to the Emperor on the future German–Polish frontier, Hindenburg wrote to the Kaiser informing him that the general in question bore no 'responsibility' in the Polish question and that the incident caused pain to 'General Ludendorff and myself', and that it had shown 'that Your Majesty disregards our opinion in a matter of vital importance for the existence of the German Fatherland'. Needless to say, the Kaiser had to give way.

The Chancellor, Bethmann-Hollweg, was dismissed in July 1917, not because the Reichstag had lost confidence in him, or because the Kaiser had lost confidence in him, but because Ludendorff had done so. His successor Michaelis, a total nonentity, was appointed because Ludendorff approved of him. Michaelis was in fact a disappointment to everyone. His successor, the aged Count Hertling, regarded himself as the representative of the army.

Approval was given to or withdrawn from ministers. The Foreign Secretary Kühlmann was dismissed after he had made a speech which did not meet with the generals' approval. In the peace negotiations with the Bolsheviks and the Ukraine the supreme command was represented and the peace was largely dictated by it.

The interference of Ludendorff extended even to the immediate entourage of the Emperor. In January 1918 he demanded that the chief of the Kaiser's civil secretariat be dismissed. His wishes were complied with. Indeed, any question of internal policy which had bearing on the military situation was subject to the approval or disapproval of Ludendorff.

The supremacy of Ludendorff was politically disastrous. Determined to subordinate everything to the successful prosecution of the war, the army command gave its approval to unrestricted submarine warfare which did not bring England to her knees, but added the United States to the enemies of Germany. The German high command also agreed with the annexationist and reactionary views of the German industrialists. They demanded vast annexations both in Europe and Africa. Belgium was to be brought into political dependence on Germany, the northern coast of France was to be annexed and so was the important coal and iron area of Briey-Longwy. In the east, the Baltic area, Finland, Poland and the Ukraine were to be separated from Russia. This was to give Germany the economic sufficiency that she needed and German capital a large field for its endeavour. The German generals, Falkenhayn, Hindenburg, Ludendorff all agreed with these aims. There is no need to see in this any particular community of interest between German industry and the German officer corps. The generals wanted the same territories in order to achieve security 'for all imaginable time'.

Moreover, both the German industrialists and the Junkers and the army were determined to oppose the democratization of Germany. They knew that an unsuccessful war would result in such democratization and that it could only be prevented by victory, which would enhance the prestige of the German military–industrial–landlord complex. The army would in the case of democratization lose its privileged position, the officers their prestigious place in society, and the semi-feudal relationship between the army and the War Lord would be broken. It is true that the officer corps changed very radically in the war. Many of the old regular officers were killed in the first year of the war. Of the Prussian contingent in the peacetime army of 22,000 officers and 30,000 reserve officers, 5,600 regulars and 7,600 reservists were killed by 15 November 1915. Indeed, for the whole German army the regulars of 1914 amounted to only one-twelfth of the total number of officers at the end of the war. Hence officers had to be found among the middle classes too. It was noted that elementary school teachers made particularly good officers. But these important changes did not in fact weaken the conservative outlook of the army. The senior officers were, without exception, regular officers. Moreover, in the latter part of the war the regulars were withdrawn more and more from the front in order that they should form the nucleus of a new post-war army.

Figure 9   Wilhelm Groener (1867–1939) (Staatsbibliothek Berlin. Preussischer Kulturbesitz Bildarchiv).

Pressure for democratization, and for a way out of the war, built up in spite of the supremacy of Ludendorff. The Russian February revolution intensified this pressure. A socialist asked the Chancellor whether he intended to postpone reforms until such time as the workers had begun 'to speak Russian'. General Groener, who was to succeed Ludendorff as Quartermaster General at the end of the war, frequently expressed the belief that the process of democratization could not be put off for ever. The course of wise statesmanship was to learn to steer the democratic movement into paths which were non-revolutionary.

Moreover, German socialism was no longer united in its support for the war. Every time a new war credits bill was placed before the Reichstag the number of socialists who abstained or voted against it increased. By the spring of 1916 German social democracy had split, in fact, though not yet formally, into three groups. The majority was still prepared to continue its support of the government until the moment of victory. A large minority, which claimed it would support Germany in a defensive war, was unhappy about a war which seemed to be imperialistic. These anti-war socialists included not only left-wingers. Many revisionist socialists, like Bernstein, were to be found in their ranks. On the other hand, basing themselves on the internationalist platform of pre-war European socialism, the left tended to gravitate towards this group. To the left of them was a small group of internationalists whose inspiration were the two anti-war socialist conferences in Switzerland, at Zimmerwald and Kienthal. They wanted to turn the war from a struggle between two sets of capitalist powers into a class war. The German Communist party originated from this group. Its two leaders were Rosa Luxemburg and Karl Liebknecht, both of whom spent much of the war in prison. They acquired the name Spartacist, after the leader of the slave revolt in Rome.

The final split occurred at a congress of the anti-war dissidents held in Gotha on Good Friday 1917. It was in Gotha that a united socialist party had been founded forty-two years before and it was ironic that in the same city it should split. The dissidents, feeling that the majority had betrayed the principles of socialism, formed the Independent Social Democratic Party (USPD). The aim of the Spartacists was to remain within the fold of the Independents, and when the time was ripe to break up the party.

It seemed in July 1917 that Germany was on the threshold of a democratic regime and also of the end of the war. Matthias Erzberger, one of the leaders of the Catholic Centre party, called upon the Reichstag to pass a resolution calling for a negotiated peace on the basis of no annexations. His speech had an immediate effect. An inter-party committee was set up, composed of all the political parties with the exception of the right and left extremes, to draft such a resolution. It did more than this. It called for the introduction of a democratic franchise in Prussia and the admission of prominent deputies to executive positions in the Reich and Prussian governments. On 19 July, by 212 to 126 votes, the peace resolution was passed. The new Chancellor, Michaelis, accepted it with the fatal emendation 'as I interpret it'. The Germans argued in March 1918 that the terms of the Treaty of Brest-Litovsk were not contrary to the resolution on the grounds that Germany was not annexing territory, simply liberating non-Russian territory from Russia.

Figure 10   Karl Liebknecht (1871–1919) in 1919 (Staatsbibliothek Berlin. Preussischer Kulturbesitz Bildarchiv).

Figure 11   Rosa Luxemburg in 1919 (Staatsbibliothek Berlin. Preussischer Kulturbesitz Bildarchiv).

74

Exercise 3

Shortly after the outbreak of war in August 1914, a German socialist deputy stated:

We stand today before the brutal fact of war, and the terrible threat of enemy invasion. The decision to be made is not whether to take sides for or against the war but rather on the means necessary for the defence of our country. Our heartiest wishes go out to our brethren, irrespective of party affiliations, who are called to the colours. Much if not all would be lost to our people and its future independence in the event of a victory for Russian despotism.

Quoted in K. S. Pinson, *Modern Germany*, Macmillan, 1955, p. 314.

Question 1

Comment on this passage as an example of German socialist attitudes, and explain these attitudes.

Specimen Answer

The statement is very typical of the majority of German socialists, who, despite their theoretical opposition to all 'capitalist wars' before 1914, in fact swung enthusiastically behind the German war effort. Once war had begun, the appeal to 'the defence of our country' was always a strong one. Harry Hanak gives two explanations of the change in attitude. First, that socialism as a political force would be destroyed if it did not accommodate to the national effort; and second, and this is brought out strongly in the last sentence of the passage quoted, the socialists saw the war primarily as a war against Russian imperialism.

5.9   GERMANY IN 1917

From the point of view of economic self-sufficiency Germany was in a poor position in 1917. Before the war the German Reich imported a quarter of its foodstuffs. The calling up of men for the army removed from agriculture much of its labour force. Food became expensive in spite of the attempt of the government to fix prices. Bread rationing was introduced in January 1915 and virtually all foodstuffs were rationed by the autumn of the same year. There was a shortage of potatoes, due largely to the transport difficulties. The shortage of animal feeding stuffs resulted in a considerable reduction of the German food and meat supply. Indeed, matters might have deteriorated even further had not a War Food Office been created in May 1916 with the duty to act as a dictator in all questions relating to the production of food. In spite of this the winter of 1916–17, the 'turnip winter', was particularly hard. The ration for an adult was reduced to 1,900 grams of bread, 2,500 grams of potatoes, 80 grams of butter, 250 grams of meat, 180 grams of sugar and half an egg per week.

Industry, like agriculture, was equally hit. The trouble was that all economic calculations were based on the likelihood of a short war. Coal and iron were in sufficient supply and were indeed increased by the exploitation of the coal and iron mines of Belgium and northern France. But virtually all other metals had to be imported from abroad and in the case of copper nine-tenths of it came from America. There was a shortage of textiles and the material used for military uniforms rapidly decreased in quality. Sulphur, nitrates, rubber and oil, had all to be imported. Substitutes were found, in particular for nitrates. The oil supply was also improved after the defeat of Rumania in 1916.

The bad economic conditions, combined with the hopes raised by the Russian revolution, produced the inevitable strikes. About 300,000 men went on strike in Berlin, Leipzig, Magdeburg, Halle and Brunswick in 1917. In Leipzig the strikers established a workers' council. This was the first time that such a council had been formed and it showed the influence of the Russian revolution. Hopes for an early peace were raised by the participation of all three socialist groups in the Stockholm Socialist conference to which the Russians also came. The socialists of the other allied countries were prevented from coming by their own governments. The lengthy negotiations for a peace with the Bolsheviks which had begun after the Russo-German armistice of 15 December 1917 further inflamed the situation. The refusal of the German military leaders to accept Trotsky's formula of 'neither war nor peace' was condemned by the Independents and the Spartacists. The strike wave of January 1918 which began in Vienna and Budapest and spread to Germany was the direct result of shortage of food and disappointment at the lack of success achieved in negotiating with the Russians. The strike was not led by any of the socialist groups but by shop stewards who in this way protested against the pro-government attitude of the trade-union leadership.

15.10   THE GERMAN 'REVOLUTION' OF 1918

In the spring of 1918 the Germans attempted to repeat their Russian triumphs on the Western front. At first the offensive which began at the beginning of March was successful but soon ground to a halt and in July Foch counter-attacked. By August the allies had broken through the German lines. Ludendorff and Hindenburg were not yet prepared to concede defeat. Indeed, as late as July, when Ludendorff was asked by the Foreign Minister whether he was certain of finally and decisively defeating the enemy, he answered that he was. Even a month later Ludendorff, though admitting that the German army was no longer capable of a great offensive, still maintained that he could force the allies to sue for peace by a skilful defensive policy. In September Ludendorff and Hindenburg announced to the Kaiser, the Chancellor and the Foreign Secretary that the war was lost. Ludendorff went further than this. He demanded the reconstitution of the government on a broader basis. Thus he inaugurated a revolution from above. Hertling resigned and the first parliamentary government of imperial Germany was headed by a south German prince and a relative of the Kaiser, Prince Max of Baden. His political adviser was Dr Kurt Hahn, who after 1933 founded Gordonstoun School in Scotland. Prince Max appointed two socialist to his government, Bauer and Scheidemann, and three members of the Centre, Trimborn, Grober and Erzberger.

On 29 October, when it had become obvious that Germany had lost the war, the navy, which apart from the submarines had not challenged the allies since the battle of Jutland, received orders to sail. The sailors had no intention of dying for a cause that everyone knew was lost. On 4 November the navy in Kiel mutinied. There had, in fact, been a minor mutiny a year previous to this. Indeed, the most characteristic aspect of the central and east European revolutions was the naval mutinies. Russian sailors mutinied on the battleship *Potemkin* in 1905, the Austrians in the Bay of Cattaro in 1918, the Russians in the naval base at Kronstadt in 1917 and again, but this time against the Bolsheviks, in 1921. The mutineers, aware of the Russian example, immediately set up a sailors' council. The government sent a Social Democratic deputy, Gustav Noske, to Kiel and he soon gained control over the council.

Figure 12   Gustav Noske
(1868–1946) in 1919
(Staatsbibliothek Berlin.
Preussischer Kulturbesitz
Bildarchiv).

Within a matter of days councils were established in many German cities. In nearly every case they made themselves responsible for law and order. The powers that be rapidly accommodated themselves to the new situation. In Cologne the mayor, Konrad Adenauer, put rooms in the town hall at the disposal of the soldiers' and workers' council.

Berlin lagged somewhat behind the other centres of revolution. Ebert and many of the Majority Socialists were prepared to accept a constitutional monarchy or alternatively they wanted the German people, as represented in a new parliament, to decide the issue. It was clear, however, that the Kaiser himself would have to abdicate. He showed much reluctance to do so and only after General Groener had carried out a kind of opinion poll among senior officers was he persuaded that the army could not be relied upon to march on Berlin led by the Kaiser. Meanwhile, the ministers in Berlin had got tired of waiting. Or to put it more precisely, if they wanted to keep control of the situation, and not go the way of their counterparts in Russia, they would have to move to the left. On 9 November Prince Max announced that the Kaiser had abdicated—he had not—and handed over the premiership to the Majority Socialist Ebert. 'Herr Ebert,' the Prince said, 'I commit the German Empire to your keeping.' 'I have lost two sons for this Empire', answered Ebert proudly. Meanwhile, the Socialist minister Scheidemann, eating his watery soup in the Reichstag building, was told that Liebknecht was about to proclaim a Soviet Republic. Scheidemann acted quickly. As he himself wrote later he had no intention that Germany should become a Russian province. 'I saw the Russian madness in front of my eyes, the replacement of the Tsarist terror regime by the Bolshevik one.' From a window of the Reichstag he made a speech to the soldiers and citzens of Berlin and ended it with the words, 'Long live the German Republic'. Then he went back to finish his soup. Ebert, as he recounts, was furious.

From that moment on, the moderates held the initiative. A government was formed and given the suitably revolutionary title of the Council of People's Commissioners: the Majority Socialists were represented by Ebert, Landsberg and Scheidemann; the Independents by Haase, Dittman and Barth. Next day a meeting of the soldiers' and workers' councils elected an executive council in which both socialist groups were equally represented. It also 'elected' the government, that is, the already existing Council of People's Commissioners. Indeed, its only vaguely revolutionary action was to send fraternal greetings to the Soviet Government, expressing its 'admiration for the Russian workers and soldiers who have opened the path to revolution'.

One of the main reasons for the failure of the German revolution was the efforts made to preserve the army. It was, of course, quite natural that the Generals should seek to preserve it. It was a little more surprising that Ebert should accept the old imperial army. On 10 November Groener, the new Quartermaster General, telephoned Ebert and told him that he and Hindenburg placed themselves at the disposal of the government but only on condition that the government combated Bolshevism. As Groener made clear later, by the term Bolshevism he meant also the soldiers' and workers' councils. From that time on Groener kept in touch with Ebert by telephone every night.

The connexion had far-reaching implications. 'We hoped through our actions,' Groener explained, 'to secure for the army and the officer corps part of the power in the new state; if we succeeded in this, then the best and strongest elements of the old Prussia were saved for the new Germany, in spite of the revolution.'

In accepting the help of the army Ebert was not simply hoping to avoid being the German Kerensky. The German high command evacuated its troops rapidly behind the Rhine. Indeed, the withdrawal was carried out with an efficiency that everyone had come to expect of the German army. Allied officers were impressed. In some cases the Germans withdrew so rapidly that the forward allied columns lost contact with them and simply came upon the neatly piled-up weapons that the Germans had left behind in accordance with the armistice agreement. It was clear to Ebert as it was clear to most soldiers that an orderly return to Germany was only possible under the army command. The soldiers' councils could cause disorder but not withdraw the army. All the six commissioners, including the three Independents, agreed that army discipline must be maintained on the retreat otherwise thousands of Germans would be made prisoners of war. All of them signed an order on 12 November which conceded to the soldiers' councils an advisory role only.

Yet the regular army was soon to receive a severe blow. On 23 December the People's Naval Division—one is reminded of the Kronstadt sailors—a rowdy, ill-disciplined group, had kidnapped a Majority Socialist who was in charge of the defence of Berlin. The army moved in and the sailors, after suffering heavy losses, asked for a truce in order to conclude arrangements for their surrender. Meanwhile, a huge crowd gathered round the soldiers. The soldiers melted away. In any case it was Christmas Eve and everyone went home. Even the Spartacists celebrated Christmas.

There was, however, no second German revolution. There was no German November. On 29 December the Communist Party of Germany was founded. Karl Radek, sent from Russia, was there. He told the hundred delegates that 'when the news of the German revolution reached us a veritable tumult of joy seized the working class of Russia . . . which knows well that without a socialist revolution in Germany it would not have sufficient strength to build anew on the ruins of capitalism'. Karl Liebknecht, a superb agitator and speaker but a poor organizer, saw himself as the leader of a Bolshevik revolution. Radek was less certain and so was Rosa Luxemburg, who urged the delegates to realize that the time was not ripe and that the comparisons made with Petrograd were false.

Tension came to a head on 6 January. The police chief in Berlin, Eichhorn, was an Independent with Spartacist tendencies and he infiltrated Spartacists into the police force. Ebert dismissed him on 4 January but Eichhorn refused to budge. A vast crowd turned up outside the police headquarters. Meanwhile, a large group of left Independents, revolutionary shop stewards and communists gathered within the building—including Liebknecht and Wilhelm Pieck, who became the head of the East German State after 1945. Impressed by the revolutionary mood of the crowd outside, they decided to call a general strike and to overthrow the government. In supporting the uprising Liebknecht was in fact going contrary to the decisions of the party, whose programme was relentless agitation among the workers. However, at first all went well. On 6 and 7 January workers occupied most of Berlin; and having done so did not know what to do next. There was no organization, no plan. A communist paper reported later:

The masses were standing from nine in the morning in the cold and fog. Somewhere their leaders were sitting and conferring. The fog lifted and the masses were still standing. Their leaders conferred. Noon came, and in addition to the cold, hunger came. And the leaders conferred. The masses were feverish with excitement. They wanted one deed, even one word to calm their excitement. But nobody knew what to say, because the leaders were conferring. The fog came again and with it the dusk. The masses went home sad.

(Gustav Noske, *Von Kiel bis Kapp.—Zur Geschichte der deutschen Revolution*, Berlin, 1920, pp. 69–70.)

It was easy under these circumstances for the energetic Noske from his headquarters in a girls' school in fashionable Dahlem—one thinks of Lenin in the Smolny, also a girls' school—to summon the Freikorps to Berlin. They acted with maximum efficiency and maximum brutality. The amateur revolution was suppressed. Rosa Luxemburg and Liebknecht were found some days later and murdered.

This was not the end of the Berlin revolution. Leo Jogiches, chairman of the German Communist party, sought to bring down the government not by an armed uprising—the Freikorps were too strong for this—but by a general strike. The Berlin strike of early March 1919 was successful but the communists had so little control over the workers that they could not prevent them resorting again to arms. The Freikorps moved in again and 1,200 were killed.

There were risings, fighting and much bloodshed in many parts of Germany and especially in some north German cities, in the Ruhr and in Saxony. It was in Bavaria especially that the revolutionary movement took the most extreme form, culminating in the establishment of a Bavarian council or Soviet Republic. The hero of the Bavarian revolution was Kurt Eisner. He was neither a Catholic nor a Bavarian but a Berliner and a Jew. This by itself made his leadership of the Bavarian revolution curious. He was not a Spartacist but an Independent and not particularly left wing at that. After a demonstration and meeting on 7 November 1918 in Munich, Eisner proclaimed a Bavarian republic and announced that power had passed into the hands of the Council of Workers' and Soldiers' and Peasants' Deputies. A coalition as in Berlin was created except that, unlike in Berlin, the Majority Socialists were in a minority. The Majority leader Erhard Auer became Minister of the Interior. One of the peculiarities of the Bavarian revolution was the support of some peasants. The Council movement spread among the peasants like wildfire and there were soon 3,555 of them. But agricultural workers were very weakly represented on them. The peasants owned land and one reason for the rapid sprouting of these councils was to prevent workers from the towns creating them. The councils were an interesting example of direct rule by the peasants. Yet they remained largely passive.

Eisner's eccentric rule was short. In the elections of 12 January 1919 his party, the Independents, got 86,000 votes (2.5 per cent and the Bavarian Peasant League which co-operated with him 310,000 votes (9.1 per cent). The Majority Socialists gained 33 per cent of the votes and the Catholic Bavarian People's party 35 per cent. For a few more weeks Eisner clung to his office. On 21 February, with his resignation in his pocket, Eisner set out to the Parliament to hand it in. He was murdered by Count Arco-Valley. An hour later, Auer, having just finished paying tribute to the dead Prime Minister, was shot in the parliament chamber by a butcher's apprentice.

Eisner was given a vast funeral procession. The workers went on a three-day strike. A new government was formed but had to flee to Nuremberg. A group of idealistic Independents led by the poet Ernst Toller, the playwright Erich Mühsam and the translator of Shakespeare, Gustav Landauer, formed a government to carry on the traditions of Eisner. They proclaimed a Republic of Councils on 6 April, very largely under the influence of the events in Hungary where a Council or Soviet Republic under Bela Kun had been established. Indeed, the plan for a union of Hungary, Austria and Bavaria was the aim of some of these men. In fact the first Bavarian Council Republic was a joke and lasted six days. Its Foreign Minister Lipp telegraphed Lenin to say that the Majority Socialist Premier had fled and taken the key of the ministerial lavatory with him.

Figure 13   Kurt Eisner (1867–1919) in 1919 (Staatsbibliothek Berlin. Preussischer Kulturbesitz Bildarchiv).

Their successors were authentic communists—but they were not the authorized representatives of the German Communist Party, which was still trying to reconstruct itself from the wreckage of the March uprising. It was impossible for the Bavarian counter-government in Nuremberg to subdue Munich. They had to call on the Reich authorities and Noske was generous in providing Freikorps. He even provided a 'Bavarian' Freikorps under Ritter von Epp. The Freikorps burst into Munich on 1 May, the day on which Lenin was telling an immense crowd in Red Square that the working class was celebrating May Day together with the Hungarian and Bavarian Soviet Republics. By 3 May Munich had been taken and then began the customary white terror.

As early as January 1919 elections were held to elect 423 members of the National Assembly. The Majority Socialists won 39 per cent of the votes and were thus by far the 'largest party. The USPD got only 22 seats to the SPD's 163. The Centre got 91. The old Progressives, now known as Democrats, got 75. There was also a resurgence of the right. Streseman's German People's Party had done badly but the old Conservatives, now known as the German National Party, got 44 seats. These results illustrated the moderation of the German electorate and its reluctance to countenance radical experiments. The Russian electorate had also shown its moderation but the Russian elections were held after, not before the Bolshevik revolution.

The failure of the second German revolution was also due to the fact that the government—from which the Independents soon resigned—was able to arm itself. The army could not be trusted to shoot down German workers but the Freikorps could. They were military formations raised by individual officers and often bearing their name whose task it was to protect Germany's frontiers in the east and to combat the internal enemy. The first were formed in December 1918 and by the end of January 1919 there were 130 of them and their number continued to increase. In the Baltic area they co-operated with the Whites against the Bolsheviks, with the approval of the British. After Noske, the Defence Minister, had shown off his troops to Ebert on 4 January the government sanctioned them five days later.

In using them against the left-wing rebels the government was using the only reliable military force at its disposal. Yet the Freikorps had views that were very different from those of Ebert, Noske and Scheidemann. This was shown in March 1920. Kapp, an obscure nationalist civil servant, together with General v. Lüttwitz, took Berlin at the head of Freikorps detachments. The government fled to Dresden. General Seeckt, commander of the army in succession to Hindenburg and Groener told the government bluntly that he would not defend the Republic. 'Troops do not fire on troops.' He withdrew to his flat and waited to see what would happen. What did happen was more laughable than serious. Kapp as Chancellor and Lüttwitz as army chief did not carry conviction. Even the head of the State bank refused to hand over the cash which the new Chancellor demanded. When one of the Freikorps leaders was asked why he did not just take it, he answered, 'What do you think I am, a bank robber?' The main reason for the failure of the putsch was, however, the general strike which Karl Legien, chairman of the largest German trade-union organization, called. Twelve million workers, white-collar employees and even civil servants went on strike. The putsch was soon over. As Seeckt was to say three years later, 'No one can make a putsch in Germany except I'.

Even after the Freikorps were dissolved they represented an actively disloyal element to the republic. It is hardly surprising that most of the men who had served in them eventually found their way into Hitler's SA.

An important element in the survival of the 'old Germany' was the continuation of its army, even though limited by the Treaty of Versailles to 100,000 men. The Germans accepted the myth that the German army had not been defeated in a battle, but it had withdrawn from occupied territory to Germany undefeated. What had then happened, that is, the dictate of Versailles, had only taken place because the German army had been stabbed in the back by socialists, communists and Jews. Even Ebert welcomed the home-coming troops to Berlin as men unvanquished in battle.

In 1919 parliament set up a committee to inquire into the war and especially the question of war guilt and the reasons for Germany's defeat. They invited Hindenburg, now in retirement, to give evidence. Hindenburg answered none of the

*Figure 14   Generaloberst
von Seeckt (1866–1936)
(Staatsbibliothek Berlin.
Preussischer Kulturbesitz
Bildarchiv).*

questions posed to him but instead read a prepared statement in which, basing himself on the supposed words of an English general, he said that the German army
had been stabbed in the back. Nobody has ever discovered who this English general
was. In any case Hindenburg in his war memoirs, published in September 1919,
had also spoken of the German army being stabbed in the back in the same way that
Siegfried had been stabbed in the back by Hagen. The stab-in-the-back legend
became accepted dogma among all nationalists.

The army was small but imbued with the ideas that had led Germany to war in
1914. It was supported by the men who had served in the Freikorps and who
were always prepared to take up their task again. The bureaucracy and judiciary
were equally nationalistic and in some cases disloyal to the republic. In 1925
the German people elected the aged Marshall Hindenburg to the presidency,
although he received a million votes less than the two candidates who opposed him.
Still, nearly half of the German electorate looked firmly backwards.

This does not mean that the collapse of Weimar was inevitable or that the rise of
Hitler to power was inevitable. The German revolution pointed the road to a democratic Germany. Many Germans did not take the road.

15.11   CONCLUSIONS

Russia went through two revolutions and a long civil war. In Germany, there was,
as one historian put it, 'a change of guard rather than a revolution'. The reasons
for this contrast should be obvious from what has been said.

Djilas records that Stalin once compared the Germans to sheep. 'I remember also,'
Stalin said, 'when I was in Germany before the Revolution: a group of German
Social Democrats came late to the Congress because they had to wait to have their
tickets confirmed, or something of the sort. When would Russians ever do that?

Someone has said well: "In Germany you cannot have a revolution because you would have to step on the lawns." '

Stalin's impromptu views need not be taken very seriously but certainly the Germans living in a state which prized discipline highly and where the rule of law was respected, showed less revolutionary fervour than did the Russians. But there are other reasons to be considered.

The inability of the Russian provisional government to fight the war successfully or to bring it to a speedy conclusion brought revolution. In Germany the army remained intact till the end of the war. Every German soldier was dependent on his officers during the period of withdrawal from the fronts. In Germany the trains ran on time and the German soldier was brought quickly home. Again the Russian army lost the loyalty of the soldiers during 1916 and was unable to re-establish new links of loyalty between the men and their officers after the February Revolution. The Russian army was an unsuccessful army. The German army was successful, even in defeat.

The German government, the Council of Peoples' Commissars, managed to arm itself. In the Freikorps the new leaders of Germany found a powerful weapon to use against left extremists. In Russia the provisional government was too weak to arm itself and the Kornilov adventure was a miserable failure.

In Germany the forces of order were lucky in their leaders: in Russia the forces of revolution possessed the ablest leadership. In Germany Hindenburg, Groener, Ebert and Noske provided the leadership which defeated the revolutionaries, none of whom possessed the abilities of Lenin. In Russia, Lenin and Trotsky were superior to all others in the art of conspiracy and in the science of revolution. How could a Kerensky stand up to them?

The links of loyalty which tied the German citizen to the German State were not broken. There was near universal indignation at the terms of the Treaty of Versailles. The Bolsheviks spent agonizing days of argument before they signed the Treaty of Brest-Litovsk. There was no popular outcry at their having done so. This does not mean that the Russians were less patriotic than the Germans. It simply shows that the Russians, citizens and soldiers, had been driven past endurance. The Germans, in spite of losses and suffering, had not yet reached this state of desperation. That they did not do so was partly due to Ludendorff's revolution. He made it clear to the officers of his staff that as the war was lost any more bloodshed was useless. The army would be needed to fight Bolshevism at home. Thus spoke Ludendorff, who in April 1917 permitted Lenin to travel to Russia through Germany.

Exercise 4

Question 1

What explanations are given for the significant role frequently played in eastern and central Europe by the navy?

Question 2

What crucial difference is stressed between the peasantry of Russia and the peasantry of most other European countries?

Question 3

What two basic explanations are given for the failure of the provisional government and, therefore, for the success of the Bolshevik take-over?

Question 4

Harry Hanak stresses the importance, in the final achievement and consolidation of Bolshevik power, of the Cheka and of the Red Army. What part do you think the war situation played in the raising of these two important organizations?

Question 5

What long-term result is indicated of the significant role played by the first of these two organizations?

Question 6

Russia and Germany were both defeated. In what sense, however, was the German army still 'successful'?

Question 7

Explain the short-term and the long-term significance of the Freikorps.

Specimen Answers

1   Living and working close together had the same effect on sailors that working together had on workmen in factories. Secondly, social distinctions between naval officers and sailors were much greater than those in the army.

2   Whereas the peasantry elsewhere was generally a conservative force, in Russia it was a radical force.

3   The provisional government was able neither to pursue the war successfully nor to bring it to an end. Secondly, there was a kind of political vacuum which neither the government nor the soviets filled.

4   The war created a situation in which men had arms, were used to using arms, and were used to all kinds of violence and cruelty. It also created a situation in which many men had no other jobs to go to, or if they did they were likely to encounter starvation conditions.

5   The Communist regime thereafter continued to depend on terror.

6   The German army was able to secure an orderly retreat without loss of prisoners of war. This contrasts completely with the utter collapse of the Russian armies.

7   The Freikorps first of all played a part in making sure that the German 'revolution' at the end of the war did not move leftwards; later, they played a part in the rise of Hitler.

15.12   SOME FURTHER REMARKS
(by A. M.)

To round off the story, you should now read *Roberts*, Chapter 13, pages 401–17, and 436–52. This will at least give you an outline knowledge of the nature of the regimes which the war, arguably, helped to establish in Germany and Russia. However, my own particular interst in history extends beyond the nature of particular political regimes. I should like to round off this unit by drawing your attention to one or two other aspects which, legitimately enough, Harry Hanak has not dealt with. I shall again give a few tentative answers at the end, but the main purpose of this section is to get you thinking about some of the other broader issues. I start off with a very broad question indeed.

Exercise 5

Question 1

Are the major changes in this period in Russia and Germany due to war or due to revolution? When have we come across this problem already in this course? How did *that* problem differ from *this* one?

Question 2

In general, did the war bring about greater or lesser social equality in Russia and Germany?

Question 3

In particular, what effects did the war have on the position of women in Russia and Germany?

Question 4

Did the war increase, or decrease, individual liberty in Russia and Germany?

Specimen Answers

1   My quick answer to this, perhaps not a completely satisfactory one, would be to say that it is scarcely possible to disentangle war from revolution at this time. Rather, I would see war and revolution as one great 'discontinuity' bringing into play the four mechanisms of social change which I have mentioned so often. That is to say, in Russia (the more significant instance) war led directly into revolution, while revolution in turn prolonged a war situation (essentially a civil war, but with outside intervention). We met this sort of problem before in Block III when we were discussing the Revolutionary and Napoleonic Wars. The difference there was that, initially, revolution led into war, rather than, as here, war leading into revolution. (Incidentally the same sort of problem crops up when we discuss modern guerrilla warfare—Unit 32.)

2   In my view, the participation effect undoubtedly strengthened the power of labour during the war in both countries. I believe this had a lasting effect in Germany, where the new constitution fully recognized all the rights of labour. It is at the same time true that the destructive effects of war meant that for a time real wages were below those of pre-war days. The war, and the Bolshevik revolution, effectively destroyed the old class structure in Russia, and, theoretically at least, established a new kind of social equality.

3   In both countries women got political rights at the end of the war. They made some social and economic gains as well in Germany; and they achieved practically full social and economic equality in Communist Russia. In my view, this was actually less due to the participation of women in the war effort, than to the way in which the war destroyed the old order in both countries, and made possible a new order in which there was an ideological commitment to the notion of women's equality. However, that is a complicated matter which need not trouble you too much just now.

4   There was almost certainly much greater individual liberty in Weimar Germany than there was in pre-war Germany. The long-term answer to the question will depend on how far you see the rise of Nazism as directly linked to the war. From 1917 onwards political liberties were undoubtedly severely curtailed in Communist Russia; some commentators would see this as being balanced, or partially balanced, by a growth in social and economic liberties.

Bibliography

There is a vast number of books on the Russian revolution. Apart from the set book, M. T. Florinsky, *The End of the Russian Empire*, the best account is probably W. H. Chamberlin, *The Russian Revolution*, 2 vols., Macmillan, 1935.

A short account which closely follows Chamberlin is by J. Carmichael, *A Short History of the Russian Revolution*, Nelson, 1966 (and Sphere paperback). An excellent account by a participant, is Leon Trotsky, *History of the Russian Revolution*, Gollancz, 1932–3. Two justly famous accounts are N. N. Sukhanov, *The Russian Revolution, 1917* (ed. J. Carmichael) Oxford University Press, 1955, and John Reed, *Ten Days that Shook the World*, 1919, reprinted Lawrence and Wishart, 1960. Important also is E. H. Carr, *The Bolshevik Revolution*, Macmillan, 1950, Pelican, 1966, especially volumes 1 and 2, L. Schapiro, *The Communist Party of the Soviet Union*, Methuen, 1960, especially Chapters 6 to 11, A. Ulam, *Lenin and the Bolsheviks*, Secker and Warburg, 1966, especially Chapters 4 to 8.

On Germany, the books in English are by no means as plentiful. A brilliant book of interpretation is Arthur Rosenberg, *Imperial Germany, the Birth of the German Republic, 1871–1918*, Oxford University Press, 1970. On the army read G. A. Craig, *The Politics of the Prussian Army*, Oxford University Press, 1955, Chapters 7 to 9. Read also the early chapters of F. L. Carsten, *The Reichswehr and Politics, 1918–1933*, Oxford University Press, 1966, and by the same author, *Revolution in Central Europe, 1918–1919*, Oxford University Press, 1972. Very useful are also A. J. Ryder, *The German Revolution of 1918. A Study of German Socialism in War and Revolt*, Cambridge University Press, 1967, K. Epstein, *Matthias Erzberger and the Dilemma of German Democracy*, Oxford University Press, 1959, Chapters 7–12. See also J. W. Wheeler-Bennett, *Wooden Titan, Hindenburg*, Macmillan, 1936, and P. Nettl, *Rosa Luxemburg*, Oxford University Press, 1969 (abridged version).

Acknowledgements

Acknowledgement is made to the following for illustrations used in this unit:

Mansell Collection; Staatsbibliothek Berlin. Preussischer Kulturbesitz Bildarchiv.

Unit 16

The West in World War 1

Prepared by Arthur Marwick for the Course Team

CONTENTS AND OBJECTIVES

Preliminaries

There was no British, French, or American 'revolution' at the end of the First World War. It is less easy, therefore, to find a convenient focal-point for a comparative study of the effects of the war on the three main Western countries. Obviously, in the week at our disposal we can only look at certain aspects of the question. Indeed, this unit raises in potent form the whole issue of how much ground you can reasonably be expected to cover. You will recall that in the very first unit I suggested that you should always aim at a minimum coverage of each unit, coupled with a really thorough study (including background as well as prescribed reading) of the equivalent of one unit in four. The main core of this unit concerns British society, and in this case 'minimum coverage' means dealing with the British topics (16.1.1–16.1.3, with *prescribed* reading, and 16.2.1 and 16.2.3). Special credit will be given to you in the exam if you show that you have followed up the comparative references and recommended reading given in the other sub-sections, but this is *far from essential*. If you are in difficulties with time the sub-section which can most readily be cut altogether is 16.1.4 (marked 'optional').

The set book for this part of the course is Arthur Marwick, *The Deluge: British Society and the First World War*[1]. In many ways it is a pity that you should have to read one of my own books in addition to having to wade through my correspondence material. Ideally, I should have preferred to get you to read a book which takes a rather different line from my own, so that we could then have a genuine discussion of the differences of approach. But the fact is that at the time of writing this unit (November 1971) no other study of the topic exists: for some time it has been announced that Professor Trevor Wilson (the distinguished authority on the history of the Liberal Party in the twentieth century) is writing a general study of Britain and the First World War for the Collins series on War and Society. Anyway, Trevor Wilson has himself informed me that there is no chance of his book being ready in time for the first students of this course. You should, however, look out for it once it is available: I hope that after you have worked through this unit you will feel confident enough to make an informed critical appraisal of the book for yourself. Apart from reading *The Deluge* you may need to refresh your knowledge of *Roberts*, Chapter IX, and *Fuller*, Chapter IX.[2]

There is an annotated list of background reading at the end of the unit.

In the main the unit is concerned with the second of the major themes for the course as a whole: *the consequences of wars*. But it also looks at, in the context of Britain and France in the First World War, one part of the third theme: *the relationship between civil and military authorities*.

Before proceeding any further you must read *The Deluge*, annotating your copy, or taking notes, as you feel to be necessary. If you have already read the book, make sure that you recall the main points made in it. Now I realize that to read the whole of *The Deluge* will take up rather more than half the time at your disposal. If you really do find yourself becoming bogged down in the reading, then, *and only then*, you may prefer to have a bash at the correspondence material, coming back to *The Deluge* as its relevance (I hope!) becomes plainer.

[1] Penguin Books, 1967.

[2] J. M. Roberts, *Europe 1880–1945*, Longman; J. F. C. Fuller, *The Conduct of War, 1789–1961*, Methuen (SET BOOKS).

6.1 BRITISH SOCIETY AND THE FIRST WORLD WAR, WITH SOME COMPARATIVE REFERENCES TO FRANCE AND THE UNITED STATES

1.1 France, Britain and the United States in 1914

In Unit 2, Section 2.2 (if you can remember back that far!) I stressed that when discussing the consequences of war 'in any real situation it will be necessary to consider the special characteristics of a given society on the eve of war, and any other variables which may be important during and after the war'. Let's take the first of these two points. If we are (however briefly) going to compare the effects of the war on Britain, France and the United States, what 'special characteristics' ought we to consider? (You could take your guidance here, if you like, from the opening section of *The Deluge*, 'Britain in 1914'.)

Specimen Answer and Discussion

If you simply note the points as they crop up on the opening pages of *The Deluge*, you will get a pretty haphazard list of 'characteristics'—something like this:

(1) geography;
(2) 'untroubled history' and 'native inventiveness';
(3) industrial power;
(4) military and naval strength;
(5) political ideas and structure;
(6) social attitudes and policies;
(7) exploitation of science;
(8) special problems (Ireland);
(9) population, urbanization, etc.;
(10) industry and agriculture;
(11) class structure;
(12) social conditions;
(13) attitudes to war and peace, etc.

Obviously, if we want to use this as a basis for comparative study we ought to try to make the list a little more systematic and less haphazard. Point (2) is a difficult one to handle: these days historians and social scientists, wisely I think, prefer to avoid talking about 'national character', so I think all we can do here is note that certain salient features of a country's history will necessarily affect the state of society at any given point in time.

Here, then, is a revised list. The square brackets indicate how I have grouped the original haphazard list of points arising from *The Deluge*.

1   Geography (to include physical size and significant characteristics, relationship to other countries, urbanization, population, etc.). [(1), (9)]

2   Significant features of previous history (a slightly question-begging phrase, but then, as you will have fully realized by this time, one of the most important skills which, I hope, will emerge from this course, is that of appreciating what, historically, is significant, in any particular context). [(2)]

3   Racial composition and social cohesion (including the Irish problem in the case of Britain). [(8)]

4   Economics (including trade, exploitation of science, balance between industry and agriculture, etc.). [(3), (7), (10)]

5 Social structure [(11)]

6 Social conditions [(12)]

7 Customs and behaviour [not previously mentioned, but obviously very important]

8 Social and economic ideas and policies [(6)]

9 Social and intellectual attitudes [(13)]

10 Political structure and ideas [(5)]

Note: I prefer to leave naval and military matters for separate treatment. Where they affect social development they can be considered under headings 9 and 10.

I am sure you won't have arrived at a final list exactly like this, but I hope you have found it worth while trying to work out the sorts of things you would have to compare in different countries, as a prelude to assessing the consequences of the war. Clearly many of the headings overlap. However, give or take a few points of detail or emphasis, I think this list makes a reasonable working basis for comparative study. What immediately follows is designed more to give you a taste of the comparative method in operation, than to provide you with essential factual information. If you feel you already have some knowledge of France and America (guidance on further reading is provided in 16.1.4) do please attempt this part as an exercise. But if you are merely aiming at 'minimum coverage' of the unit, you are quite at liberty to read through it with great haste, or even to miss it out altogether. Please note that in presenting my 'Comparative study of France, Britain and the U.S.A. in 1914' I have not stuck rigidly to the order in which the ten points are listed above, since I am trying to write reasonably polished prose. But you should, if you attempt the exercise at all, stick to note form.

France, Britain and the United States in 1914

France, Britain and the United States can be contrasted in various obvious ways. First of all in sheer size: America is enormous compared with the two European countries, with a total area of 3,002,387 square miles; though a large country by European standards, France's total area is a mere 212,961 square miles; Great Britain is less than half the size of France with an area of only 88,755 square miles. If, however, we turn to the question of relative geographical isolation, the order is slightly different. France has been closely involved in most of the great European upheavals, and already by 1914 knew well what it was to suffer invasion and defeat. Britain, though separated from the continent by only a narrow channel, had for many centuries been insulated from the worst upheavals of continental Europe, and had thus been able to develop without interruption her own relatively close-knit society—from which, however, Ireland remained significantly apart. The United States, with the whole breadth of the Atlantic between her and Europe, naturally had remained most isolated from European conflicts. In a real sense, America had grown up as an experiment in creating a new society away from the storms and stresses of old Europe. But against this we must place a third comparison: while France was racially an extremely homogeneous country and while Britain across the centuries had become so, America in 1914 was still very much a country of mixed immigrant population. Indeed, the period from 1903 to 1914 saw immigration reach its peak with more than six million people (mainly from Italy, south-eastern Europe and Russia) entering the country annually. And as a historical relic of the institution of slavery America had a substantial Negro population. Though in some respects the most free and democratic of all the nations under review here, America was the least homogeneous racially.

In 1914 France's greatest industry was agriculture. More than half the population, over twenty-two millions in all, lived and worked on the land. The most important agricultural product was wheat, particularly in the northern areas, although sugar beet, potatoes, apples and other products were also grown in these regions. The south-west was an area of vineyards and of dairy farming. Further to the south and south-east, vineyards dominated. Around the Massif Centrale soil conditions and altitude made farming difficult. The highland plateaux were left to cattle rearing; the lower areas were used to grow rye, oats, potatoes and fruit. The Mediterranean coast was covered in vineyards and olive groves.

After almost a century of European industrialization, France was suffering from her poverty of natural resources. Her coal output in 1913 was 41 million tons, compared with Germany's 279 million tons and Britain's 292 million tons. France, indeed, had to import much of her coal. The continued and growing importance of luxury goods for export, and the tendency of French industry in general to concentrate on the home market, meant that her industries were, on the whole, comparatively small. Such big industry as she had was confined to five *départements* in the north, the edges of the Massif Centrale, and a few cities such as Paris, Lyons, and Marseilles. By 1914 her main exports were textiles, iron ore and luxury goods.

In the race towards industrialization and commercial strength France was losing in comparison with Britain, Germany and the United States, though she did, at least, lead Britain in some of the new technological industries, such as the manufacture of the motor car (but, at that time, this too was a luxury). France was also falling behind in regard to population growth. In 1880 she had had 15·7 per cent of the European population; in 1900 she had only 9·7 per cent. The rate of increase of the French people between 1880 and 1910 was 5 per cent, for Germany it was 43 per cent, and for Britain 26 per cent. France's total population in 1914 was 39,600,000; this compared with 40,200,000 in Great Britain, and with 92,228,496 in the United States. American industry was undoubtedly expanding; Britain's was giving some cause for concern: but overall as the situation stood in 1914 Britain was certainly still far ahead of France industrially and indeed she was still enjoying the fruits of economic primacy, even if that was now being challenged by Germany and by the United States.

Many of the raw materials which Britain lacked could be drawn from her overseas empire which outbid that of France in terms of size and wealth in raw materials. With 35 per cent of all world trade in 1900, Britain was still the world's greatest trading nation.

The greatest geographical variety, physical and climatic, naturally, is to be found in the United States: from east to west, America stretches for 2,700 miles and from north to south for a maximum of 1,600 miles. It is possible, however, in the first instance, to divide the country roughly by the three great mountain ranges. Starting from the east they are: the Appalachians, the Rockies, and the Sierra Nevada in the far west. East of the Appalachians are the Atlantic coastlines. Between the Appalachians and the Rockies lies the 'central valley', stretching from the great lakes to the Gulf of Mexico. The central valley itself is divided and watered by the Mississippi–Missouri rivers and their tributaries. West of the Rockies lies an area of desert, separated from the fertile Pacific coastline by the Sierra Nevada and the Cascade mountains. But this rough division fails to describe the variety of regions in the country, although the regions are in some degree governed by this basic division. In the extreme north-east lies New England, an area of mountains, lakes, rocky headlands, and a climate similar to, but colder than that of its namesake. Further west are the mid-Atlantic states, New York, Delaware, Pennsylvania, etc., which are not quite so bleak in terrain as New England, but

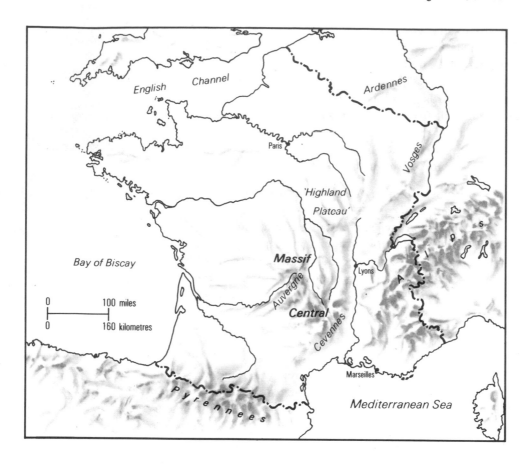

Figure 1   Map of France, physical regions

which suffer considerable extremes of climate. By 1914 these two regions formed the industrial heart of America. Further west again lie the states of the Mid-West and the great plains, the great farming and cattle raising regions of America.

To the east these states enjoy a fairly temperate climate, but farther west there are great extremes of heat and cold, and the constant threat of drought. The far west consists of mountains, the arid deserts, and also the fertile, warm, fruit-growing Pacific coastlands. The south, the area from Texas to the east coast, from Maryland to Florida, has a climate ranging from Mediterranean to tropical, suitable for the cotton, tobacco, rice and sugar grown there in small farmsteads. The southern areas have always been particularly prone to such major natural hazards as typhoons and floods. In 1914 the South was one of the most backward areas of the United States, lacking in major industry, deficient in transport facilities, and still suffering in the shadow of defeat in the Civil War, which still cast divisive influences over the whole of American Society.

American natural resources already could be seen to surpass those of any comparable area in the world. Her rich supplies of coal and minerals, mainly along the Appalachians and in Kentucky and Illinois, had still to be fully exploited in 1914, but had already supplied the basis for the American industrial revolution which had accelerated after 1865.

All three of the major Western countries shared in certain common trends, particularly the trend towards urbanization. Thus far this trend had gone furthest in Britain; it had gone least far in France. America was beginning rapidly to embark on the process of urbanization in the last decades before 1914. In 1880 the number of cities with a population of 100,000 or more was nineteen; in 1900 it was thirty-six; and in 1910 it was fifty. By 1914 more than a third of the total population of America had congregated in the urban areas; but in Britain well over half the population had been living in towns and cities since the middle of the nineteenth century.

94

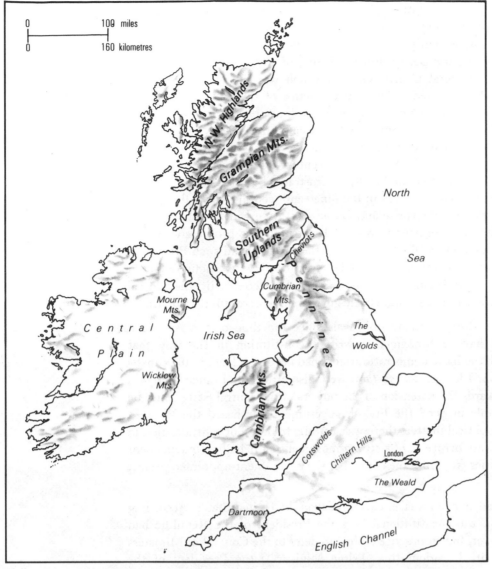

Figure 2   Map of Great Britain, physical regions

In many ways Great Britain had the most rigid social hierarchy, with a city-based proletariat, amounting to about eighty per cent of the total population, sharply cut off from the middle and upper classes. Political, social and economic power was largely concentrated in the hands of a ruling class made up of the old landed aristocracy and the more successful products of the business and commercial class. In France there was a well-defined conflict of interest between the relatively small industrial proletariat and the peasant proprietors, whose economic position might not be very strong. The old aristocratic interests still had considerable influence in the army and in certain other professions; because of the complex revolutionary history through which France had gone politics were probably more open to genuine middle-class influences than they were in Britain. In most respects the United States was a much more open and mobile society than either of these two European countries. In theory at least, there was no traditional aristocracy, though in practice in certain areas local ascendancy had certainly been achieved by long-established groups (this was particularly true of the White Anglo-Saxon Protestants —WASPS—in New England and the Planters in the South). Against the undoubted opportunities for social mobility must be set the depressed position of Negroes and of many recent European immigrants; furthermore, sharp conflicts were already apparent between the employing classes and labour.

Unlike Britain or France of the Third Republic, the government of the United States was based on a constitution. That constitution had been written in 1788 and had been continuously in effect, with minor amendments, since 1789. It certainly had not been written with the conditions of twentieth-century urbanized industrial life in mind. The federal government of the United States was divided into three branches: the executive, in the form of the President; the legislature, consisting of two houses, the Senate and the House of Representatives; and the Judiciary, that is the Federal Courts, chief of which was the Supreme Court. Government was still conducted strictly by the letter of the constitution; and although the President and the Congress were free to interpret as they wished, the courts had the last word. Thus the Supreme Court could declare any executive or legislative act unconstitutional. The theory was that of 'checks and balances', the theory thought to have operated in eighteenth-century Britain; any attempts at strong action by the President could usually be frustrated by the legislature. This was a not unsatisfactory state of affairs in the nineteenth century when the fundamental principles of private enterprise and *laissez-faire* were widely upheld as the basis upon which American prosperity rested. Trends towards progressivism and even socialism were apparent at the beginning of the century; and such Presidents as Theodore Roosevelt had attempted to take stronger executive action; but in 1914 the principles of *laissez-faire* and of minimal interference by the federal government in the affairs of the separate State governments were still paramount.

France, having gone through many upheavals since the time of the American revolution, did not have a fundamental written constitution in the way that America had, though the basic democratic system had been stabilized in the constitutional laws of 1884. Ideas of *laissez-faire* were also strong in France though a slight movement towards the extension of the powers of the central State could be discerned: for example in 1908 the French government purchased the Western Railway system. In political matters there was a strong tradition of centralization in France, and in the years before 1914 a strong movement on behalf of independent powers for the localities free from the control of the government-appointed prefect was growing up.

France in practice had an even weaker executive than the United States. According to the strict letter of the constitutional laws the President of the Republic had considerable real power, but in practice he had to defer to the Council of Ministers (the 'Cabinet') and its President (the 'Prime Minister'); the President of the Council of Ministers, in his turn, found himself very much at the mercy of the changing whims of the French parliament. The continuous procession of temporizing coalition governments was already a notorious feature of the French political scene. When discussing American or British politics in the First World War it is meaningful to speak of 'a Democratic President', or 'a Liberal prime minister', in France there were all sorts of labels, 'Radicals', 'Radical Socialists' and so on, all in fact standing for the bourgeois middle, which was flanked on one side by various kinds of 'Socialists' and 'Syndicalists', and on the other by ultra-Catholics and monarchists. Many French publicists were fully alive to the dangers of a weak executive, particularly at a time when a major war seemed imminent: in 1913, despite the fact that monarchism represented the ultimate in right-wing politics, a socialist deputy, Marcel Sembat, actually published a book with the title *Make a King, or else Make Peace.*

Britain had no written constitution as such (though much constitutional theory was embedded in various Acts of parliament). But the system of Prime Minister and cabinet government which had developed throughout the nineteenth century did permit stronger executive government. Against this, Britain was in practice less democratic than either the United States or France. In 1911 only fifty-nine per cent of the adult male population of Britain had the franchise. France had universal male suffrage, while the different States of America had different qualifying clauses, many of them designed to exclude Negroes. Save for a few States in America, no women had the vote. In a small country like Britain there was no equivalent of the considerable powers possessed by the separate States which made up the United States of America; on the other hand, there was greater respect for the rights of local government than there was in France. However, this is perhaps to concentrate attention too much on the superficial appearance of the political machine; arguably, below the level of the overt powers of the prefects there was more genuine participation in local government in France, as in America, than in Britain.

These are complicated contrasts and parallels. On the question of social ideas, it would probably be true to say that the principles of individualism and *laissez-faire* were about as strong in Britain as in the United States. France, on account of an older tradition rather than because of recent developments, was most prepared to accept centralized control. All countries had begun the introduction of piecemeal social welfare legislation in the years before the war. The Liberal government in Britain after 1906 had set the pace: yet even this legislation must, I believe (though many other historians would disagree), be seen as falling within the context of traditional individualist ideas. There was a socialist movement as well as a strong middle-class 'Progressive' movement in the United States, and in Britain there had appeared the still very small Labour party advocating socialist policies. There was a strong Socialist party in France, where, however, the conflict between Catholics and anti-clericals tended to divert attention and energies from positive social reform. There was a very strong women's suffrage movement in the U.S.A., which had already made prohibition of alcohol one of its planks. The suffragists and suffragettes were very active in Britain too: rather less so in France.

To conclude this brief comparative survey let me turn away from 1914 to stress the other vital point made at the beginning of this section, the need to consider 'any other variables which may be important during and after the war'. What, at the very least, we do have to bear in mind is the differing way in which the First World War as an actual historical reality affected the different countries.

Here let us reduce that question to its simplest form:

Exercise 1
In the light of what you know about the course of the First World War from Unit 14 and from your reading in Fuller and in Roberts, say which country was most affected, and which country was least affected, by the war as an actual historical reality.

Figure 3   Map of the U.S.A., physical regions

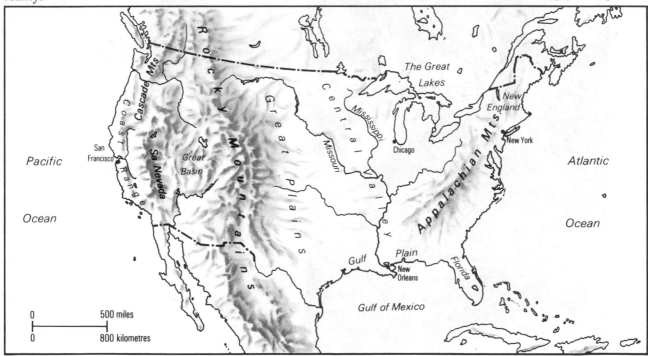

Specimen Answer and Discussion

France was most affected, because part of the war was in fact fought over her territory. America was least affected, because she did not come into the war until 1917, and even then, her entire resources were never involved in the war effort in the way in which the resources of both France and Britain were.

16.1.2   British Society and the First World War

At the beginning of the previous sub-section we settled for nine headings which might be used in trying to pin down the character of any society on the eve of war. We can now use the same list to pin down the changes which, as argued in *The Deluge* (though, of course, not all historians would agree with the arguments presented in *The Deluge*) took place during the war. Actually two of these headings would, at first sight, seem to be less relevant and useful in this connection than the other seven.

Exercise 1

Say which they are.

Specimen Answer and Discussion

1 Geography. But this could well be affected by transfers of territory. And urbanization, population and other aspects of economic and social geography would almost certainly be affected. So let us retain this heading.

2 Significant features of history. This isn't likely to be very relevant here. We are looking at the whole history of the war and then seeing how it is significant in regard to our other headings. Still, perhaps we'd better retain this heading too in

Figure 4   Tram-conductress in Glasgow (Imperial War Museum)

case there is any really outstanding feature of the history of the war which, though of undoubted social significance, cannot be accommodated to any of the other headings.

Exercise 2

On the basis of your reading of *The Deluge* note against each of the ten headings the main changes which did come about in Britain over the period of the First World War.

Specimen Answer

1   Southern Ireland gained independence in 1921. In Britain itself there was a new population drift to the south, and a further decline in the birth rate.

2   Under this heading one might place the 'traumatic' effect of trench warfare, the inequalities of sacrifice between civilian and soldier, and the feuding between generals and politicians, all of which left scars on British society.

3   It is hard to detect any changes one way or another in this respect. (If anything, the Irish situation was further inflamed.) There was much violence in the pre-war period: there doesn't seem to have been more in the post-war period.

4   There were great developments in chemicals, electricity, and the exploitation of the internal combustion engine, and the basis was laid for the development of broadcasting. Undue emphasis was placed on the old heavy industries in time of war, which were now set for a long period of decline. The war disrupted the pattern of Britain's overseas trade, and her international banking activities, laying the scene for economic depression, and recurrent financial crises.

5   The really deep gulf between the working class and the rest of the community was partially bridged by the experience of the war. The total working class declined slightly, whereas the middle class increased. While there remained a definable ruling class, the composition of this changed in favour of the non-landed elements. There was a decline in servant-keeping.

6   Real wage rates went up twenty to twenty-five per cent. According to A. L. Bowley, the war accomplished 'the pressing social task' of raising the wages of the worst-paid workers. In State-subsidized housing, baths became a normal fixture (though the majority continued to live in nineteenth-century housing). Some sections of the working classes had acquired a taste for such consumer goods as pianos, gramophones, motor-bicycles during the 'affluence' of the war period: this 'taste of affluence' in itself became an agent of further change in material conditions. The war fostered a technologically based society creating a common basis of consumer goods shared by all classes. But, it must be noted, unemployment—itself a product of the disruptions of war—nullified many of those changes.

7   In general there was a liberalizing of attitudes and activities as far as manners and morals were concerned. Many of the older formal symbols of dress also tended to disappear in the war period. The old prevalence of heavy drinking was drastically diminished. There was a new popular craze for dancing, and also for the poor man's form of 'the sport of kings', dog-racing. The cinema became a prime agent in the standardization of social behaviour.

8   The war provided many examples of the efficacy of State intervention in social and economic matters and through the other mechanisms by which war operates on society created a situation where at the end of the war there was for the first time a Housing Act which brought State subsidies into play to provide housing at less than economic rents; there was for the first time a Ministry of Health charged with looking after the health and housing of the community; and there was a great extension in social insurance policies.

The old theories of unrestricted *laissez-faire* had been convincingly challenged and henceforth there would always be men, some of whom became influential in the '30s and '40s, ready to argue that only through State management could the economic crisis be solved. A striking example of the coming together of technological and collectivist developments is the establishment of the B.B.C. in 1926.

9   The war marked a final challenge to Victorian authorities and orthodoxies, gave an impetus and a wider currency to modernism in the arts (here refer as appropriate to your Anthology[1]) and dealt severe blows to religious belief and church attendance.

10   There was less change in political structure than elsewhere, though the country did, for the first time, become a full democracy (save for women under thirty). Socialist ideas advanced at the expense of liberal ones. The land-based elite was giving place to the urban commercial and industrial elite and labour was throwing up a political elite of its own.

Do bear in mind that this exercise, and my answers, involve providing very potted summaries which (I hope) cannot do justice to the complex and detailed arguments of *The Deluge*. In particular we have said nothing here of *how* these changes came about. In this connection you may have been surprised, since I have probably bored you into the ground with my constant references to my four-tier model, to find that there was no mention at all of such a model in *The Deluge*.[2]

Exercise 3

Where in the book do I come nearest to building such a structure?

Specimen Answer

At the beginning of Chapter IX where I list seven 'direct consquences' of the war.

In fact these were the conclusions I arrived at, working in the early 1960s, in accordance with the traditional methods of the historian. The four-tier model is essentially intended as a refinement and simplification of this sevenfold list of 'consequences'.

Exercise 4

Take each of the seven 'consequences' listed at the beginning of Chapter IX and explain how I have reduced them to four, as expressed in the four-tier model.

Specimen Answer

First consequence fits into the first tier, *destruction and disruption*.

So does the second consequence.

So does the third consequence.

The fourth consequence has been rephrased and forms part of the second tier, *the test of war*.

The fifth consequence, more obviously, belongs to this second tier as well.

---

[1] J. Ferguson (ed.) *War and the Creative Arts*, Macmillan, The Open University Press.

[2] In case you are sitting on a bus at the moment, the four tiers of the model, fully discussed in Unit 2, are (1) *destruction–disruption*, (2) *test*, (3) *military participation*, (4) *psychological*.

The sixth consequence again fits into the first tier: it is the paradoxical result of destruction, the 'building again, and building better than before' syndrome.

The seventh consequence becomes the fourth tier of the model.

Exercise 5

What sorts of points could be made in arguing against the general view of the effects of the First World War presented in *The Deluge*?

Specimen Answer and Discussion

That social change does not take place as suddenly as the book seems to imply. That the changes would have come about anyway, being part of 'long-term trends'. Or, that the crucial period of rapid change came in the years immediately before the war. Or both. That the changes were designed purely for a temporary situation, and had little lasting effect.

Think about these points and decide for yourself how successfully, if at all, I meet them in *The Deluge*. One very readable book which makes the case for the major social changes having in fact taken place just *before* the war is S. L. Hynes, *The Edwardian Turn of Mind*. An example of a good solid textbook which plays down the influence of the war is A. F. Havighurst, *Twentieth Century Britain*.

1.3 Some Primary Sources for the Study of British Society and the First World War

To do this section you will need to have beside you the twentieth-century collection of documents sent to you as part of Unit 5. We shall be concentrating on Section D, the section concerning Britain in the First World War. In answering the various questions you are expected to bring in the knowledge acquired from reading *The Deluge*.

Exercise 1

I want you now to read carefully Documents 1 and 5 in that collection.

Question 1

What points about women's employment, and about the conditions under which they worked emerge from a comparison of these two documents? (I noted four points.)

Specimen Answer

1   There was nothing new about the employment of women in factories before the war.

2   Conditions, as far as sanitation and so on were concerned, were pretty deplorable.

3   Attempts were being made, particularly by the Factory Inspectors, to improve these conditions (this is further evidence for the Liberal social reform movement already in being well before 1914).

4   Conditions had considerably improved after one year of war and we can see here the direct effect of the war in that the influx of women into the factories led to an improvement in welfare conditions.

Question 2

What other primary evidence have we already seen for this question of women's employment and welfare in factories?

Specimen Answer

Film evidence in the programme 'Women in Two Wars', and 'Consequences of the War for Britain, 1914–1930'.

Exercise 2

Now read Document 2, *The British Labour Movement and the War*, 1915.

Question 1

Different individuals and different groups gave different theoretical justifications for their support of the British effort: for instance, some simply said that they were fighting 'for King and country'. What is the basic theoretical justification for the Labour Party's support for the war?

Question 2

Why, according to the document, was it necessary for the Labour movement to make this statement? In fact, there is a more simple reason which made the leaders of the Labour movement feel that they must clarify their position. What is this?

Exercise 3

Now read Document 6, *The Child and the War*, 1917.

Question 1

What general conclusions about the impact of war would you derive from this document?

Question 2

For what reasons should you hesitate to draw final conclusions about the consequences of war from this document?

Exercise 4

Now read Document 9, *Extracts from the Cabinet Minutes 1st August 1917*. I have deliberately not given any further title to this document because I want you, doing what the historian must do when approaching any document, to bring in the knowledge that you have acquired from other sources, to tell me what the central issue is which is being discussed in this document. What is this central issue?

Exercise 5

Now read Document 10, *Fisher's Speech introducing his Education Bill, House of Commons Debates*, 10 August 1917.

Question 1

How reliable is this document for telling us about the motivation which lay behind educational reform at the end of the First World War?

Question 2

What arguments are put forward in favour of educational reform which do not relate directly to the war?

Question 3

What arguments are put forward which do suggest a direct relationship between the experience of war and educational reform?

Exercise 6

Now, instead of getting you to turn to your documents unit, I want you to consider these statistical tables.

Occupied Population of Great Britain in 1921 (thousands)

	Men and Boys	Women and Girls
Wage-earners	10,526	4,182
Salaried	1,637	1,071
Independent workers	841	366
Employers, farmers, professional	652	83
Total occupied	13,656	5,702

Occupied Population of the United Kingdom in 1911 (thousands)

	Men and Boys	Women and Girls
Wage-earners	11,000	4,650
Salaried	1,120	550
Independent workers	650	
Employers, farmers, professional	1,530	650
Total occupied	14,300	5,850
Present area of S. Ireland	1,060	390
Present area of U.K.	13,240	5,460

Question 1

What general points can be made about the utility or otherwise of these tables for the historian?

Question 2

On the basis of the tables, what points can be made about the changing social structure as between 1911 and 1921?

Exercise 7

You will recall that in Unit 14 I described how I would like you to go about writing a full commentary on a document, dividing your answer into

1 general introduction to the document making points of source criticism and so on;

2 a point-by-point commentary on particular points of difficulty or interest in the body of the document; and

3 a general summing up of the historical significance of the document.

I want you therefore to turn to Document 11, *Extracts from the War Cabinet Report for the Year 1917*, and I want you to write a commentary on the third paragraph of that document.

*Figure 5 'It's our Flag',
First World War poster
(Imperial War Museum)*

Specimen Answers
Exercise 2
Question 1

The key idea is the defence of democracy.

Question 2

The reason given is the spread of misleading and often entirely false statements about Labour's views in this country and abroad. The more simple reason is that the Labour movement was in fact divided, with a small but important minority opposed to the war: it was really this which gave rise to misunderstandings and led the official Labour leadership to try to clarify its pro-war position.

Exercise 3

Question 1

One would conclude that the consequences of war were extremely bad, leading to disruption of family life and increased juvenile delinquency.

Question 2

As always, one would not rely on one document alone, but would demand supporting evidence from other sources. Apart from that it would have to be noted that this report relates to 1915; it might be that the consequences of war in this respect were rather different in the later years of the war. Above all it is possible that the creation of the very problems described here might stimulate a desire to reform the conditions leading to juvenile delinquency. [Having said all this, I think I should comment that overall there is little doubt that the effect of modern war is to create conditions conducive to a rise in juvenile delinquency.]

Exercise 4

The issue here concerns the holding of an international socialist conference at Stockholm, to be attended by German as well as allied and neutral delegates. Arthur Henderson, both a member of the War Cabinet and Secretary of the Labour Party, had come down in favour of this conference. As can be seen from the document the remainder of the War Cabinet were very upset by this decision. Because of this, Arthur Henderson was in fact forced out of the War Cabinet, his place being taken by a duller and more solid Labour member, G. N. Barnes.

Exercise 5

Question 1

Political speeches have always to be taken with some caution, yet it is reasonable to accept that the man who framed the Education Bill would be a reliable source in explaining the motives which lay behind the bill. It may be, though, that Fisher did, for obvious reasons, rather go out of his way to stress the relationship between his proposed reforms and the war which so much monopolized the attentions of parliament at that time.

Question 2

The relationship between education and physical efficiency; the lack of a scientific correlation between different parts of the system, leading to erratic, unequal provision as between one council and another. Fisher also refers to what he sees as a growing demand from the workers (the industrial army, as he calls them) for education purely as a means to a fuller more civilized life.

Question 3

The deficiencies which have been revealed by the war; the intellectual wastage which has been caused by the war; the growing industrial pressure upon children during the war. The increased feeling of social solidarity created by the war, leading to an extension of the idea of citizenship.

Exercise 6

Question 1

One problem is that the census categories 'wage-earners', 'salaried', etc., do not directly coincide with social classes as usually understood by the historian. You will recall that after 1921 Southern Ireland was no longer part of the United Kingdom, hence the little subtraction sum which has to be done at the end of the 1911 table in order to try to make the figures as nearly comparable as possible. In fact, because of changes in definition, as well as for other reasons, it is very difficult to get exact comparability.

Question 2

Two points are clear: the slight decline in the size of wage-earners ('the working class'), and the increase in size of the salaried class in general ('the middle class'), and, above all, in salaried women. On the basis of the table alone it is difficult to interpret the drop in 'employers, farmers, professional', which may be partly due to the loss of Eire. From other sources we know that businesses were tending to combine, and that many farmers were setting up as owners of their own land (*The Deluge*, p. 325).

Exercise 7

In December 1916 the Asquith government, which had been attacked for its lack of vigour in dealing with the problems of reorganization necessitated by the war, was replaced by a new coalition under the energetic leadership of Lloyd George. One of the basic issues in the political crisis concerned the question of setting up a small War Cabinet, which in fact Lloyd George proceeded to do when he came to power. This document is part of an official report on the first year of the new War Cabinet. Since it is an official document it will tend to present official views, and perhaps to exaggerate the achievements of the new War Cabinet government. On the other hand the British Civil Service which would be responsible for preparing the actual text of the document does have a reasonably justified reputation for objectivity. Thus, although we will have to take the opinions expressed very cautiously, we can regard the document as providing a reasonably reliable, and of course very informed, record of the main happenings in regard to the War Cabinet in the year 1917. 1917 was, of course, a very difficult year as far as military history is concerned: the submarine crisis reached a peak in the early autumn, and the year ended with the terrible losses of Passchendaele.

The extract begins by referring to the introduction of the War Cabinet system as a result of the change of government. It explains that the essence of the War Cabinet system lay in the setting up of a small body directly responsible for the direction of the war and separate from the large group of other ministers who continued to be responsible for their own departments. All of the members of the War Cabinet, except one, were completely free from departmental responsibilities so that they could devote themselves entirely to the question of directing the war. Although the disagreements which lay behind the December 1916 crisis went much deeper, it was this proposal which formed the actual occasion for the crisis. Lloyd George had proposed the War Cabinet idea with the implication that although Asquith could continue to have the name and style of Prime Minister, he would not be a member of this small War Cabinet. The members of the original War Cabinet are listed: they are, of course, Lloyd George; Curzon, a former Viceroy of India and one of the strongest Conservative figures in the country; Milner, who had started as a Liberal, but who was strongly in favour of a form of economic and social reorganization, often called 'social imperialism' which at times verged on what was later known as Fascism; Bonar Law the leader of the Conservative Party, and the man whose consent had been essential in ensuring that Lloyd George was successful in ousting Asquith; and Arthur Henderson, representing Labour in the War Cabinet and demonstrating how important it was for the government to have the co-operation of Labour. Of the new members, Carson was a leader of the Ulster Unionists: his presence in the War Cabinet necessarily upset and antagonized the Irish Nationalists who had previously looked upon Lloyd George as a friend to the aspirations of Ireland, and G. N. Barnes was a rather less distinguished Labour leader who took the place vacated by Henderson after the Stockholm incident. If the inclusion of first, Henderson, and then Barnes, represents the participation effect as far as Labour is concerned, the attendance of Smuts shows the same participation effect in regard to the Empire countries which played an important role in the war. The point made about Bonar Law is not specially significant;

eventually he too gave up being Chancellor of the Exchequer so as to confine his energies to the war effort.

The significance of this extract lies in the way in which it pins down the important governmental changes which came about when Lloyd George took over from Asquith. The implication is that this was a much more rational and efficient way of running the war effort. Undoubtedly Lloyd George was more effective than Asquith, but it should be noted that not all of the experiments of the new government were completely successful. Asquith had been an obstacle to the changes which many others had been advocating for many months; Lloyd George was not the originator of these changes, but at least he did not obstruct them. In other words, the successful conduct of the war was rather less due to governmental reorganization than this extract would suggest. But, in general, the change in cabinet government, and more important the reorganization throughout society which went with it, was an important stage in the economic, social, and (in lesser degree) political, transformation brought about by the war.

1.4   Hints towards a Comparative Study of the Effects of the War on Britain, France and America

(OPTIONAL SUB-SECTION)

Do this sub-section only if you have the time and the inclination. Ideally, I do think it important that having studied the British experience in some depth you should be able to relate and compare that experience to the experience of the other major Western countries; however, let's face it—life is short. A small but important portion of the American experience is taken up again in Unit 28 when, in discussing the effects of the Second World War on the Afro-American, Neil Wynn refers back to the Negro's earlier history. In the next section I look at another aspect of French war-time history, and in the next unit Merryn Williams discusses Henri Barbusse's novel of life in the French trenches, *Under Fire*,[1] which is also one of your prescribed texts. Later in the course quite detailed attention is paid to France in the Second World War. If you want to make a choice, I think you will find further reading in American history slightly more useful at this moment than further reading in French history.

Here now are some suggestions as to what books you should read if you are going to develop a comparative study of France and America in the First World War.

France

The best reasonably short account in English is Chapter XXV of Gordon C. Wright's *France in Modern Times*; Professor Wright stands well within the tradition of liberal historians who find it difficult to attribute any social change (save in the form of misery and chaos) to war. Yet, as is even more apparent from *The Ordeal of Total War*,[2] the general textbook of the Second World War which is a prescribed book for later parts of this course, Professor Wright is too good a historian to ignore altogether the evidence of social change brought about by war. The chapter in *France in Modern Times*, then, is a careful, judicious account, which refrains from drawing any very sweeping conclusions.

[1] H. Barbusse, *Under Fire*, Dent (SET BOOK).
[2] G. Wright, *The Ordeal of Total War*, 1939–45, Harper and Row.

Figure 6 French reservists leaving the Gare du Nord to report to depots, August 1914 (Radio Times Hulton Picture Library)

Chapter IX of D. W. Brogan's *The Development of Modern France*, provides a pretty full account, while the most useful brief summary is in J. P. T. Bury, *France 1815–1950*.

Other general accounts are just too sketchy for our purposes, so that for real detail you have to turn to various specialist studies, of which several are to be found in the multi-volume *Social and Economic History of the War*, published by the Carnegie Foundation shortly after the end of the war: among the volumes available in English, Charles Gide, *Effects of the War on French Economic Life* (1923), Arthur Fontaine, *French Industry During the War* (1926), and Pierre Renouvin, *The Forms of War Government in France* (1927) all bring out the effects of war quite strongly, but, of course, lack the perspective of later studies. Shepherd B. Clough, *France: A History of National Economics*,[1] stresses the influence of the war in furthering measures of State control.

Finally, Jere C. King, *Generals and Politicians: Conflict Between France's High Command, Parliament and Government, 1915–1918*, though it only touches incidentally on social topics, forms a bridge between this section and the next, where it is an important piece of recommended reading.

America

A judicious summary, comparable in length and approach to the Gordon Wright chapter on France, is Chapter XVI in Volume 2 of *The Growth of the American Republic* by S. E. Morison, H. S. Commager and W. E. Leuchtenburg. A stimulating article which refers ahead from the war to the 1930s, and so links up with Unit

[1] New York, Scribner, 1939.

19, is W. E. Leuchtenburg's 'The New Deal and the Analogue of War'[1] (this article is supplied as an Appendix to this unit: if you read nothing else on America, please sometime read this). Charles Hirschfeld has a short essay on 'The Transformation of American Life' in a collection of essays (first delivered in 1964 as a series of lectures) entitled *World War I: A Turning Point in Modern History*, ed. Jack J. Roth. An important book which argues that the critical changes in twentieth-century American society took place before America's entry into the war is H. F. May, *The End of American Innocence*.

In any additional reading along these lines that you are able to do, I should like you to keep two questions firmly in mind:

1   How far is any particular development due to the war, and how far is it due to other circumstances?

2   How does it compare with what you know about developments in Britain, and about the social consequences of war in general?

To help you in answering these two questions, let me remind you of the relevant points made so far, which you should also keep firmly in mind:

3   What, in regard to a particular development, was the state of French or American society *before* the war?

4   What was the nature of the impact of the war as an actual historical reality? (Bombing, invasion, merely supplying arms and equipment?)

5   Is the four-tier model of any use or relevance in explaining particular developments?

6   Finally: always ask yourself how far the historian you are reading is really *analysing* the effects of war, and how far he is merely *narrating* a list of changes. Here, to conclude this brief guide, is an example of that sort of narration, which tells us much, but doesn't really explain anything:

As for the war, it had raised the living standard of factory workers and built a powerful labor movement; it had created great shifts in population and accompanying tensions. It had given a temporary bonanza to the farmer, stepped up mechanization of agriculture, and brought the plow to tens of thousands of acres of semi-arid prairie grasslands. Much of this transformation had been painful, and led to further difficult adjustments in the twenties. War also had changed styles and fashions, and molded consumer demands into new channels. In little ways (such as in the introduction of wrist watches for men, shorter skirts for women, and cigarettes for both) and in major ways that involved basic shifts in the economy, it was changing the pattern of life for most Americans.

(Frank Friedel, *America in the Twentieth Century*, New York, Knopf, 1959, p. 21.)

6.2   RELATIONS BETWEEN ARMY AND GOVERNMENT IN FRANCE AND BRITAIN 1914–18

.2.1   The General Problem

The differences in geography and in history meant that civil–military relations operated in slightly different contexts in France and in Britain. None the less there are certain basic common problems which would usually hold true for all countries in all periods. Within the broad general problems, there are of course sharp variations in accordance with which of the models of the military elite described by

[1] In John Braeman, R. H. Bremner and Everett Walter (eds.) *Change and Continuity in Twentieth-century America*, New York, Harper and Row, 1966.

Janowitz is most nearly applicable. Though we may in fact detect some differences in degree, we have already agreed that for the period of the First World War the aristocratic model is still largely applicable, though in both Western countries the situation is complicated by the fact that the war came at the beginning of a time of transition to the democratic model.[1] Of course, any theoretical discussion of civil–military relations depends upon the acceptance of the premise that armies are necessary. Pacifist views on this issue will be discussed elsewhere in this course (Unit 29). Here we simply take it as a fact that in both Britain and France there was acceptance for the notion that armies were necessary. However, that doesn't quite settle that problem. Over the centuries in both countries there had been some debate over whether there should be a permanent professional army, or whether an army, which was no more and no less than the citizens in arms, should be raised only when immediate danger threatened.

The Thirty Years War in the seventeenth century had made it abundantly clear in France that a continental country with vulnerable frontiers must have a permanent professional army. Because Britain was protected from invasion by the sea and by her navy, resistance to the establishment of a permanent professional army continued much longer. It was a much vaunted part of English 'liberty' that there should be no standing professional army, though it has to be noted that there was a professional navy, and that conditions within the navy were illiberal in the extreme. In France the revolution of 1789, and the post-revolutionary period, gave rise (as we saw in Unit 6) to the notion of citizen armies. Thereafter the matter was one of constant debate in France. Liberal politicians, who distrusted professional soldiers, argued for the maintenance of the revolutionary tradition of the citizen army; professional soldiers distrusted the idea of a citizen army as both inefficient and politically suspect. Professor Michael Howard and Professor Robert Blake, in separate essays in a volume edited by Professor Howard, which forms invaluable supplementary reading for this part of the unit, point out that there was never quite this sort of ideological debate in Britain.[2] They are perhaps led, as many British historians are, to overstress the pragmatic quality of all political debate in this country; in fact, within the separate contexts set by history and geography, one can see that some of the essential problems in both countries are the same. The two poles of the essential conflict are these: complete control of the professional army by the government; and complete independence from the government for the professional army. Both of these extreme resolutions of the conflict have their dangers.

Exercise

What are these dangers?

Specimen Answer and Discussion

Complete political control of the army could lead to a total dictatorship on the part of the government of the day. Complete independence for the army could lead to what is called Caesarism; that is to say the taking over of political government by the all-powerful leader or leaders of the army.

---

[1] See Unit 2. Section 2.3.1 for a discussion of M. Janowitz, 'Military Elites and the Study of War' in your set book, *War: Studies from Psychology, Sociology, Anthropology*, Basic Books Harper and Row.

[2] M. Howard, 'Introduction: the Armed Forces as a Political Problem', and Robert Blake, 'Great Britain from the Crimea War to the First World War', in *Soldiers and Governments: Nine Studies in Civil–Military Relations*, ed. Michael Howard. Some of the problems raised in this section have, of course, already been discussed in Units 10–13.

In fact, in both countries the theory was that it was the responsibility of the civilian government to determine all matters of strategic policy, whereas it was for the professional army to work out the details of its execution. Rank and promotion within the army depended very much upon internal army considerations; but the actual allocation and disposition of posts of command lay in the hands of the civilian government. Effectively, too, the ideal of the professional army reigned supreme in both countries, even though France had a highly inequitable form of a selective conscription which provided the basis of the army reserve, whereas Britain had no conscription at all. The big problem that was always bound to loom up in time of war was where did broad strategy (the prerogative of the politician) end, and where did detailed execution (the prerogative of the soldier) begin?

There were other ways, too, in which division of responsibility could become blurred. In both countries by 1914 the government spokesman on military matters was the Secretary of State for War (or War Minister): but sometimes instead of, as theory would have demanded, a professional politician being appointed to this post it was in fact occupied by a soldier (though of course his responsibility was to his civilian colleagues in the cabinet). One irony that frequently emerged in France during the war was that soldier War Ministers were often more resolute in standing up to the demands of their Commander-in-Chief than civilian ones, who often saw their function as defenders of, and yes-men for, the military command in face of the criticisms of other members of the government. On what, theoretically, was the purely military side, there could also be conflict between the Chiefs of Staff on one side and the Commander in the field on the other. Sometimes the political government would adopt the device of trying to strengthen the powers of the General Staff at the expense of those of the Commander-in-Chief.

2.2   France

With regard to the social composition of elites, the crucial fact in France was that by and large the generals and the leading politicians were brought up in totally different traditions. The professional soldiers very much maintained the ideals of the old aristocracy, whereas the politicians saw themselves much more as the representatives of the bourgeois victors in France's revolutionary struggles (if we confined ourselves to the models presented by Janowitz, we would say that the military elite was 'aristocratic', whereas the political elite was 'democratic'). However, the ultimate disgrace of the military elite in the Dreyfus Affair (Dreyfus, a young Jewish officer was wrongly sentenced in 1894 for allegedly betraying secrets to the Germans; by 1906 it was triumphantly demonstrated by the 'Dreyfusards'—among them the novelist Zola and the journalist and politician Clemenceau —that the military had gone to extraordinary lengths to try to cover up the original miscarriage of justice) enabled the republican politicians to purge the army of extreme monarchists. The new hero of the politicians was General Joffre whose own appearance was that of a portly, ruddy-complexioned bourgeois. In 1911 Joffre was appointed to a powerful new post which combined the functions of the Vice-President of the Supreme Council of War and Commander-in-Chief of General Headquarters.

In the last crises weeks before the outbreak of war the political government was weakened by the absence in Russia of President Poincaré and Prime Minister Viviani (a Radical Socialist). The Council of Ministers found it hard to resist Joffre's claims that the French armies must be ready to take an immediate initiative, and that he himself should have maximum freedom of action, especially since the War Minister Messimy acceded to Joffre in all things. On 1 August Joffre was able

to force approval for general mobilization by hinting that otherwise he might resign. This weapon of threatened resignation was always to prove a potent one in the hands of military leaders faced with politicians who in the last analysis were the victims of their own ignorance of military affairs and hence their dependence on the leading professionals. Joffre got what he wanted on 2 August when, after reports of German violations of French frontiers, Messimy telephoned him to say that the government 'gave to the Commander-in-Chief *absolute liberty* of action for the execution of his plans, even if these should lead to crossing the German frontier'.

Figure 7   Joffre, Haig and Foch at Beauquesne, 12 August 1916 (Imperial War Museum)

When the German declaration of war was actually delivered on 3 August France was not equipped with any cut-and-dried definition as to how military responsibilities were to be allocated in time of war, though the broad theory remained as described in the previous section. On 2 August Poincaré proclaimed a 'state of siege' which meant that eight *départements* were placed in Joffre's 'zone of the armies' and so subject to an amalgam of civilian and military control. The 'state of siege' was confirmed by parliament when it met on 4 August. It then adjourned *sine die*, while, on 2 September, mainly on Joffre's insistence, the government moved from Paris to Bordeaux. On 10 August a proportion of these *départements* were declared to be in a 'state of war', which meant that summary military methods were now applicable there. On 6 September military control in the 'zone of the armies' was stepped up: justice could now be administered by summary courts martial. Furthermore, the 'zone of the armies' was extended to cover thirty-three *départements*.

The fact was that, expecting a short war, the politicians had completely abdicated their responsibilities to the professional soldier, Joffre. In this first period of the war Joffre himself deliberately kept the government in ignorance of military developments, and he even instituted a scheme whereby soldiers in the 'zone of the armies' were set to work manufacturing munitions.

Joffre was one of the leading exponents of the view, widely held in France before the war, that the way to victory lay in headlong offensive. Because he was convinced that the Germans would not put their reservists into the front line, Joffre completely underestimated the threat of a German right wing breakthrough on the lines of the Schlieffen plan. However, Joffre's part in the 'miracle of the Marne' when the German advance was halted was sufficient to preserve his reputation untarnished for the time being (much of the most recent military scholarship is inclined, anyway, to defend Joffre's generalship).

The battle of the Marne effectively prevented a rapid German victory; but it did not seem to have brought a French victory much closer. On 7 December the government returned to Paris and on 22 December a one day special session of parliament was held, followed by the opening of the regular parliamentary session on 12 January 1915. Certain of the politicians, having now refound their voices, began to suggest that the stalemate which had now established itself in the West might be broken by opening up a new front in the Balkans or in Turkey. Joffre was easily able to overrule any such suggestions. But there were now many reports of inadequacies in the supply of munitions and other materials of war, and certain politicians began to press for an investigation of these matters by parliamentary commissions. Early in 1915 a direct struggle between these politicians and the military authorities broke out over the rights of the parliamentary commissioners to conduct their enquiries in the 'zone of the armies'.

If Joffre was generally acceptable to bourgeois politicians, the Left, for no terribly strong reason, had a special hero of their own in General Sarail, Commander of the Third Army. In the spring of 1915 anonymous memoranda began to circulate arguing that Sarail would be a better Commander-in-Chief than Joffre. Joffre was able to secure Sarail's dismissal and eventual transfer to the ill-fated Salonika expedition. Although towards the end of the year politicians were reasserting themselves more and more, so that, for instance, on 10 December 1915 the enhanced military control over the 'zone of the armies' which Joffre had acquired in September 1914 was abolished, Joffre's own position *vis-à-vis* all other generals was strengthened: on 2 December he was elevated from 'General in Chief of the Armies of the North and North-east' to the rank of 'Commander-in-Chief of the French Armies' (only the colonial corps in Algeria, Tunis and Morocco being excluded from his command). Reassertion of political authority also meant re-establishment of much of the instability inherent in the French political system. On 25 October a new Prime Minister, Briand (a one-time Socialist, now firmly established as a bourgeois Radical politician of liberal sympathies) took office. As War Minister, he appointed a professional soldier, General Galliéni.

At the turn of the year there were many rumours about the inadequacies of the French defences round the historic fortress town of Verdun. Joffre, however, continued to maintain that all the defences were sound, forcing the government into the traditional dilemma of having either to accept his advice, or else to dismiss him. On 21 February 1916 the German attack on Verdun, deliberately designed to bleed the French armies to death in defence of a historic position which really had little strategic value, began. Just at this time General Galliéni was taken ill, and he was replaced by Joffre's own personal choice, General Roques. By that curious irony which I referred to in the previous section, General Roques, a professional soldier and the personal choice of Joffre, proved to be far tougher in standing up to Joffre than any civilian War Minister had been. The terrible French losses at Verdun greatly weakened Joffre's prestige, and made it possible for Roques to reassert political control over military appointments. Veiled criticism of Joffre was now permitted in the press. And on 16 June 1916 the first secret parliamentary session of the war was held. The disasters of Verdun were followed in the summer by the failure of the Somme offensive, by the collapse of the Salonika expedition, and by severe Allied set-backs in Romania. A second secret parliamentary meeting was held on 28 November 1916. In December Briand replaced the large cabinet by a small War Cabinet. He also replaced Roques by another soldier, the ultra-conservative General Lyautey. But most important he pressed Joffre for his resignation, replacing him by General Nivelle, who appealed to the anti-clerical members of parliament because he was a Protestant.

Nivelle's great ambition was to mount a big offensive against the Germans. His plans seemed impossible to Lyautey (a soldier doing a politician's job remember), so again the basic problem arose of what do the politicians do when they disagree with their Commander-in-Chief, but, since he'd only just been appointed, were reluctant to fire him. Briand got himself out of the difficulty by resigning as Prime Minister: he was replaced by another of the leading bourgeois politicians, Ribot, with Painlevé (a civilian) as War Minister. Painlevé completely shared Lyautey's doubts about the feasibility of Nivelle's offensive, so that the whole difficult problem of civilian control over military policy was now glaringly illuminated. On 6 April the French government took the unprecedented step of holding a special Conference (the Compiègne Conference, 16 April, 1917) at which Nivelle's plans were subjected to detailed scrutiny by the politicians. On behalf of this apparent violation of the division of responsibility described in the previous section, it could be argued that by this stage military questions were intimately bound up with questions of international politics. Russia might drop out of the war, America might come into it; and these vital decisions might well depend upon the course of military events on the Western Front. Ribot and Painlevé would have preferred to call off the proposed offensive, but Nivelle was able to argue that he had already, with great difficulty, made joint arrangements with the British, which it would now be difficult to withdraw from. In face of the lukewarm attitude of the political leaders, Nivelle offered his resignation. The politicians were still reluctant to see another Commander-in-Chief go so quickly, so they finally allowed him to go ahead with his offensive.

The offensive was not a success, so Painlevé now tried to weaken Nivelle's position by the device of turning to the General Staff: he had General Pétain created Technical Counsellor to the Government, as well as Chief of Nivelle's General Staff. This was merely a prelude to Nivelle's being eased out on 15 May, to be replaced by Pétain as Commander-in-Chief, with General Foch taking the post of Chief of Staff and Technical Counsellor to the Government.

Exercise 1

Here is how the British General E. L. Spears summed up the entire Nivelle episode in his book *Prelude to Victory* published in 1939. Comment on the general tone of this passage, and say whether you agree with its conclusion. The whole episode, Spears said,

Stands as a monument to the inefficiency of democracy at war, to the helplessness of ministers facing technicians, and their total inability to decide between professional opinions. . . . The Prime Minister and Painlevé . . . had power to override the Commander-in-Chief in whose plan they had no faith; yet they were incapable of pointing out the failings of that plan or suggesting alternatives, impotent even to call a halt. The Cabinet . . . supreme in name only . . . was hobbled by its lack of technical knowledge and fettered by public opinion which, aware of its ignorance in military matters, would have been intolerant of civilian intrusion in the military sphere. April 16th, 1917, epitomizes the terrible disability from which democracies, even when fighting for their existence, are unable to free themselves.

(E. L. Spears, *Prelude to Victory*, Jonathan Cape, 1939.)

Specimen Answer and Discussion

While in general this is quite a shrewd and a not unfair analysis of the state of civilian–military relations highlighted by the Nivelle episode, it is informed by a traditional military hostility to democracy.

Spears is right when he refers to the difficulty of dealing with public opinion, which certainly did tend in the First World War to side with the generals as against political interference. But his conclusion, that the sort of civil–military dilemma which it is hard to escape from, is entirely the fault of democracy does not seem to me to be valid. Actually the real conclusion of his passage would rather seem to be that difficulties arise due to the ignorance of professional military matters on the part of civilians. This is undoubtedly true, but could equally be true under dictatorship as well as under democracy. What is missing from this appraisal is a realization of the basic fact that whatever the shilly-shallying of the politicians the real failure lay in Nivelle's own misguided appraisal of the situation and his quite wrong-headed plans for an offensive which in fact was, as the politicians suspected, doomed to failure.

The terrible sufferings of the French armies at Verdun and in the Nivelle Offensive led on to the mutinies of 1917. Basically these mutinies took the form of front line soldiers simply refusing to take part in any further offensive actions. It fell to Pétain to deal with them. He took the following actions:

(i)   the system introduced in April 1916 whereby courts martial and summary sentences were replaced by *conseils de guerre* which allowed rights of appeal against sentence, was abolished.

(ii)   150 of the mutineers were sentenced to death; twenty-three sentences were actually carried out.

(iii)   on 2 June commanders were instructed to improve food and sleeping accommodation; to avoid unnecessary exercises; and to keep front line duty for any individual to a minimum.

(iv)   periods of leave were restored.

These were the actions Pétain actually took, and they were in fact successful in taking France through the dangerous mutiny period, and restoring something of army morale. However, Pétain publicly explained the mutinies as being due to the following factors:

(i)   the corrupting influence of degenerate persons who met the troops on leave at Parisian railway stations;

(ii)   the actions of *agents provocateurs*, disguised in military uniforms, who frequented the trains and even the army camps;

(iii)   restrictions upon the severity of the sentences which could be issued by the *conseils de guerre*, with the result that persons of criminal intent could hope to get off with nominal punishment;

(iv)   drunkenness caused by the ready availability of wine and troops receiving bonuses for trench duty;

(v)   the reports received by troops at the front, describing the attendance of soldiers and even certain officers at pacifist meetings held in the 'zone of the interior';

(vi)   strikes in Paris and other industrial centres;

(vii)   the example of the Russian brigades stationed in France, which formed soviets;

(viii)   the articles in the French press describing in detail the Russian committees of workers and soldiers.[1]

Exercise 2

How would you describe the attitude of mind behind this diagnosis, and how does it compare with the measures Pétain actually took as described above?

Specimen Answer and Discussion

This is very much a traditional military view blaming degenerate persons, *agents provocateurs*, lack of severity in punishing wrong doers, drunkenness, pacifists' meetings and reports thereof, strikes, the example of Russian brigades, and the newspapers; indeed everything except the real grievances suffered by the men. Pétain's actual actions show that he did realize that the men had genuine grievances, so to some extent this diagnosis is a face-saving exercise, and also, of course, an attempt to hit back at the army's civilian assailants. It is probable that Pétain both believed his diagnosis and also realized that there were other very real sources of grievance which he had to attend to. It is also typical of the traditional military attitude not to want to wash dirty linen in public.

Of the actual detailed points in his explanation, point (iii) is certainly dealt with in the abolition of the *conseils de guerre*. On the other hand, the restoration of home leave seems to be in flat conflict with his first point that troops were menaced by degenerate persons meeting them at railway stations.

The balance of power had now shifted away from the military dictatorship asserted by Joffre at the beginning of the war back towards control by the politicians. But in July and August of 1917 there was a series of shabby political scandals which suggested that within parliament itself there were defeatists and even traitors to the French cause, so that politicians once again were discredited. First Ribot and then Painlevé, who took his place as Prime Minister, fell from office. The Painlevé ministry was significant as being the weakest in the entire war: socialists and left-wing politicians, who from the day war broke out had joined with conservatives in the 'Union Sacrée', giving their support to the government of the day, now went into vociferous opposition. Painlevé was replaced by Clemenceau, the former Dreyfusard, described by J. P. T. Bury as 'a Jacobin Radical in the classical tradition of 1893'.[2] Clemenceau quickly built up semi-dictatorial powers over parliament and civilian life; but he also stood for civilian control over the military.

Now, however, there came a new twist to the story of conflict of powers. There had never been any formal means of co-ordinating the British and French military effort in France, though from early 1917 Lloyd George had been preoccupied with schemes of this sort, partly because he wanted to do something to diminish the authority of his own Commander in Chief, General Haig. As a direct result of the German successes in March 1918, General Foch was finally appointed as Co-ordinator to the Allied Armies. Further German successes in April led to Foch being elevated to the position of 'Commander in Chief of the Allied Armies operating in France'. But up to a point this diminished the authority of Clemenceau, since Foch was to be answerable to the Supreme War Council rather than to the French Prime Minister. There was a further limitation on Clemenceau's authority in that Foch was in fact reluctant to issue commands to the other allied generals.

---

[1] Here, and elsewhere in this section, I have drawn heavily on Jere C. King, op. cit.
[2] J. P. T. Bury, op. cit., p. 249.

Figure 8   Clemenceau
(Mansell Collection)

On the other hand, after the third great wave of German successes in June 1918 Clemenceau was able to prevail upon Foch to dismiss some of his older generals.

Out of this patchy, and possibly difficult, narrative, we can, perhaps, discern a pattern of three phases in civil–military relations:

(i)   from the outbreak of war till the spring or summer of 1915 when Joffre exercised a virtual military dictatorship;

(ii)   from 1915 till the autumn of 1917 when the civilian politicians gradually recovered some of their authority, to the extent that they tried to limit Nivelle's freedom of action and, finally, were able to secure the dismissal of Nivelle.

(iii)   semi-dictatorial civilian rule by Clemenceau from autumn 1917 to the end of the war.

Exercise 3

How far does this changing pattern reflect the basic conflicts which we outlined at the beginning of this discussion, and how far was it governed by the actual military and political events? Could one draw conclusions as to what settles the particular balance of power during any given period of time?

Specimen Answers and Discussion

In terms of basic conflict it could be argued that Joffre went too far in defiance of the theory of proper spheres of influence for military and civilian authorities, and that therefore there was necessarily a civilian reaction against the military dictatorship. It could be argued, too, that since, in their period of growing ascendancy, the politicians did not succeed in preventing such gross military errors as Nivelle's offensive, thus a stiffening of civilian authority, as represented by Clemenceau, was still necessary. But, personally, I think that we must give much greater weight to the actual military and political circumstances. Foch failed to achieve the quick victory which he promised, and he compounded this with his blunderings over Verdun. More than this, the new style of total war needed the co-operation of civilians so that the politicians really had to be involved in a way that Foch, with his ideas of setting soldiers to make munitions, was not prepared to allow for. Foch, therefore, had to accede to greater parliamentary control. Parliamentary rule, however, was disgraced by the scandals of 1917, and (more important in my view) was still not successful in bringing about the total reorganization needed for victory. (It was also characterized by the Nivelle fiasco and the mutinies.) Hence the emergence of strong civilian rule under Clemenceau. Finally the German victories in 1918 forced further changes in regard to the problems of allied co-operation.

One conclusion about what settles the particular balance of power at any given time, and one that seems to be accepted by Professor Jere C. King, is that the balance is determined by the extent of military and political success. Professor King writes:

France, which had entered the war in the circumstances of parliamentary deference to the military, emerged from the conflict with a strong-minded president of the council in the ascendant over both command and parliament. The nation had groped its way from the initial military dictatorship through a gradual recovery of parliamentary authority until it came out with virtually a civilian dictatorship in the hands of the chief of the executive power. The reason for this backing and filling lay principally in the failure of Joffre to win a quick and decisive victory, and in parliament's inability to do any better when it and the government narrowly circumscribed the command during the Nivelle epoch. The loss of face by the military was equalled by the tarnished prestige of civilian politicians when it transpired during the lenient Painlevé administration that traitors, near traitors, and defeatists were in the very midst of parliament, if not of the government itself. Through default, therefore, power shifted from Joffre to parliament until it finally resided with the figure whose name symbolised the will to victory, Georges Clemenceau.

(J. C. King, *Generals and Politicians: Conflict between France's High Command, Parliament and Government, 1914–1918*, University of California Press, 1951, p. 192.)

Undoubtedly, relative success must be a factor in determining any pattern of relationships. But in my view King underplays the importance of the need in this war for efficient organization of the home front. Quite possibly a military leader with a real appreciation of the needs in this area might have succeeded in asserting himself, but on the whole, given the nature of French society and the need to maintain civilian morale, the emergence of a form of civilian dictatorship does seem a logical outcome of the peculiar needs of this first total war. In other words, I am suggesting that the needs of the particular type of war, as well as the degree of success attending upon any particular experiment, will help to determine the pattern of civil–military relationships.

.2.3 Britain

In Britain it was much more the case that the military elite was drawn from the same social class as the political elite, though some differences were appearing with the rise of the latest generation of liberal politicians. One bad old tradition, which on the whole had had the beneficial effect of preventing the development of a chasm between military and political leaders, had been the system whereby commissions in the army were purchased, so that service in the army was almost a hobby for the upper-class, rather than a separate profession and tradition in its own right. Purchase of commissions was finally abolished (despite strong resistance) in 1871: but right down to 1914 it did remain true that the army was not yet a completely separate caste. In general the fairly easy-going theory was that the army should not meddle in politics, but equally that politicians should not meddle with the army. Campbell-Bannerman, Liberal Minister of War, and, later, Liberal Prime Minister, said cynically that the basic principle governing military affairs in the nineteenth century was 'leave the old army alone and don't make a war'. One privilege, felt to belong to the army, which lasted into the First World War, was that the army had a right to make direct representations to the monarch.

Exercise 1

Can you see what reputable principle might lie behind this apparently rather astonishing idea?

Specimen Answer

The idea is really related to the danger of dictatorship which I mentioned at the very beginning of this discussion: the army should be the servant of the entire nation (of whom the king is the head) not the instrument of any one politician or political party.

The first decade of the twentieth century was a period of reorganization and professionalization in the British army. In 1904 the old solo post of Commander-in-Chief was abolished: instead a new body, the Army Council, was created together with the new post of Chief of the General Staff (renamed Chief of the Imperial General Staff—C.I.G.S.—in 1908). The very fact of these reforms being carried through meant that the theoretical separation of military affairs from politics had to be broken. Admiral Sir John Fisher, First Sea Lord from 1904 (that is to say the professional non-political head of the Navy—the political head is the First Lord of the Admiralty) carried through many important technical reforms in the Navy, though being a violent and opinionated man he also stirred up a good deal of controversy. He was a stout upholder of the traditional view that Britain's defences could rest entirely on the navy—that is to say he was a member of the 'blue water school' against the supporters of a larger army, what he called the 'blue funk school'. Referring to the navy's sobriquet, 'the silent service', Robert Blake remarks that 'a less appropriate description of the Edwardian navy could hardly be conceived'.

Army reforms were carried through by the more tactful Liberal Secretary for War, R. B. Haldane. By reducing the army estimates and firmly rejecting any idea of conscription, while at the same time creating a more efficient army with a European Expeditionary Force at the ready, Haldane secured wide support for his reforms.

The Irish crisis just on the eve of the war revealed another aspect of the complicated story of civil–military relations. The Liberal Government of the day was committed to giving Home Rule to Ireland: for the strongly pro-British Ulster Protestants in the North this would involve being governed by the Catholic majority from Dublin. In face of the determined resistance of Ulstermen who were openly forming a volunteer army of their own, the British government would need the loyal support of the British army in carrying through its declared policies. But in fact all the sympathies of the overwhelmingly Conservative army lay on the side of the Ulstermen. This is the background to the famous Curragh incident (or Curragh mutiny) of 1913 when British officers in Ireland made it clear that they would prefer to resign their commissions rather than carry through any action against Ulstermen. Robert Blake agrees that this action was unconstitutional but gives it his approval. He then continues:

Whatever one thinks of the Curragh incident, it would be agreed that it is quite abnormal. It is the only instance in modern times where the army has been pulled into politics in respect of what was a wholly non-military issue, whereas both before and after 1914 such intervention, when it occurred, has always concerned matters of military significance.

(M. Howard (ed.) *Soldiers and Governments*, Eyre and Spottiswoode, 1957, p.30.

Exercise 2

Do you agree with this dismissal of the significance of the incident as being quite abnormal?

Specimen Answer

As a matter of historical fact what Blake says about the 'abnormality' of the incident is completely true. Yet, to my mind, his dismissal of it is a little light. Ideally, in accordance with the norm of civil–military relations described in Section 16.2.1, one would want an army which could be relied on to support the civil authority even when its sentiments were affected.

Exercise 3

Moving to the actual outbreak of war, Blake points out that now there was raised 'a series of major problems about relations between the leaders and the armed forces and the civil authorities'. He then asks (p. 39): 'Why were these relations so much more difficult than in any previous war?' Try to answer this question.

Specimen Answer

Blake's answer to his own question is: 'chiefly, I think, because the 1914–18 war was the first total war, involving in the end, complete mobilisation of the entire nation in order to achieve victory'. I hope you got that point all right. Blake also adds the point that in previous wars there were only small professional armies fighting far away from home. Now, of course, there was to be a mass army, whose field of operations lay just across the Channel in France.

In keeping with what was said in the opening section, the theory of civil–military relations in Britain was pretty simple. It was for the Cabinet to decide broad outlines of strategy: for example whether the war should be fought primarily in the German overseas colonies, at sea, or through an expeditionary force sent to the Western front. Cabinet decisions were to be communicated through the War Minister and the Chief of the Imperial General Staff to the Commander in a particular area. It was his job to carry out his general instructions. If the Commander made a mess of things then the Cabinet had the right to dismiss him; but otherwise he should be free from interference from politicians in carrying out his instructions. As we have already noted, in practice it was always extremely difficult to draw the exact line between broad strategy and the military execution of it. It was not, therefore, altogether surprising if politicians should sometimes wish to interfere in areas which soldiers might regard as being purely concerned with detailed execution of policy. By the same token leading soldiers would sometimes wish to press their own ideas on strategy upon the Cabinet, or more subtly by playing off different ministers against each other, or against the Prime Minister, or, as we have remarked, by appealing direct to the King. Two further problems arose from the actual events of Britain's First World War experience, and from the nature of the personalities involved therein:

1   A number of the leading soldiers (Kitchener, Haig and Robertson) acquired a great popular following, so that they attained positions of considerable power as against the politicians.

2   Strategy and politics in Britain during the First World War was marked by the great divide between the supporters of concentration on the Western front (the 'Westerners') and the 'Easterners' who believed in opening up a new front in the Balkans or Turkey.

Exercise 4

We saw that there was a similar movement in France, though in fact it was never so important in France as in Britain. Why not?

Specimen Answer

French politicians, even those most enthusiastic for an Eastern offensive, could never escape from the fact that the Germans were on French soil and that therefore much of the fighting must take place there. British politicians were not limited by this patriotic consideration.

Let us now look at the chronology of civil–military relations in Britain during the First World War.[1] The War Secretary in the Liberal Government in office in the years before the war, Colonel Seely, had resigned because of the Curragh incident, and the Prime Minister, Asquith, had for the time being taken over his duties. When war broke out there was a great outcry in the press in favour of Lord Kitchener, the most prestigious of all Britain's military leaders, being appointed to the office of War Secretary. Bowing in a characteristic way to the appeal of military prestige, and also influenced by the notion that Kitchener's appointment would lend to his government a certain national, non-party, character, Asquith duly made the appointment. Unlike most other experts, Kitchener did appreciate that the war might well last for three years or more. But in all other respects his ideas were completely outmoded and he had few gifts as an administrator. At best, he was as someone remarked, 'a magnificent poster'. Most critically from the point of view of the subject-matter of this section, he failed to provide the appropriate link between political government on one side and the army on the other. He rather seems to have seen himself as occupying the role of the old solo Commander-in-Chief. Certainly he outraged the Commander-in-Chief of the British Expeditionary Force in France, Sir John French, by arriving in France wearing his Field-Marshal's uniform, and thus blatantly outranking French.

[1] The best single account is Paul Guinn, *British Strategy and Politics 1914–1918*.

In the matter of the British Government's failure to provide the army with sufficient munitions, French had rather stronger grounds for complaint against Kitchener. In May 1915 French in effect launched his attack on Kitchener by means of *The Times* military correspondent, Colonel Repington, who published a dispatch in *The Times* referring to the shortage of munition supplies. There was also at this time a crisis at the Admiralty between the political head, the First Lord of the Admiralty, Winston Churchill, and the professional head, the First Sea Lord, Admiral Fisher. (It is highly relevant to the central issue of this section that Churchill—then a Liberal—was viciously attacked in Conservative circles for exceeding his purely political functions: on 21 October 1914 the ultra-Tory *Morning Post* declared that Churchill should recognize 'that his proper function was to represent the Government in the Admiralty and the Admiralty in the Government and to be guided in matters of warfare by his expert advisers. But we have now sufficient evidence to demonstrate that the First Lord seeks to guide the operations of war.'[1]) There has been a good deal of argument among historians as to which of the two crises, the munitions crisis touched off by Repington, or the Admiralty crisis, was responsible for the replacement of the Asquith Liberal government by a coalition of Liberals and Conservatives with Labour representation, still under Asquith. In my view, as you will have seen from *The Deluge*, the crucial point was the general failure of the Asquith Liberal government to carry through the social, economic and political reorganization needed to meet the challenge of war. In this view the two crises merely provided the occasion for the change of government which deeper discontents would have brought within a matter of months in any case.

Figure 9   The King with British Army Commanders at Buckingham Palace, 19 December 1918. Left to right: Sir William Birchwood, Sir Henry Rawlinson, Sir Hubert Plumer, the King, Sir Douglas Haig, Sir Henry Horne, Sir Julian Byng (Imperial War Museum)

[1] Quoted in Martin Gilbert, *Winston S. Churchill*: Volume III, *1914–1916*, p. 144.

Asquith contemplated getting rid of Kitchener, but, in a familiar way, decided that his prestige was too high with the general public to make this possible. Instead, towards the end of 1915, Asquith hit upon the expedient of reviving and augmenting the powers of the Chief of the Imperial General Staff. The last important holder of this office had died in October 1914 and Kitchener had deliberately chosen a nonentity to fill the post. Asquith now appointed Sir William Robertson as Chief of the Imperial General Staff, while at the same time restricting Kitchener's powers to those traditionally exercised by a War Minister, that is to administration and supply. Robertson, on the other hand, was to attend Cabinet meetings, give the Cabinet strategic advice independent of the War Secretary, and was to be the sole channel for conveying Cabinet instructions to the armies in the field. At the same time Sir John French was replaced as Commander-in-Chief of the British forces in France by Sir Douglas Haig.

Figure 10   Kitchener recruiting poster (Imperial War Museum)

The military events of 1916 scarcely provided any glorious vindication for this reallocation of military authority. However, when further crisis came in December 1916 it was in no sense caused by conflict between civil and military authorities. Robert Blake sees the 'underlying issue' as 'one of personalities'—the energetic Lloyd George arrayed against the lethargic Asquith. Again, as you will see from *The Deluge* (pp. 192–200) I would put much less emphasis on personalities and much more on the further build-up of pressures for drastic economic and social reorganization.

As far as civil–military relations are concerned, the last two years of war present an almost classic instance of the situation in which the civil authority (Lloyd George) distrusts the aims and ability of the military, but feels unable to risk a direct confrontation. On strategic aims Lloyd George, by conviction, remained an 'Easterner', while Haig, naturally, was an absolute 'Westerner'. One possible way of diminishing Haig's influence was through the establishment of a unified Allied Command, but Lloyd George's first attempt to achieve this, at the Calais Conference of February 1917, succeeded only in arousing further mistrust on Haig's part towards the Prime Minister. The 'Passchendaele' campaign in the last months of the year (244,897 casualties, many of them literally drowned in the mud of the battlefield, for microscopic gains) seemed to justify all Lloyd George's mistrust of Haig. Yet still Lloyd George did not dismiss his Commander-in-Chief.

Exercise 5

Try to give some of the reasons why he did not do so.

Specimen Answer

Because, in general, Haig's prestige still stood high with the 'public'—i.e. his dismissal would have led to a great, and politically dangerous, outcry in the newspapers. More specifically, it would have led to resignations from Lloyd George's government (in particular, though I would hardly expect you to know this, from the War Secretary, Lord Derby: Lloyd George felt he could not survive the loss of both Commander-in-Chief and War Secretary). Finally, Lloyd George had the problem that there was no obvious successor for Haig. Any Commander-in-Chief would have to be able to command a certain respect and to maintain morale among the troops.

When the Supreme Allied Council was established at Versailles, Lloyd George was able partially to circumvent Sir William Robertson, by seeking alternative advice from the British representative there, General Sir Henry Wilson (who was, incidentally, an extreme Ulster conservative and, seemingly, an opponent of all the political principles professed by Lloyd George; Haig's own comment on Wilson was that 'he seems to acquire a more evil look each time I see him'). But in reality this was not more than a most indirect attack upon Haig; Robertson, as C.I.G.S., was a slightly less difficult target than Haig, who had all the prestige of a commander in the field. In February 1918 there were press attacks on the Versailles organization, and the *Morning Post* (11 February) published a vigorous attack on Lloyd George, penned by Repington (briefed, he claimed, by Clemenceau):

My opinion is that by starving our Armies in the field, by advocating adventures contrary to the advice of his legitimate military advisers, and by approving a decision which deprives our Commander in France of his full command, Mr Lloyd George has clearly and finally proved his incapacity to govern England in a great war. This is the situation which Parliament must clear up in such manner as it thinks best.

This charge against Lloyd George, that he deliberately starved the Western Front of men was one often repeated then and since. It fits well into the pattern of civil authorities arrayed in bold confrontation on one side, against military authorities on the other. Actually the position was not as simple as that. There is no evidence that Lloyd George ever said that he 'would not be Haig's butcher', or that he ever deliberately tried to hold men back. It seems that the holding back of some men in reserve in Britain was largely due to the War Office's own bureaucracy.[1] Anyway, Lloyd George had further minor victories in that he succeeded in forcing Robertson's resignation (replacing him by Wilson), and a few weeks later he was able, without incident, to replace Lord Derby as War Secretary by Lord Milner.

When the Germans achieved a series of remarkable, and frightening, victories in the early months of 1918, Lloyd George pointedly tried to place the blame on the military leadership. General Gough, Commander of the Fifth Army was recalled, and in a speech in the House of Commons the Prime Minister asserted that the army in France was numerically stronger in 1918 than it had been a year previously. This was not in fact true, but it does seem that Lloyd George had genuinely been misled by erroneous figures supplied by the War Office. In May General Sir Frederick Maurice, who had been Director of Military Operations at the War Office until Robertson's resignation brought his own dismissal, entered the fray. In a letter sent to several newspapers Maurice (among other things) accused the government of straight dishonesty in its claims about the numerical strength of the army in 1918. For a serving soldier this action was entirely against King's Regulations; it was also a sincere and courageous one. In the upshot no disciplinary action was taken against Maurice.[2]

The 'Maurice letter' was followed by the 'Maurice debate' in the House of Commons. This was the only occasion in the entire war in which there was an open parliamentary debate which could have resulted in the destruction of the government of the day. But again the occasion scarcely fits any pattern of civil–military confrontation. Extreme right-wingers, the most enthusiastic upholders of military authority, would have liked to see Lloyd George defeated, but they had little enthusiasm for the man upon whom it fell to issue the parliamentary challenge— the ousted Prime Minister Asquith. In fact the debate simply turned into another oratorical triumph for Lloyd George, and the majority he achieved (293 to 106) ensured that his position as Prime Minister was unassailable till the end of the war—save that he was still stuck with Haig!

2.4   Some Conclusions

Controversy over the rights and wrongs of the 'brass hats' and the 'frocks' in the First World War has continued ever since. The outstanding military thinker and historian, Sir Basil Liddell Hart, published many works which were highly critical of the British generals for their inflexible strategy which produced such bloodshed for apparently tiny results. Dr Paul Guinn has generally followed the line established by Liddell Hart, but specialist military historians, such as John Terraine, have recently offered reasoned defences of the Western strategy. It would seem to me that all the serious charges that can be laid against the generals—in particular overweening confidence in face of overwhelming contrary evidence, on the part of Haig—have not been answered entirely satisfactorily. But that is not to

[1] See A. J. P. Taylor, *English History 1914–1945*, p. 98.
[2] For a full account of the Maurice affair see my article in *History of the First World War*, Vol. 7, No. 2, London, BPC, 1971.

say that the politicians should have had more control over the military effort. It is true that, in the case of the navy, Lloyd George was right when he forced the professional sailors, against their own judgement, to adopt the convoy system as a defence against submarine attacks. But it seems clear that the politicians simply did not have the knowledge to be able to take over control of military strategy; and so, in not finally dismissing Haig, Lloyd George seems to have recognized this.

Exercise 1

Imagine you are Prime Minister in time of war and you have developed grave doubts about the abilities of your Commander-in-Chief, who, however, remains highly popular in the public eye.

Question 1

What moves should you make prior to contemplating his dismissal?

Question 2

What moves could you make to diminish his influence short of actually dismissing him?

Question 3

What factors could you hope to have on your side if you did dismiss him?

Exercise 2

What were the main influences making for differences between civil–military relations in France and Britain, 1914–18?

Specimen Answers
Exercise 1
Question 1

Make sure that you have the support of your War Secretary. If not, try to replace him with someone who will support you (try anyway to avoid losing Commander-in-Chief and War Secretary simultaneously). Make sure you have a credible alternative Commander-in-Chief in mind. Try through the press, etc., to undermine the position of the present Commander-in-Chief.

Question 2

Strengthen the General Staff at the expense of the Commander-in-Chief. Try to place the Commander-in-Chief under the authority of an allied commander.

Question 3

That in a country with liberal institutions it is accepted that the political power is superior to the military. (If your country had no such tradition you might well be running the risk of a *coup-d'état* on the part of the ousted general.) That, in time of war, the ranks will usually close behind the government of the day—provided that government is successful. Through censorship you will probably have a pretty thorough control of the press.

Exercise 2

From the war itself, the fact that it was fought on French soil, not British, seems to me very important in explaining why French politicians became more involved in military matters than did British politicians. Other differences arise from the slight variations in the nature of the civil and military elites in the two countries.

Background Reading

Beaverbrook, Lord, *Men and Power: 1917, 1918*, London, Hutchinson, 1956 and *Politicians and the War*, 1914–1916, London, Oldbourne Book Co. Useful for British civil–military relations. Accounts by an 'insider' with all the virtues and vices that implies.

Brogan, D. W., *The Development of Modern France*, London, Hamish Hamilton, 1940. Includes quite a full account of World War I.

Bury, J. P. T., *France 1814–1940*, 4th edition, London Methuen (University Paperback), 1969. Good straight-forward textbook.

Carrington, Charles, *Soldier from the Wars Returning*, London, Hutchinson, 1965. The best introduction to the realities of trench life.

Fontaine, Arthur, *French Industry During the War*, New Haven, Carnegie Endowment, 1926. Detailed monograph.

Gilbert Martin, *Winston S. Churchill:* volume III *1914–1916*, London, Heinemann. Fascinating, but immensely long.

Guinn, Paul, *British Strategy and Politics 1914–1918*, London, Oxford University Press, 1965. The most recent standard authority on this subject.

Hart, Liddell, *The War in Outline, 1914–1918*, London, Faber, 1936. The briefest of his several classic denunciations of the Western generals.

Havighurst, A. F., *Twentieth Century Britain*, 2nd edition, New York, Harper and Row, 1966. Reliable textbook. Useful antidote to the 'Marwick' view.

Howard, Michael, (ed.), *Soldiers and Governments: Nine Studies in Civil–Military Relations*, London, Eyre and Spottiswoode, 1957. Howard's introduction, and Blake on Britain are superb. The essay on France is of little value.

Hynes, S. L., *The Edwardian Turn of Mind*, London, Oxford University Press, 1968. Argues that social change took place *before* the First World War.

King, Jere C., *Generals and Politicians: Conflict between France's High Command, Parliament and Government, 1914–1918*, Berkeley and Los Angeles, University of California Press. The standard work on its subject.

Leuchtenburg, W. E., 'The New Deal and the Analogue of War' in John Braeman, R. H. Bremner and Everett Walters (1966) (eds.), *Change and Continuity in Twentieth-century America*, New York, Harper and Row, 1966. Useful and stimulating article.

May, H. F., *The End of American Innocence*, New York, Knopf, 1959. Argues that social change took place *before* the First World War.

Milward, Alan, *The Economic Effects of the World Wars on Britain*, Macmillan, 1970. A useful bibliographical pamphlet, marred by some inaccuracies and irrelevancies.

Morison, S. E., Commager, H. S., and Leuchtenburg, W. E., *The Growth of the American Republic*, Volume 2, 6th edition, New York, Oxford University Press, 1969. Excellent chapter on World War I.

Roth, Jack J., (ed.), *World War I: A Turning Point in Modern History*, New York, Knopf, 1967. Interesting; but doesn't quite live up to promise of its title.

Taylor, A. J. P., *English History 1914–1945*, Oxford, The Clarendon Press, 1965. Good chapters on World War I.

Terraine, John, *The Western Front, 1914–1918*, London, Hutchinson, 1964. One of several books by the most convincing defender of Haig and the Western generals.

Wright, Gordon C., *France in Modern Times*, London, John Murray, 1962. Excellent chapter on World War I.

ACKNOWLEDGEMENTS

Acknowledgement is made to the following for illustrations used in this unit:

Imperial War Museum; Mansell Collection; Radio Times Hulton Picture Library.

Appendix

THE NEW DEAL AND THE ANALOGUE OF WAR*

WILLIAM E. LEUCHTENBURG

The metaphors a nation employs reveal much about how it perceives reality. The unconscious choice of symbols bares the bedrock of its beliefs. Moreover, the words people use are not neutral artifacts; they shape ideas and behavior. Just as the psychoanalyst listens for slips of the tongue or strange incongruities of ideas to help him understand the patient, or the literary critic studies the symbols in a poem or novel, so the historian finds it rewarding to explore the imagery a particular period has used, consciously or unconsciously, to interpret its experience.

In the months and years that followed the stock market crash of 1929, America searched for some way to make comprehensible what was happening. Sometimes people thought of the Great Depression as a breakdown of a system, sometimes as the product of the machinations of evil or stupid men, sometimes as the visitation of a plague like the Black Death. But from the very first, many conceived the depression to be a calamity like war or, more specifically, like the menace of a foreign enemy who had to be defeated in combat. Occasionally, the analogue of war was a general one, more often it referred specifically to World War I. When President Hoover summoned the leading industrialists to meet in Washington, one financial journal commented: ' "Order up the Moors!" was Marshal Foch's reply at the first battle of the Marne. . . . "Order up the business reserves," directed President Hoover as pessimistic reports flowed in from all quarters, following the stock market crash.'[1]

For the rest of his years in office, Hoover resorted constantly to the imagery of war to describe the depression.[2] In one of his addresses, he claimed that the country had just won its 'battle of Chateau-Thierry' and must 'reform [its] forces for the battle of Soissons.' 'Again and again he used military terms in describing the struggle in which he was engaged,' recalled one of his aides. 'He was the commanding officer at general headquarters, so visualized himself.'[3] Hoover's advisers perceived the crisis in the same terms. In June, 1931, after the President unfolded his reparations plan, Secretary of State Henry Stimson confided to his diary: 'We have all been saying to each other the situation is quite like war.'[4]

In addition to employing the metaphor of war to explain the meaning of the depression, the 1930s drew on the experience of the economic mobilization of World War I for instrumentalities to combat hard times. These are two discrete themes. Some who

* The writer is indebted to David Brody, Clarke Chambers, Bernard Cohen, Paul Conkin, Robert Cross, Bertram Gross, Charles Hirschfeld, Richard Hofstadter, Robert Holt, Henry Kaiser, Val Lorwin, Warren Miller, Carl Resek, James Shideler, and Rexford Tugwell for helpful comments on an earlier draft of this essay. The essay was originally presented as a paper at the meetings of the American Historical Association in New York in December, 1960, and was substantially revised when the writer was a Fellow at the Center for Advanced Study in the Behavioral Sciences, Stanford, California, 1961–62.

[1] *Magazine of Wall Street*, XLV (1929), 264, cited in J. Kenneth Galbraith, *The Great Crash*, Boston, 1929, p. 143.

[2] Hoover, observed Georges Seldes, 'repeatedly used the figures of speech of war in his description of the depression. It was a skillful association of ideas, for the war was a difficult time which ended happily; it was exciting; and it was the last time the whole nation was united.'—Seldes, *Years of the Locust*, Boston, 1933, p. 258. The conviction of political leaders and publicists that reference to the war would evoke a favorable response suggests some modification of the view that the 'pacifist thirties' thought of World War I only with abhorrence. While they viewed war as a wasteful, inhuman social institution, many progressives also recalled World War I as an ennobling experience of sacrifice for the national welfare and as a time of economic advance. In 1931 Richard Ely wrote: 'A marked difference between the general situation in the World War and our situation during Hard Times must be noticed. A war may at first be attended by a good deal of economic confusion and distress, but very soon the wages and profits mount upward and people are apparently more prosperous than ever. Returns of capital in many lines of activity are large and wages are apt to mount up to levels heretofore unknown.'—Ely, *Hard Times—The Way In and the Way Out*, New York, 1931, p. 110.

[3] *Literary Digest*, CXIV (September 10, 1932), 4–5; *New Republic*, LXXII, 1932, 86; Theodore Joslin, *Hoover Off the Record*, Garden City, N.Y., 1934, p. 63. 'Fighting this depression is becoming more and more like waging a war,' Hoover observed. 'We have the combats, if against an unseen foe of inestimable strength. We have our men and we have our casualties among them.'—*Ibid.*, p. 182.

[4] Henry Stimson MS Diary, June 15, 1931. Sterling Memorial Library, Yale University, New Haven, Conn., Stimson MSS. For similar assessments of the depression, see *Report of Proceedings of the Fiftieth Annual Convention of the American Federation of Labor*, Washington, D.C., 1930, p. 366; Henry Morrow Hyde MS Diary, December 17, 1931, Alderman Library, University of Virginia, Charlottesville, Va., Hyde MSS; Justice Brandeis' dissent in *New State Ice Co.* v. *Liebmann*, 285 U.S. 306, 1932; *Rocky Mountain News*, March 1, 1933.

resorted to the analogue of war had no interest in the precedent of the wartime mobilization, and a few who turned to the example of the mobilization did not employ the imagery of war. Hence, it would be possible to examine these strands separately. But so closely did most Americans associate the metaphor of war with the specific legacy of the war mobilization that it has seemed more fruitful to discuss both these themes in a single context.

In the New Deal years, the two strands were inseparable. As early as his 'forgotten man' speech in the 1932 campaign, Franklin Roosevelt manipulated the analogue of war to his advantage. In that same address, he referred to the specific operations of the war mobilization, a heritage he was to acknowledge on many occasions after his election to the presidency. But the legacy of the war was to prove a mixed blessing. Useful as a justification for New Deal actions, it also served to limit and divert the reformers in ways that had not been anticipated.

In tracing the genealogy of the New Deal, historians have paid little attention to the mobilization of World War I. Instead, they have centered their interest on two movements: populism and progressivism. Both were important antecedents—a reasonably straight line may be drawn from the Populist sub-treasury plan to the Commodity Credit Corporation, from the Pujo committee to the Securities and Exchange Commission. Yet in concentrating on populism and progressivism, writers have given too little attention to the influence of the wartime mobilization, which may have been as great as the example of the Progressive era and certainly was more important than populism.[5]

Much of the experience of the Progressive era proved irrelevant to the task facing Roosevelt in 1933. Very little in the Populist and Progressive periods offered a precedent for massive federal intervention in the economy. Many of the reforms of the prewar generation were modest ventures in regulation or attempts to liberate business enterprise rather than ambitious national programs of economic action. Moreover, in these years, reformers thought the state and the city more important arenas than the national capital.

World War I marked a bold new departure. It occasioned the abandonment of laissez faire precepts and raised the federal government to director, even dictator, of the economy. The War Industries Board mobilized production; the War Trade Board licensed imports and exports; the Capital Issues Committee regulated investment; the War Finance Corporation lent funds to munitions industries; the Railroad Administration unified the nation's railways; the Fuel Administration fixed the price of coal and imposed 'coal holidays' on eastern industry; and the Food Administration controlled the production and consumption of food. The Lever Food and Fuel Control Act of 1917 gave the President sweeping powers: to take over factories and operate them, to fix a maximum price for wheat, and to license businesses in necessaries. By a generous interpretation of its powers, the War Industries Board supervised pricing, compelled corporations to accept government priorities, and forced companies to obey federal edicts on how to dispose of their products. 'This is a crisis,' a War Industries Board representative scolded steel-industry leaders, 'and commercialism, gentlemen, must be absolutely sidetracked.'[6] Actions of this character, as well as the proliferation of public corporations ranging from the United States Housing Corporation to the Spruce Production Corporation, proved important precedents for New Deal enterprises fifteen years later.[7]

---

[5] One cannot, of course, distinguish sharply between the relative influence of World War I and progressivism since the war mobilization was, in some respects, a logical outgrowth of the Progressive movement. (There were, too, other antecedents of the New Deal, notably the experiments of the 1920s.) Some historians of the New Deal, it should be noted, have been sensitive either to the indebtedness of the Roosevelt administration to the war mobilization or to the use the New Deal made of war imagery. See, especially, Frank Freidel, *America in the Twentieth Century*, New York, 1960, p. 312; Arthur Schlesinger, Jr., *The Crisis of the Old Order (The Age of Roosevelt)* Boston, 1957, pp. 37–39; Schlesinger, *The Coming of the New Deal (The Age of Roosevelt)* Boston, 1959, p. 176; Paul Conkin, *Tomorrow a New World: The New Deal Community Program*, Ithaca, N.Y., 1959, pp. 50–54, 67. Most narratives, however, have not only ignored this relationship but have minimized the significance of the political and economic events of the war years. With respect to the war, historians have been chiefly interested in what happened *before* our intervention (the submarine crisis) and what happened *afterwards* (the League of Nations fight), not with the substance of the war experience itself.

[6] David Brody, *Steelworkers in America: The Nonunion Era* ('Harvard Historical Monographs,' XLV, Cambridge 1960), p. 206; *Iron Age*, May 9, 1918, pp. 1206–13.

[7] If, by later standards, the experiment in controls was embryonic, it nonetheless represented an unprecedented degree of government intervention. In the immense literature on the war mobilization, see Benedict Crowell and R. F. Wilson, *How America Went to War*, 6 vols.; New Haven, 1921; Bernard M. Baruch, *American Industry in the War*, New York, 1941; Woodbury Willoughby, *The Capital Issues Committee and War Finance Corporation*, ('The Johns Hopkins University Studies in Historical and Political Science,' LII [Baltimore, 1934]); M Hsin Chiang, 'The United States War Industries Board, 1917–1918' (Master's thesis, Stanford University, 1937); William Clinton Mullendore, *History of the United States Food Administration 1917–1919*, Palo Alto, Calif., 1941; Waldo G. Leland and Newton D. Mereness, *Introduction to the American Official Sources for the Economic and Social History of the War*, New Haven, 1926.

The field of labor relations may serve as a single example of the difference in importance of the Populist and Progressive experience and that of World War I. Prior to the war, no serious attempt had ever been made to empower the federal government to uphold the right of collective bargaining.[8] Federal action was limited to peripheral areas. When class lines were drawn in labor disputes, progressives frequently aligned themselves against the unions.[9] But in World War I, the War Labor Board proclaimed its support of union rights and, to the discomfiture of businessmen, enforced these rights. Many of the labor policies pursued in the war months would have been inconceivable a short while before. When the Smith & Wesson Arms Company of Springfield, Massachusetts, insisted on its prerogative to require workers to sign yellow-dog contracts, the War Department commandeered the plant, even though the Supreme Court had upheld the legality of such contracts.[10] The government even dared to seize Western Union when the president of the firm denied his employees the right to join the Commercial Telegraphers Union.[11] The panoply of procedures developed by the War Labor Board and the War Labor Policies Board provided the basis in later years for a series of enactments culminating in the Wagner National Labor Relations Act of 1935.

The war gave a home to the new class of university-trained intellectuals which had emerged in the generation before the war. While some of them had found a career in public service in state governments before 1917, few had worked in the national government, chiefly because there was so little in Washington for them to do. After the United States intervened, Washington swarmed with professors, until, one writer noted, 'the Cosmos Club was little better than a faculty meeting of all the universities.'[12] In all countries, he observed, professors 'fought, and they managed affairs, thus refuting the ancient libellous assumption that they constituted an absent-minded third sex. . . .'[13]

Public administrators of this type represented a new force in American politics. They were advisers and technicians but, more than that, men of influence and even of power. At a time when class conflicts were sharpening, they did not reflect particular classes so much as the thrust for power of *novi homines* who had a significant role to play on the national stage. Some like Gifford Pinchot had made their appearance in Washington before the war, and still more like Charles McCarthy had been active in such reform capitals as Madison and Albany, but it was the war which offered them an unparalleled opportunity. Randolph Bourne noted perceptively the 'peculiar congeniality between the war and these men. It is as if the war and they had been waiting for each other.'[14] Phenomena almost wholly of the twentieth century, they came by the 1930's to have a crucial part in shaping legislation and in manning the new agencies which their legislation developed. The passage of the Wagner Act in 1935, for example, resulted less from such traditional elements as presidential initiative or the play of 'social forces' than from the conjunction of university-trained administrators like Lloyd Garrison within the New Deal bureaucracy with their counterparts on senatorial staffs like Leon Keyserling in Senator Wagner's office.

This new class of administrators, and the social theorists who had been advocating a rationally planned economy, found the war an exciting adventure. The *New Republic* liberals rejoiced that the war produced a novel kind of democratic state which was creating a radical new order based on the democratization of industry. '. . . During the war we revolutionized our society,' the *New Republic* boasted.[15] These liberals distinguished themselves sharply from the New Freedom reformers who aimed only to achieve minor changes in the nineteenth-century tradition. Nationalists and collectivists, they looked toward a centralized state which would use its powers to reshape the economy in the interests of labor and other dis-

---

[8] The most ambitious federal program was the investigation conducted by the U. S. Commission on Industrial Relations (Graham Adams, 'Age of Industrial Violence.' PhD. dissertation, Columbia University, 1962).

[9] See, for example, George E. Mowry, *The California Progressives*, Berkeley and Los Angeles, 1951, pp. 294–99.

[10] 'Springfield and Bridgeport.' *New Republic*, XVI (1918), 185–86; Henry F. Pringle, *The Life and Times of William Howard Taft*, 2 vols.; New York, 1939, II, 921.

[11] 'Snubbing the War Labor Board,' *Survey*, XL, 1918, 292–93; 'The Western Union and the Government,' *New Republic*, XV, 1918, 163–64; Pringle, *The Life and Times of William Howard Taft*, II, 919–20. For the wartime labor experience, see 'Final Report of the Chairman of the Labor Division, War Industries Board, 1919,' copy in Library of Congress, John P. Frey MSS, Box 15; Brody, *Steelworkers in America*, Chap. X; U.S. Department of Labor, Bureau of Labor Statistics, 'National War Labor Board,' in *Bulletin No. 287*, Washington, D.C., 1922; Gordon S. Watkins, *Labor Problems and Labor Administration in the United States During the World War* ('University of Illinois Studies in the Social Sciences,' VIII, Urbana, Ill., 1919); Felix Frankfurter, 'New Labor Ideas Taught by War,' in Edwin Wildman (ed.) *Reconstructing America*, Boston, 1919, pp. 239–44.

[12] Gordon Hall Gerould, 'The Professor and the Wide, Wide World,' *Scribner's Magazine*, LXV, 1919, 466.

[13] *Ibid.*, p. 465.

[14] Bourne, *Untimely Papers*, ed. James Oppenheim, New York, 1919, p. 129.

[15] 'The Uses of an Armistice,' *New Republic*, XVII, 1918, 60.

advantaged groups.[16]

Many progressives believed that Wilson's war measures signified both a fulfillment of Progressive hopes and a happy augury for the future. Enormously impressed by 'the social possibilities of war,' John Dewey observed that in every warring country, production for profit had been subordinated to production for use. 'The old conception of the absoluteness of private property has received the world over a blow from which it will never wholly recover.'[17] Thorstein Veblen, who worked for the Food Administration in 1918, thought the war created new possibilities for far-reaching social change.[18] Economists viewed the War Industries Board as 'a notable demonstration of the power of war to force concert of effort and collective planning,' and anticipated that lessons from the war could be applied in times of peace.[19] When Wesley C. Mitchell closed his lectures at Columbia University in May, 1918, he remarked that peace would bring new problems, but 'it seems impossible that the countries concerned will attempt to solve them without utilizing the same sort of centralized directing now employed to kill their enemies abroad for the new purpose of reconstructing their own life at home.'[20] 'What we have learned in war we shall hardly forget in peace,' commented Walter Weyl. 'The new economic solidarity, once gained, can never again be surrendered.'[21]

The end of the war left the administrators with a sense of incompletion. One writer noted unmistakable shadows of annoyance at the Cosmos Club when 'the dark cloud of peace' lowered in October, 1918.[22] After the war, to the chagrin of the planners, the economic machinery was quickly dismantled, but the lesson that the war had taught—that the federal government could mobilize the nation's resources in a planned economy—was not forgotten.[23] Throughout the 1920s, the more advanced Progressives looked back fondly toward the war mobilization which seemed to have drawn a blueprint for America's future. In 1927, Rexford Tugwell lauded the war as 'an industrial engineer's Utopia.' He wanted to co-ordinate the economy as it had been under the War Industries Board in 'America's war-time socialism.' 'We were on the verge of having an international industrial machine when peace broke,' he wrote ruefully. '. . . Only the Armistice,' he lamented, 'prevented a great experiment in control of production, control of price, and control of consumption.'[24]

The fascination the war example held for the Progressives was a consequence of the fusion of nationalism and reform in the previous generation. Heralded by Bismarck in Germany and Joseph Chamberlain in Great Britain, this conjunction appeared in America in the martial fantasies of Edward Bellamy, in Francis Walker's critique of classical economics, in the 'industrial armies' of men like Jacob Coxey, in the military forms of the Salvation Army, and in the response of certain reformers to the imperialist issues of the 1890s.[25] In the Progressive era, this association was starkly revealed in the career of Theodore Roosevelt who

[16] Charles Hirschfeld, 'American Reform and World War I,' paper delivered at the convention of the Mississippi Valley Historical Association, Denver, Colo., April 25, 1959, pp. 3, 12–13.
[17] John Dewey, 'What Are We Fighting For?' *Independent*, XCIV, 1918, 480, reprinted as 'The Social Possibilities of War,' in Joseph Ratner (ed.), *Characters and Events* (2 vols.; New York, 1919), II, 555. See, too, John Dewey, ' A New Social Science,' *New Republic*, XIV, 1918, 293.
[18] David Riesman, *Thorstein Veblen*, New York, 1953, p. 119; Joseph Dorfman, *Thorstein Veblen and His America*, New York, 1934, pp. 380–95.
[19] Curtice N. Hitchcock, 'The War Industries Board: Its Development, Organization and Functions,' *Journal of Political Economy*, XXVI, 1918, 566; Irving Fisher, 'Some Contributions of the War to Our Knowledge of Money and Prices,' *American Review, Economic* VIII, 1918, Supplement, 257–58; Joseph Dorfman, *The Economic Mind in American Civilization*, 5 vols.; New York, 1946–59, III, 485–94.
[20] Dorfman, *The Economic Mind in American Civilization*, III, 490.
[21] Walter Weyl, *The End of the War*, New York, 1918, pp. 303–4. Cf. Sidney Kaplan, 'Social Engineers as Saviors: Effects of World War I on Some American Liberals,' *Journal of the History of Ideas*, XVII, 1956, 347–69. The war experience casts doubt on the familiar generalization that war is always fatal to reform. In some ways, the war dealt a severe blow to the progressive movement; in other ways, it opened up new possibilities for reform. No doubt the war resulted in more harm than good for progressivism, but it was not the totally unusable experience it has frequently been represented to be.

[22] 'The Demobilized Professor,' *Atlantic Monthly*, CXXIII, 1919, 537.
[23] In the months after the armistice, economists like Wesley Mitchell sought to preserve the activities begun during the war, and men like Senator William S. Kenyon of Iowa attempted to keep alive and even expand the work of war agencies, but in vain. See Dorfman, *The Economic Mind in American Civilization*, IV, 9–11, 365; Lucy Sprague Mitchell, *Two Lives: The Story of Wesley Clair Mitchell and Myself*, New York, 1953, p. 303; Welsey C. Mitchell, *The Backward Art of Spending Money and Other Essays*, New York, 1937, pp. 42–57.
[24] Rexford G. Tugwell, 'America's War-Time Socialism,' *Nation*, CXXIV, 1927, 364–65. Cf. Donald Richberg. *Tents of the Mighty*, New York, 1930, p. 82. Even the social security movement of the 1920s was affected by the wartime precedents of government insurance and of the care and rehabilitation of veterans (Clarke Chambers to the writer, June 23, 1962). The Railroad Administration was to provide the model for the New Deal's Coordinator of Transportation.
[25] In some respects, this relationship had even earlier antecedents, for example, in the special place that Lincoln and the Union cause had in the hearts of postbellum reformers. It might even be traced back as far as the congruence of reform and imperialism in the Jefferson administration.

thought social justice and military preparedness to be two aspects of a common program.

While the confluence of nationalism and reform fascinated a number of progressive theorists, notably Brooks Adams, it was Herbert Croly who, in his seminal *The Promise of American Life*, explored the relationship most extensively. Croly set down the deep dissatisfaction of the Progressives with the quality of life in America. The homogeneity of the early republic, he wrote, had been fragmented by a century of individualism run riot. So long as the market place determined values, so long as each individual or interest was permitted to pursue its own ends with no commitment to a common ideal, the result could not help but be unsatisfying, Croly reasoned. Reform had foundered because it lacked a sense of national purpose. 'In this country,' he observed, 'the solution of the social problem demands the substitution of a conscious social ideal for the earlier instinctive homogeneity of the American nation.'[26]

The war offered just such a 'conscious social ideal' Through war priorities, as Bernard Baruch later explained, the economy could be 'made to move in response to a national purpose rather than in response to the wills of those who had money to buy.'[27] The nationalistic demands of war denied, if only for a time, the claims of the profit system. '. . . When production and distribution became really a matter of life and death, immediate and dramatic, every warring nation, after a few months of appalling waste, threw laissez-faire out of the window,' noted Stuart Chase. 'Wars must be won, and it was painfully obvious that laissez-faire was no help in winning them.'[28] The individualistic, competitive economy of the prewar years had to submit to the discipline of conscious government direction. Not business profit but the national interest was to determine how resources were to be allocated. The old system of competition, Rexford Tugwell wrote jubilantly, 'melted away in the fierce new heat of nationalistic vision.'[29]

When the stock market crash of 1929 precipitated the Great Depression of the 1930s, progressives turned instinctively to the war mobilization as a design for recovery. The War Industries Board, Stuart Chase pointed out, had, like the Soviet *Gosplan*, demonstrated that 'super-management' could replace 'industrial anarchy.'[30] George Soule contended that the war had shown that planning was neither beyond human capacity nor alien to American values. 'Many of those who now advocate economic planning have been doing so, in one way or another, ever since the experiences of 1917–18, and mainly as a result of the possibilities which those experiences suggested for better performance in times of peace.' The same 'deliberate collective effort' which had made possible a tremendous expansion of production could be turned to peace-time ends, he argued. 'If that military and industrial army had been mobilized, not to kill, burn and shatter, but to substitute garden cities for slums, to restore soil fertility and reforest our waste regions, to carry out flood control, to increase the necessities of life available for those in the lower income groups, we could have achieved in a short time a large number of really desirable objectives,' Soule claimed.[31]

Such men as Gerard Swope of General Electric, a veteran of the war mobilization, and Otto T. Mallery, the leading advocate of public works in the World War I era, recommended floating large federal bond issues like Liberty Bonds to finance a massive public-works program.[32] Swope wrote President Hoover: 'If we were faced with war, the President would immediately call a special session of Congress to declare war and to raise armies. This unemployment situation in many ways is more serious even than war. Therefore it is suggested that an extra session of Congress be called and the President request it to issue a billion dollars of bonds, bearing a low interest rate, and that then a campaign be organized to sell these bonds, much as the Liberty Bond campaigns were organized when

[26] Croly, *The Promise of American Life*, New York, 1909, p. 139. Croly rejoiced that the Spanish–American War and the subsequent imperial expansion had given 'a tremendous impulse to the work of national reform' (*ibid.*, p. 169). See William E. Leuchtenburg, 'Progressivism and Imperialism: The progressive Movement and American Foreign Policy, 1898–1916,' *Mississippi Valley Historical Review*, XXXIX, 1952, 483–504.
[27] Baruch, *American Industry in the War*, p. 29. See, too, J. M. Clark's perceptive article, 'The Basis of War-Time Collectivism,' *American Economic Review*, VII, 1917, 772–90.
[28] Stuart Chase, *A New Deal*, New York, 1933, pp. 84–85.
[29] Tugwell, 'America's War-Time Socialism,' p. 365.

[30] Stuart Chase, 'The Heart of American Industry,' in Fred J. Ringel (ed.), *America as Americans See It*, New York, 1932, p. 30.
[31] George Soule, *A Planned Society*, New York, 1933, pp. 184–87. See, too, J. Russell Smith, 'The End of an Epoch,' *Survey*, LXVI, 1931, 333.
[32] Mallery had headed a division of the War Labor Policies Board charged with developing public works during the postwar transition. For the proposals of Mallery and Father John O'Grady, see the *New York Times*, December 30, 1931. The economist Arthur Gayer recommended profiting from the Liberty Bond example by floating bonds for public works 'in a war on growing suffering and distress' (Arthur D. Gayer, 'Financing the Emergency Public Works Program,' *American Labor Legislation Review*, XXII, 1932, 75).

we entered the war thirteen years ago.'³³ The Wisconsin economist Richard T. Ely went a step farther. He proposed the creation of a peacetime army which, when a depression struck, could be expanded by recruiting from the ranks of the unemployed. Under the direction of an economic general staff, the army, Ely urged, 'should go to work to relieve distress with all the vigor and resources of brain and brawn that we employed in the World War.'³⁴

By the middle of 1931, both businessmen and politicians were calling on President Hoover to adopt the procedures of the War Industries Board to pull the country out of the depression. When William McAdoo, who had headed the wartime Railroad Administration, proposed a Peace Industries Board in June, 1931, he found ready support. The War Industries Board, one correspondent wrote McAdoo, 'accomplished wonders during the war, and there is no question but that a board established now to coordinate things in our national industries will also do wonders. This historical precedent is a great asset and ought to guide us in our national planning for the benefit of all.'³⁵ A month later, Charles Beard urged the creation of a National Economic Council with a Board of Strategy and Planning which would follow the pattern of 'the War Industries Board and other federal agencies created during the titanic effort to mobilize men and materials for the World War.'³⁶ The following month, Representative Chester Bolton of Ohio advanced a similar proposal. 'If we could have another body like the old War Industries Board,' he wrote the head of Hoover's voluntary relief agency, 'I believe the situation today could be greatly bettered.'³⁷ In September, 1931, Gerard Swope came forth with the most influential of all the pre-New Deal proposals: the 'Swope Plan' to stabilize employment and prices through a constellation of trade associations under a national economic council.³⁸ Early in 1932, a group of more than a hundred businessmen requested Hoover to declare a

two-year truce on destructive competition and urged him 'to consider a return to war-time experience by bringing into existence A National Economic Truce Board.'³⁹

The cornucopia of proposals included suggestions with widely differing ideological implications. Some called on the war example to support radical recommendations for national planning; others used the war precedent simply as a stratagem to free business of the encumbrance of the trust laws. Most of them had in common a demand for greater initiative by the federal government, and many of them—especially the public-works proposals—called for a sharp increase in government spending.

Such proposals ran far ahead of anything President Hoover and his followers would contenance. Most businessmen seemed chary of taking the War Industries Board as a model for peacetime.⁴⁰ The President himself gave little indication of a readiness to have the federal government assume a larger role. To be sure, he signed an Employment Stabilization Bill in 1931, and gave a major share of credit for the measure to Mallery.⁴¹ But he deplored recommendations for lavish federal spending. Ventures of this sort, the President protested, would unbalance the budget and destroy business confidence in public credit.

These doctrines received small credence from men who recalled the war expenditures. 'If it is permissible for government to expend billions in wartime in the organization of production, it is no less legitimate for government in a great emergency of

³³ Swope to Hoover, October 2, 1930, Columbia University, New York, Gerald Swope MSS.
³⁴ Richard T. Ely, *Hard Times*, pp. 103–6.
³⁵ Raphael Herman to William McAdoo, June 10, 1931, Library of Congress, McAdoo MSS, Box 359.
³⁶ Charles A. Beard, 'A "Five-Year Plan" for America,' *Forum* LXXXVI, 1931, 5. He also proposed gigantic agricultural and housing programs to be 'financed by Freedom Bonds and sold with the zeal of war issues' (*ibid.*, p. 11).
³⁷ Representative Chester Bolton to Walter Gifford, August 24, 1931, Library of Congress, Newton Baker MSS, Box 192.
³⁸ J. George Frederick (ed.), *The Swope Plan*, New York, 1931; Gerald Swope, Columbia Oral History Collection, pp. 123 ff. The Collection will be cited henceforth as COHC.

³⁹ 'A Plea from 123 Representatives of Independent Industrial Units and of Labor for the Trial of a Two Years' Truce in Destructive Competition,' to Herbert Hoover, February 11, 1932, copy in Harvey Williams to Robert Wagner, March 24, 1932, Wagner MSS, Georgetown University, Washington, D.C.
⁴⁰ For the wariness of businessmen about using the War Industries Board as a model, see U.S. Congress, Senate, *Establishment of a National Economic Council*, Hearings before a Subcommittee of the Committee on Manufactures, U.S. Senate, 72d Cong., 1st Sess., on S. 6215, October 22 to December 19, 1931, Washington, D.C., 1932, p. 174. William Appleman Williams sees men like Gerard Swope as representative of a new group of corporation executives who came out of the war with a more sophisticated approach to industrial problems, and views Herbert Hoover as their most important spokesman (Williams, *The Contours of American History*, Cleveland and New York, 1961, pp. 425–26). While this judgment seems valid for the 1920s, especially during Hoover's tenure as Secretary of Commerce, it is hardly pertinent for Hoover's presidency. The differences between Swope and President Hoover, sharply revealed by their divergent evaluations of the relevance of war to the depression, were more significant than their area of agreement.
⁴¹ Dorfman, *The Economic Mind in American Civilization*, IV, 7. Moreover, Hoover had stepped up public works right after the crash. Still, this represented far less than the progressives demanded.

peacetime to do what it is also impossible for private individuals to accomplish,' reasoned the distinguished economist Edwin R. A. Seligman.[42] The popular economic writer William Trufant Foster scolded:

If any one still doubts that our economic troubles are mainly mental, let him consider what would happen if the United States declared war today. Everybody knows what would happen. Congress would immediately stop this interminable talk and appropriate three billion dollars—five billion—ten billion—any necessary amount. . . .

Some day we shall realise that if money is available for a blood-and-bullets war, just as much money is available for a food-and-famine war. We shall see that if it is fitting to use collective action on a large scale to kill men abroad, it is fitting to use collective action on an equally large scale to save men at home.[43]

Although Hoover rejected the demand that he draw on the war legacy to mount a program of public works, he could not resist for long the clamor for government initiative to expand relief to the jobless. By the summer of 1931, the number of unemployed totaled eight million. William Allen White wrote: 'Hundreds of thousands of men, women and children are going to suffer terribly this winter in spite of all that the natural laws of economic change can do, however soon change may start, however rapidly it may move. Yet the situation is not hopeless, for if we can recreate the dynamic altruism outside of government which moved us during the war, we can harness forces that will bring relief and make us a better and nobler people.' If Hoover could arouse the 'latent altruism' of the people, White believed, great sums could be raised for relief 'as we raised the Liberty Loan, Red Cross and Y drive funds during the war.'[44]

On August 19, 1931, President Hoover named Walter S. Gifford, president of the American Telephone and Telegraph Company, to head the President's Organization on Unemployment Relief. A week later Newton Baker, a member of the Advisory Committee of the POUR, noted that Gifford seemed to be planning to organize the country along the lines of the Council of National Defense, and added: 'I am going a step farther and suggest that as far as possible men with military experience in the World War be used. They have had lessons in effective and disciplined action which will be valuable.'[45] That fall, the Gifford committee launched a 'mobilization' to win support for local fund-raising drives. National advertisements proclaimed: 'Between October 19 and November 25 America will feel the thrill of a great spiritual experience.' A few weeks later, when Senator Edward Costigan of Colorado questioned the advisability of employing such techniques, Gifford responded: 'We certainly did it in the war. I do not know that I like it, but, as I say, it is more or less the established practice. . . .'[46]

President Hoover made much more forceful use of the war precedent to meet the financial crisis of the autumn of 1931. In December, 1931, Hoover asked Congress to create a Reconstruction Finance Corporation frankly modeled on the War Finance Corporation.[47] The proposal appeared to originate at about the same time in the minds of several different men: Hoover, Federal Reserve Governor Eugene Meyer, who had been managing director of the WFC, Louis Wehle, who had been the WFC's general counsel, and Senator Joseph Robinson of Arkansas.[48] All drew their inspiration from the WFC. 'The RFC was a revival of the War Finance Corporation, that's all, but with expanded powers,'

---

[42] *Ibid.*, V, 672. During the fight over the sales tax in 1932, an Oklahoma congressman hooted at the idea that budget-balancing was a patriotic duty. 'Those who are so anxious to balance the budget at this time either forget or ignore the fact that we have in times past raised vast sums in emergencies to carry on wars without resorting to the general sales tax.' he noted ('Soak the Poor,' University of Oklahoma, Norman, Okla., Wilburn Cartwright MSS).

[43] Foster, 'When a Horse Balks,' *North American Review*, CCXXXIV, 1932, 10. John Maynard Keynes wrote: 'I hope that in the future we shall . . . be ready to spend on the enterprises of peace what the financial maxims of the past would only allow us to spend on the devastations of war.'—Keynes, 'The World's Economic Outlook,' *Atlantic Monthly*, CXLIX, 1932, 525. See, too, Lewis Kimmel, *Federal Budget and Fiscal Policy, 1789–1958*, Washington, D.C., 1959, pp. 170–72.

[44] White to David Henshaw, August 10, 1931, Library of Congress, William Allen White MSS, Box 135.

[45] Baker to Representative Chester Bolton, August 26, 1931, Newton Baker MSS, Box 192.

[46] U.S. Congress, Senate, *Unemployment Relief*, Hearings before a Subcommittee of the Committee on Manufacturers, U.S. Senate, 72d Cong., 1st Sess., on S. 174 and S. 262, December 28–30, 1931, and January 4–9, 1932, Washington, D.C., 1932, p. 327. A year later, when Newton Baker was named to head the National Citizen's Committee for the Welfare and Relief Mobilization of 1932, the *Literary Digest* explained: 'The concentrated effort is under the direct command of Newton D. Baker, who, as Secretary of War under President Wilson, mobilized the forces of the country for the war in Europe. The campaign is to be the Armageddon of the Great Depression.' (*Literary Digest*, CXIV, October 8, 1932, 20).

[47] William Starr Myers (ed.), *The State Papers and Other Public Writings of Herbert Hoover*, 2 vols.; Garden City, N.Y., 1934, II, 6.

[48] Accounts of the origin of the RFC vary in detail. Cf. Eugene Meyer, COHC, pp. 612–13; Jackson Reynolds, COHC, pp. 152–53; Louis Wehle, *Hidden Threads of History*, New York, 1953, p. 77; U.S. Congress, Senate, *Creation of a Reconstruction Finance Corporation*, Hearings before a Subcommittee of the Committee on Banking and Currency, U.S. Senate, 72d Cong., 1st Sess., on S. 1, December 18, 19, 21, 22, 1931, Washington, D.C., 1932.

Meyer recalled.[49] Observers were astonished by the speed with which Congress approved the RFC bill. 'It puts us financially on a war basis,' noted the *New Republic*.[50] When the RFC began operations, it employed many of the WFC's old staff, followed its pattern and that of the wartime Treasury in financing, and even took over, with slight modifications, the old WFC forms for loan applications.[51]

The RFC, declared one periodical, was to be the 'spearhead of the economic A.E.F.'[52] But Hoover and his aides insisted that the intervention of the RFC be held to a minimum. Hoover's reluctance to use the RFC as an agency in a new kind of mobilization suggested that the war analogy meant different things to different men and that it could be turned to conservative purposes as readily as to those envisaged by the progressives. While the progressives thought of the war as a paradigm for national planning, Hoover remembered it as a time when the government had encouraged a maximum of voluntary action and a minimum of disturbance of the profit system.[53] He wished the crucial decisions to be made, as they had been in wartime, by corporation leaders. He employed the metaphor of war to serve a conservative function: that of draining internal antagonisms onto a common national enemy.[54] In his address to the Republican national convention in 1932, the permanent chairman, Bertrand Snell, declared in defense of Hoover: 'He solidified labor and capital against the enemy.'[55]

New York's Governor Franklin D. Roosevelt sought to reap political advantage from these different perceptions of the war experience.[56] In his campaign for the Democratic presidential nomination in 1932, Roosevelt contrasted Hoover's performance with the achievements of the war mobilization. In his 'forgotten man' address in Albany on April 7, 1932, Roosevelt declared that American success in the war had been due to leadership which was not satisfied with 'the timorous and futile gesture' of sending a small army and navy overseas, but which 'conceived of a whole Nation mobilized for war, economic, industrial, social and military resources gathered into a vast unit.' The United States in 1932, Roosevelt asserted, faced 'a more grave emergency than in 1917,' and in meeting that emergency the Hoover administration had neglected 'the infantry of our economic army.' 'These unhappy times,' the Governor observed, 'call for the building of plans that rest upon the forgotten, the unorganized but the indispensable units of economic power, for plans like those of 1917 that build from the bottom up and not from the top down, that put their faith once more in the forgotten man at the bottom of the economic pyramid.'[57] Less than two weeks later, at the Jefferson Day Dinner at St. Paul on April 18, Roosevelt repeated that the nation faced an emergency 'more grave than that of war' and once more derided Hoover's efforts to meet the crisis. He added pointedly:

Compare this panic-stricken policy of delay and improvisation with that devised to meet the emergency of war fifteen years ago.
We met specific situations with considered, relevant measures of constructive value. There were the War Industries Board, the Food and Fuel Administration, the War Trade Board, the Shipping Board and many others.[58]

The 1932 election brought the Democrats to power for the first time since Wilson's war administration. It was 'only natural,' as Swisher has observed, 'that some of the World-War leaders should return to federal office and that others should become unofficial advisers of the administration. They, like the President, thought in terms of the dramatic concentration of power in the federal government

---

[49] Eugene Meyer, COHC, p. 613. Meyer's initiative, and the WFC model, is also stressed in Gerald Nash, 'Herbert Hoover and the Origins of the Reconstruction Finance Corporation,' *Mississippi Valley Historical Review*, XLVI, 1959, 455–68.

[50] *New Republic* LXIX, 1932, 291.

[51] W. Randolph Burgess, 'Plans for Financial Reconstruction,' Address at the Century Association of New York, April 7, 1932, Library of Congress, Ogden Mills MSS, Box 9; J. Franklin Ebersole, 'One Year of the Reconstruction Finance Corporation,' *Quarterly Journal of Economics*, XLVII, 1933, 468; Wehle, *Hidden Threads of History*, p. 77.

[52] *Literary Digest*, CXII, February 13, 1932, 9. Congress, reported the *Philadelphia Record*, had given the new agency 'two billion dollars' worth of ammunition. The people are waiting to see how straight it can shoot' (*ibid*).

[53] For the determination during the war to refrain from interference with business, see Randall B. Kester, 'The War Industries Board, 1917–1918; A Study in Industrial Mobilization,' *American Political Science Review*, XXXIV, 1940, 683; and Herbert Stein, *Government Price Policy in the United States during the World War*, Williamstown, Mass., 1939, p. 13.

[54] The integrative function of war is discussed in W. Lloyd Warner, *American Life: Dream and Reality*, Chicago, 1953, p. 20.

[55] *Official Report of the Proceedings of the Twentieth Republican National Convention, 1932*, New York, 1932, p. 89.

[56] As the country entered the election year of 1932, the tempo of demands for a return to the war spirit quickened. See Baker Brownell to Gifford Pinchot, January 10, 1932, Library of Congress, Gifford Pinchot MSS, Box 320; John J. Pershing, 'We are at War!' *American Magazine*, CXIII, June, 1932, 15–17, 72, 74; *B.E.F. News*, July 2, 1032.

[57] *The Public Papers and Addresses of Franklin D. Roosevelt*, ed. Samuel I. Rosenman, 13, vols; New York, 1938–1950, I, 624–25. At a Roosevelt rally in Salem, Massachusetts, James Michael Curley made effective use of the war analogue to berate Hoover (*Salem News*, April 6, 1932, Holy Cross College Library, Worcester, Mass., Curley Scrapbooks).

[58] Roosevelt, *Public Papers*, I, 631–32.

which they had helped to bring about for the defeat of a foreign enemy. It is not surprising that modes of procedure were carried over from one period to the other.'[59] In the interregnum between Roosevelt's election in November, 1932, and his inauguration in March, 1933, war recollections became even more compelling. The whole political system seemed doomed to self-asphyxiation. The discords of party, the deadlock in Congress, the maxims of the classical economists, the taboos of the Constitution all seemed to inhibit action at a time when action was desperately needed. In contrast, the war was remembered as a time of movement and accomplishment.[60]

During the interregnum, the country debated a series of new proposals for utilizing the war experience to vanquish the depression. Daniel Roper, who would soon be Roosevelt's Secretary of Commerce, suggested a few days after the election that the new President "appoint one 'super' secretary with the other secretaries assistant to him and organize under this 'super' secretary the plan of the National Council of Defense composed of, say 21 men working without compensation as they did in War times."[61] Many believed the crisis could be met only by vesting in the President the same arbitrary war powers that Woodrow Wilson had been given.[62] The depression, declared Alfred E. Smith on February 7, 1933, was 'doing more damage at home to our own people than the great war of 1917 and 1918 ever

did.' 'And what does a democracy do in a war?' Smith asked. 'It becomes a tyrant, a despot, a real monarch. In the World War we took our Constitution, wrapped it up and laid it on the shelf and left it there until it was over.'[63] Four days later, Republican Governor Alf Landon of Kansas inquired: 'Why not give the President the same powers in this bitter peacetime battle as we would give to him in time of war?'[64]

As early as the spring of 1932, weeks before Roosevelt had even been nominated, his brain trust had requested Joseph D. McGoldrick and Howard L. McBain to prepare a memorandum on presidential war powers, for they anticipated Roosevelt would need them as authority for emergency acts.[65] Early in January, 1933, the President-elect asked Rexford Tugwell to explore the possibility that the Trading with the Enemy Act of 1917 might provide the basis for an edict embargoing gold exports. Tugwell's research quickly involved him in a comedy of errors in which the New Dealers sought both to obtain the necessary information without letting the Hoover Administration learn what they were up to and at the same time to persuade themselves that a statute that had been amended many times gave them the legal authority to do what they intended to do anyway.[66] Governor Roosevelt's legal aides could not have been more co-operative. Senator Thomas Walsh, Roosevelt's choice to be Attorney General, promised that, if the President-elect found he needed the powers, he would quiet his doubts and rule that the old statute gave him the authority he required. When, after Walsh's death, Roosevelt picked Homer Cummings for the post, he turned over to him the folder on the Trading with the Enemy Act. Cummings obligingly found the statute was still alive.[67]

As the day of Roosevelt's inauguration approached, the epidemic of bank failures drove governors in state after state to proclaim bank holidays and raised fears that the economic system was on the verge of collapse. 'A blight has fallen over all American industry,' declared the Akron *Beacon-Journal* on March 3. 'A foreign invader making easy

---

[59] Carl Brent Swisher, *American Constitutional Development* (Boston, 1943), p. 878. Senator James F. Byrnes of South Carolina later wrote: 'In our efforts to find a remedy for this situation, we had no guideposts. I recalled that when I went to the House of Representatives I had firm convictions about federal-state relations and the wisdom of preserving local governments, the necessity of maintaining a balanced budget, and like subjects; but when we entered World War I in 1917, I recognized that, in a war emergency, principles as well as policies had to be temporarily subordinated to the necessity of some experimentation in order to preserve the government itself. The economic crisis now demanded a similar attitude.'— Byrnes, *All in One Lifetime*, New York, 1958, pp. 69–70.

[60] The President's Research Committee on Social Trends pointed to the 'surprising energy and efficiency' that had emerged in 1917, and noted explanation for this 'development of governmental art': 'the subordination of private to public interest, the facility in recruitment of the necessary talent when the boycott on government service was lifted, the indifference to established precedent in administrative or other method, the freedom from hairsplitting judicial restraint the unification of leadership. . . . '—The President's Research Committee on Social Trends, *Recent Social Trends in the United States* (New York and London, 1933), p. 1539. Cf. Max Lerner, 'The State in War Time,' in Willard Waller (ed.), *War in the Twentieth Century*, New York, 1940, pp. 409–28.

[61] Daniel Roper to William Dodd, November 16, 1932, Library of Congress, Dodd MSS, Box 41.

[62] Key Pittman to Franklin D. Roosevelt, June 16, 1932, Library of Congress, Pittman MSS, Box 16; Henry Morrow Hyde MS Diary, January 4, 1933.

[63] *New York Times*, February 8, 1933.

[64] Willis Thornton, *The Life of Alfred M. Landon*, New York, 1936, p. 84.

[65] Raymond Moley, *After Seven Years*, New York, 1939, pp. 22–23.

[66] Tugwell, 'Notes from a New Deal Diary,' January 4, 1933, February 27, 1933, Franklin D. Roosevelt Library, Hyde Park N.Y., Tugwell MSS; Key Pittman to Roosevelt, February 28, 1933, Pittman MSS, Box 16.

[67] Ernest K. Lindley, *The Roosevelt Revolution*, New York, 1939, p. 78; Rexford Tugwell, COHC, pp. 37–40.

conquest of our shores could do no worse.'[68] As Roosevelt took the oath of office, the atmosphere in Washington, wrote Arthur Krock, was like that 'in a beleaguered capital in war time.'[69]

Roosevelt's inaugural address on March 4, 1933 reflected the sense of wartime crisis. The nation, he resolved, must move 'as a trained and loyal army willing to sacrifice for the good of a common discipline.' He would ask Congress to adopt his legislative program, but if Congress failed to act and the emergency continued, the new President announced: 'I shall not evade the clear course of duty that will then confront me. I shall ask the Congress for the one remaining instrument to meet the crisis—broad executive power to wage a war against the emergency, as great as the power that would be given to me if we were in fact invaded by a foreign foe.'[70]

During the 'Hundred Days,' President Roosevelt sought to restore national confidence by evoking the mood of wartime: the feeling of national unity above any claim of partisan or private economic interest because the very existence of the country was imperiled. The opposition press suspended criticism of the President; business corporations, labor unions, and farm organizations pledged their cooperation; and Republican leaders urged the country to rally around the Democratic chief executive. Governor Landon declared: 'If there is any way in which a member of the species, thought to be extinct, a Republican Governor of a mid-western state, can aid [the President] in the fight, I now enlist for the duration of the war.'[71]

The New Deal hoped to arouse the same sense of devotion to the nation and the same spirit of sacrifice that had been displayed in the war. 'It is important,' wrote Rexford Tugwell, "that we should again explore the possibilities of what William James called 'the moral equivalents' of

war."[72] 'The ordeal of war,' he told Dartmouth students, 'brings out the magnificent resources of youth. . . . The ordeal of depression ought to try your mettle in similar ways. . . . The feeling which shook humanity during the War and which after the War reshaped the entire civilization of mighty nations is called for again.'[73]

When the planners of the thirties looked back at the war, they were most impressed by how much had been accomplished once the nation had been unified by allegiance to a common purpose. Writers like Rexford Tugwell and George Soule argued that the effective functioning of 'a regime of industrial democracy' required the same spirit of 'loyalty to larger aims' that the War Industries Board had exploited.[74] Nationalistic to the core, unabashedly patriotic, they believed that if the country could once again give fealty to a transcendent ideal, the depression would be conquered as once the armies of the Kaiser had been. Charles Beard proposed a 'heroic national effort' that would leave people 'richer in goods—and still more important, in patriotic spirit.'[75] Many conceived the New Deal not simply as a new kind of economic mobilization but also, as the war had been, a venture in 'nation-saving.'[76] One of the New Deal experiments was later to be lauded because it had led to 'a new baptism of patriotism and an increased consciousness of national unity.'[77]

Roosevelt's first important official act was to use the authority of the Trading with the Enemy Act

[68] Cited in Ruth McKenney, *Industrial Valley*, New York, 1939, p. 71.

[69] *New York Times*, March 5, 1933.

[70] Roosevelt, *Public Papers*, II, 14–15. The task of putting people to work, the President stated, could be 'accomplished in part by direct recruiting by the Government itself, treating the task as we would treat the emergency of a war' (*ibid.*, p. 13).

[71] Schlesinger, Jr., *The Coming of the New Deal*, p. 3. One periodical noted: 'The country was in an exalted mood. It rose to greet the new President as if to support him in the repulsion of invading armies.'—*Review of Reviews and World's Work*, LXXXVII, April, 1933, 10. In April, 1933, a Democratic senator completed a volume which was a sustained use of the war as a parable for the depression (Millard Tydings, *Counter-Attack: A Battle Plan to Defeat the Depression*, Indianapolis, 1933).

[72] Rexford G. Tugwell, *The Battle for Democracy* (New York, 1935), p. 75.

[73] *Ibid.*, p. 296. Thurman Arnold noted that in war, democracies 'achieve unity to an extent which seems extraordinary to one viewing the wartime economy from the tangled confusion of peacetime values.' Arnold added: 'Thus, in peacetimes, when the lack of cooperation between men is distressingly evident, and when the endless argument about the contradictions involved in our symbols seems to have no hope of ending, we look back to the unity of the time when nations were drawn up in battle lines and we demand a moral substitute for war.'— Arnold, *The Symbols of Government*, New Haven, 1935, pp. 243–45.

[74] The words are Tugwell's (Tugwell, *The Industrial Discipline and the Governmental Arts*, New York, 1933, p. 100). See, too, George Soule, *A Planned Society*, pp. 196–97.

[75] Beard, 'A "Five-Year Plan" for America,' p. 11.

[76] George N. Peek, with Samuel Crowther, *Why Quit Our Own*, New York, 1936, p. 123. Raymond Moley, it might be noted, had directed Americanization activities in Ohio under Governor James Cox during World War I.

[77] Alfred C. Oliver, Jr., and Harold M. Dudley, *This New America*, London, 1937, p. viii. See, too, the reference to 'nation-building' in John L. Christian, 'America's Peace Army,' *Current History*, XLIX, 1939, 43.

of 1917 to proclaim a national bank holiday.[78] When he sent his banking bill to Congress, the House received it with much the same ardor as it had greeted Woodrow Wilson's war legislation. Speaker Rainey said the situation reminded him of the late war when 'on both sides of this Chamber the great war measures suggested by the administration were supported with practical unanimity. . . . Today we are engaged in another war, more serious even in its character and presenting greater dangers to the Republic.'[79] After only thirty-eight minutes debate, the House passed the Administration's banking bill, sight unseen.[80]

On March 10, Roosevelt sent his second message to Congress, a plea for plenary powers to slash government spending. To the dismay of progressive Republicans and liberal Democrats, Roosevelt proved to be as orthodox on fiscal matters as his predecessor. When Senator Tom Donnally of Texas talked to Roosevelt in December, 1932, the President-elect had stressed the importance of balancing the budget by cutting federal spending and had dwelt upon the constitutional limitations of the President. 'If it was constitutional to spend forty million dollars in a war,' Connally told Roosevelt angrily, 'isn't it just as constitutional to spend a little money to relieve the hunger and misery of our citizens?'[81] The President-elect brushed aside such remonstrances and chose instead to heed the counsel of his conservative choice for Budget Director, Lewis Douglas. After studying the wartime authority Congress had granted Woodrow Wilson, Roosevelt decided to ask the new Congress to renew those powers in order to enable the President to balance the budget.[82]

The spirit of war crisis speeded through the economy bill. 'It is true this bill grants a great deal of power,' conceded Representative John McDuffie of Alabama, 'but this country is in a state of war—not against a foreign enemy but war against economic evils that demanded some sacrifice on your part and mine.' Representative John Young Brown of Kentucky spoke even more bluntly when he scolded fellow Democrats:

> . . . I may say to you that we are at war today, and the veterans of this country do not want you, in their name, to desert the standards of the President of the United States.
> I had as soon start a mutiny in the face of a foreign foe as start a mutiny today against the program of the President of the United States. [Applause.] And if someone must shoot down, in this hour of battle, the Commander in Chief of our forces, God grant that the assassin's bullet shall not be fired from the Democratic side of this House. [Applause.][83]

Many Congressmen disliked the Administration's economy bill, but feared to oppose the President. When Senator Wallace H. White, Jr., spoke out against the proposal, a Maine constituent warned him that he was 'riding out to certain death.' He agreed that White's position was logically sound, yet he cautioned that since 'a state of war does exist,' the Senator would be foolish to sacrifice himself by disregarding the war spirit.[84] After only two days debate, Congress voted the Economy Act. Senator Henry Fountain Ashurst of Arizona explained: 'The conditions are as serious as war and we must follow the flag.'[85]

There was scarcely a New Deal act or agency that did not owe something to the experience of World War I. The Tennessee Valley Authority—the most ambitious New Deal experiment in regional planning—grew out of the creation of a government-operated nitrate and electric-power project at Muscle Shoals during and after the war. In his message asking for creation of the TVA, President

[78] Roosevelt, *Public Papers*, II, 18. Tugwell, who worked on the banking proclamation, referred to it as 'this rather doubtful executive act' (Tugwell, 'Notes from a New Deal Diary,' March 31, 1933). See, too, Rixey Smith and Norman Beasley, *Carter Glass*, New York, 1939, pp. 341–42.

[79] *Congressional Record*, 73d Cong., 1st Sess., LXXVII (March 9, 1933), 70.

[80] 'It was a grim Congress which met today, the most momentous gathering of the country's legislators since war was declared in 1917. It is trite to say that they declared war but it is nevertheless true that they hurled against the enemy of depression and despondency a weapon which they hoped would penetrate the subtle armour of an allegorical or Bunyan-like antagonist.'—*New York Times*, March 10, 1933. Roosevelt's new banking act was deliberately framed to use the 'war power' to overcome possible objections to its constitutionality. The President's extraordinary powers were granted 'during time of war or during any other period of national emergency declared by the President' (Gustav Cassel, *The Downfall of the Gold Standard*, Oxford, 1936, p. 117.

[81] Tom Connally, as told to Alfred Steinberg, *My Name Is Tom Connally*, New York, 1954, p. 148.

[82] Schlesinger, Jr., *The Coming of the New Deal*, pp. 9-10.

[83] *Congressional Record*, 73d Cong., 1st Sess., pp. 201, 209.

[84] Wingate F. Cram to White, March 18, 1933, Library of Congress, Wallace White MSS, Box 1.

[85] *New York Times*, March 11, 1933. 'The President has been elected as Commander-in-Chief to pull us out of this financial crisis and it is my purpose to stand by him,' agreed Rep. Sam McReynolds of Tennessee (McReynolds to George Fort Milton, March 27, 1933, Library of Congress, Milton MSS, Box 13). At a homecoming meeting for the Nevada Congressional delegation, following the historic session of the Hundred Days, Senator Pat McCarran stated: 'On March 9 of this year to the astonishment of many, war was officially declared. . . . The war was against fear, fear that the entire government would go into bankruptcy.' Clipping, n.d., Scrapbook 44018, Nevada State Historical Society, Reno, Nev., James Scrugham MSS

Roosevelt concluded: 'In short, this power development of war days leads logically to national planning. . . . '[86] When the TVA bill was introduced in April, 1933, it seemed appropriate to refer it to the House Military Affairs Committee. Although war considerations played an inconsequential part in the birth of the Authority, the TVA Act of 1933 stipulated that in case of war or national emergency, any or all of the property entrusted to the Authority should be available to the government for manufacturing explosives or for other war purposes. The original World War I nitrate plant, which was turned over to the TVA, was to be held as a standby which might be needed in a future war.[87] When foes of the TVA challenged it in the courts, Chief Justice Charles Evans Hughes found constitutional authority for the construction of the Wilson Dam by resting his ruling, in part, on the war power.[88] The TVA was only one of a number of resources operations—from soil conservation to public power development—that employed the war rhetoric or drew from the World War I experience.[89]

The public-housing movement of the thirties had first come of age during the war. In World War I, Congress authorized the Emergency Fleet Corporation and the United States Housing Corporation to provide housing for war workers. The war established the principle of federal intervention in housing, and it trained architects like Robert Kohn, who served as chief of production of the housing division of the U.S. Shipping Board.[90] After the armistice, Kohn observed: '. . . The war put housing 'on the map' in this country.'[91] In 1933, President Roosevelt named Kohn to head the New Deal's first public-housing venture.

Imaginative wartime experiments with garden-city ideas paved the way for the greenbelt towns of the thirties, while the rural resettlement and subsistence homestead projects of the New Deal reaped the harvest of seeds planted by Elmwood Mead and Franklin K. Lane in the war years.[92] Roy Lubove has pointed out:

In such residential communities as Yorkship Village (New Jersey), Union Park Gardens (Delaware) and the Black Rock and Crane Tracts (Bridgeport, Connecticut), the Emergency Fleet Corporation and the United States Housing Corporation offered American architects and planners their first opportunity to apply garden city principles in comprehensive fashion: curvilinear street systems and street sizes adapted to function; park and play facilities; row-house design; the skillful spacing of mass and volume for maximum aesthetic effect and maximum sunlight and ventilation. The memory of the federal war-housing program persisted over the next two decades, a reminder of the potentialities of non-speculative, large-scale site planning for working-class housing.[93]

The New Deal's program of farm price supports owed something to the wartime Food Administration and even more to a decade of proselytization by George Peek, a hard-bitten farm-belt agitator who had served as 'a sort of generalissimo of

[86] Roosevelt, *Public Papers*, II, 122. Cf. Sarah Elizabeth Boseley Winger, 'The Genesis of TVA,' Ph.D. dissertation, University of Wisconsin, 1959, pp. 580–81; Judson King, *The Conversion Fight: From Theodore Roosevelt to Tennessee Valley Authority*, Washington, D.C., 1959, chaps. vii–viii; Norman Wengert, 'Antecedents of TVA: The Legislative History of Muscle Shoals,' *Agricultural History*, XXV (1952), 141–47; Kenneth McKellar to George Fort Milton, May 17, 1933, Milton MSS, Box 13. The special form of the TVA—the government corporation endowed with many of the powers and much of the flexibility of a business corporation—had first found wide acceptance in the war.

[87] Tennessee Valley Authority, *To Keep the Water in the Rivers and the Soil on the Land*, Washington, D.C., 1938, p. 44.

[88] *Ashwander et al., v. Tennessee Valley Authority et al.*, 297 U.S. 288, 1936; Joseph C. Swidler and Robert H. Marquis, 'TVA in Court: A Study of Constitutional Litigation,' *Iowa Law Review*, XXXII, 1947, 296–326.

[89] In arguing the case for passage of the Taylor Grazing Act, a former senator claimed: '. . . The remaining public domain is vital to the nation from a standpoint of national defense. . . . Without an adequate supply of meat and wool the nation would be considerably handicapped in case of war.'—Holm Bursum to Charles McNary, April 16 1934, Bursum MSS, University of New Mexico, Albuquerque, N. M., Box 1. The public-power reformers of the New Deal were schooled in wartime agencies like the Power Section of the Emergency Fleet Corporation (Morris L. Cooke, 'Early Days of Rural Electrification,' *American Political Science Review*, XLII, 1948, 437); 'U.S. War Industries Board, 1918,' folder, J. D. Ross MSS, University of Washington, Seattle, Wash. One conservationist commented on his work on the Mississippi Valley Committee with Morris Cooke: 'To all of us it was a great experience . . . epoch-making. . . . The exper. was as valuable to me as to you; it was similar to an enriching exper. I had under the same leadership back in 1917–18, during the war.' Harlow Person to Donald Bower, December 9, 1935, 'Quasi Official and Personal Correspondence of Morris L. Cooke,' National Archives, REA Files (notes of Jean Christie).

[90] Timothy L. McDonnell, S. J. *The Wagner Housing Act* Chicago, 1957, pp. 7–9; Curtice N. Hitchcock, 'The War Housing Program and Its Future,' *Journal of Political Economy*, XXVII, 1919, 241–79; Miles Colean, *Housing for Defense*, New York, 1940, chap. i.

[91] Robert D. Kohn, 'Housing in a Reconstruction Program,' *Survey*, XLII, 1919, 341. The most intense interest in government housing, however, came not so much in the war as in the reconversion period, although it was triggered by the war experience. (McDonnell, *The Wagner Housing Act*, pp. 12–15).

[92] Conkin, *Tomorrow a New World*, pp. 50–54, 67; Roy Lubove, "Homes and 'A Few Well-Placed Fruit Trees': An Object Lesson in Federal Housing," *Social Research*, XXVII, 1960, 469–86.

[93] Roy Lubove, 'New Cities for Old: The Urban Reconstruction Program of the 1930's.' *Social Studies*, LIII 1962, 205.

industry' under the War Industries Board.[94] Peek's war experience with the ways government could benefit industry had led him to argue that the government should give the same measure of aid to the distressed farmer.[95] Frustrated in the twenties by Republican presidents in his campaign to win support for McNary-Haugenism, Peek pinned his hopes on the election of Franklin Roosevelt in 1932. 'It looks to me as though in the campaign for Roosevelt for President we are in the last line of trenches and if he is not elected that agriculture is doomed to peasantry,' Peak wrote.[96] Roosevelt's victory touched off a serious debate over how to curb farm surpluses which, after months of wrangling, ended in the passage of the Agricultural Adjustment Act in the spring of 1933.[97] To head the new Agricultural Adjustment Administration, Roosevelt named George Peek.[98] 'To him, with his war experience, this whole thing clicks into shape,' Peek's wife noted, 'and some of the fine men of the country are coming to his call as they did in 1917, and with the same high purpose.'[99]

Consciously devised to provide the moral equivalent to war that men like Tugwell sought, the Civilian Conservation Corps aimed to install martial virtues in the nation's youth.[100] When the CCC enlisted its first recruits, it evoked memories of the mobilization of the AEF. 'By the fifteenth of July we shall have 275,000 people all actually at work in the woods,' Roosevelt reported a few weeks after Congress adopted the CCC proposal. 'It is a pretty good record, one which I think can be compared with the mobilization carried on in 1917.'[101] 'America has a new army and has sent it to war,' observed one writer that summer. 'In two brief months 300,000 men have enlisted, been trained, transferred to the front, and have started the attack. The battle is on in earnest.'[102]

---

[94] James Shideler, 'Wilson, Hoover, War and Food Control. 1917–1918,' paper delivered at the convention of the Mississippi Valley Historical Association, Denver, Colo., April 25, 1959; Grosvenor Clarkson, *Industrial America in the World War*, Boston and New York, 1923, p. 239.

[95] Gilbert Fite, *George N. Peek and the Fight for Farm Parity*, Norman, Okla., 1954, p. 32.

[96] George Peek to Earl Smith, October 18, 1932, Western Historical Manuscripts Collection, University of Missouri, Columbia, Mo., Peek MSS.

[97] During the debate, Senator Smith Wildman Brookhart of Iowa advocated a 'war emergency' plan in which the surplus would be 'commandeered' by the government (*Jackson* [Miss.] *Daily Clarion-Ledger*, January 23, 1933). When Roosevelt sent his farm message to Congress, Secretary of Agriculture Henry Wallace announced: 'In no case will there be any gouging of the consumer. We hope to revive the Wartime spirit in everyone to put this thing across.' *Time*, XXI (March 27, 1933), 12. A study of Wallace's rhetoric has noted his fondness for military terminology in his speeches (Robert Gene King, 'The Rhetoric of Henry Agard Wallace,' Ph.D. dissertation, Department of Speech and Drama, Teachers College, Columbia University, 1963). The farm protest movement employed similar metaphors. One farmer told an Iowa county agent bluntly that 'the Word War [had] its slackers,' and that, sixteen years after the war, the country was plagued by 'yellow pups running around in the shape of nincom-poop-flatheaded County Agents.' Jesse Sickler to Milo Reno, April 16, 1933, Reno MSS (privately held).

[98] Roosevelt had first offered the post to Peek's 'boss', Bernard Baruch, who, as head of the War Industries Board was regarded as the most important of the war administrators, J.F.T. O'Connor MS Diary, May 13, 1933, Bancroft Library, University of California, Berkeley, Calif., O'Connor MSS.

[99] Georgia Lindsey Peek MS memoir, 'Early New Deal,' Peek MSS. For Jerome Frank's first experience with farm issues in the United States Food Administration, see Jerome Frank, COHC, pp. 52–53. 'It was the greatest thing that ever happened when the government took charge of the wheat situation and told the big and little barons what price the farmers should get for their wheat,' a Florida newspaper stated that summer. 'Everyone knows what the government was able to do with the price of wheat during the war.' 'Why Not Government Control of Citrus Fruit?', *Lakeland* (Fla.) *News*, July 1, 1933, clipping in P. K. Yonge Library, University of Florida, Gainesville, Fla., Spessard Holland MSS, Box 52.

[100] There had been widespread agitation for offering such an alternative to groups like the 'wandering boys of the road' and the bonus marchers (George Rawick, 'The New Deal and Youth,' Ph.D. dissertation, University of Wisconsin, 1957, p. 40; Pelham Glassford, 'Training Camps for the Unemployed,' Institute of Industrial Relations Library, University of California at Los Angeles, Los Angeles, Calif., Glassford MSS, Box 1; James Harvey Rogers, 'Sound Inflation,' *Economic Forum*, I, 1933, 127.

[101] Roosevelt, *Public Papers*, II, 238. Schlesinger points out that Louis Howe's original plan for the CCC called for 'a large-scale recruiting effort, bands playing and flags flying, leading to a mass exodus of the unemployed to the forests' (Arthur Schlesinger, Jr., *The Coming of the New Deal*, p. 337). See, too, 'Memorandum for the Secretary of War: Subject: Civilian Conservation Corps,' April 3, 1933, Franklin D. Roosevelt Library, Hyde Park, N.Y., Louis Howe MSS, Box 59. The Third Corps Area, it was observed, enrolled the first recruit in the 'peace time army' on the anniversary of America's entrance into World War I (Charles Price Harper, *The Administration of the Civilian Conservation Corps*, Clarksburg, W. Va., 1939, p. 24).

[102] Harrison Doty, 'Our Forest Army at War,' *Review of Reviews and World's Works*, LXXXVIII, July, 1933, 31. 'It represented the greatest peacetime demand ever made upon the Army and constituted a task of character and proportions equivalent to emergencies of war,' Chief of Staff Douglas MacArthur wrote in a communiqué to all Army Corps Area Commanders. 'It was well done, Army. MacArthur.'—Rawick, 'The New Deal and Youth,' p. 66. See, too, 'Extracts from Address of Honourable George H. Dern, Secretary of War,' n.d., Library of Congress, Dern MSS, Box 1.

While the agency was under civilian direction, the Army ran the camps.[103] CCC recruits convened at army recruiting stations; traveled to an Army camp where they were outfitted in World War I clothing; were transported to the woods by troop-train; fell asleep in army tents to the strain of 'Taps' and woke to 'Reveille.'[104] A stanza of a poem by a CCC worker made clear the Army's role:

Uncle, he says to his Army,
'You did a good job before
When you took three million rookies
And polished 'em up for war,
Now if you can handle the civvies
Like the Doughboys and the Gob,
And stiffen their ranks till they're tough as the yanks
I'll give 'em a great big job.'[105]

The CCC newspaper, frankly modeled on *Stars and Stripes*, offered a prize for the best nickname for a CCC worker: 'You know—some word that has caught on in your camp—the way the word 'dough-boy' was used to describe the American soldier in France.'[106] *Happy Days* recounted the work of the 'Tree Army' in the language of military communiques: 'Company 217 at Beachy Bottoms, N.Y. has been filled to full Gypsy-moth-fighting strength,' or, in Montana, 'Depression Warriors Holding Western Front.'[107] On July 1, *Happy Days* reported:

The big drive has begun. Uncle Sam has thrown his full C.C.C. strength into the front lines of the forest. ... The entire reforestation army has landed in the woods—and has the situation well in hand.
In all sectors the reforestation troops are moving ahead. Battle lines of the Gypsy moth are beginning to crack and fall back in New York and New England. Yellow pine beetles are retreating from the mountains of Colorado and California before the onslaught of the C.C.C. Forest fires ... are being repulsed on all flanks the moment they show their smudgy red heads through the trees.[108]

Of all the New Deal agencies, the CCC was probably the most popular, because it united two objectives: 'the conservation of America's natural resources and the conservation of its young manhood.'[109] Many observers believed that the 'forestry army' embodied James's proposal for an army of youth enlisted in a 'warfare against nature,' although Roosevelt himself may not have been directly affected by James.[110] The Corps, it was claimed, had rescued young men from meaninglessness, rebuilt bodies and character, and given men a soldier's pride of accomplishment.[111] Speaker Rainey wrote: 'They are also under military training and as they come out of it they come out improved in health and developed mentally and physically and are more useful citizens and if ever we should become involved in another war they would furnish a very valuable nucleus for our army.'[112]

While the CCC, the AAA, the TVA, housing, economy, and banking legislation all shared in the war legacy, it was the National Recovery Administration that was the keystone of the early New Deal, and the NRA rested squarely on the War Industries Board example. The National Industrial Recovery bill, modeled on WIB procedures, wove together a series of schemes for government-business co-ordination of the kind that had prevailed in the war.[113] One of the most influential recovery designs, sponsored by Meyer Jacobstein, a Rochester (New York) banker, and H. G. Moulton, president of the Brookings Institution, recommended the creation of 'a National Board for Industrial Recovery, with powers similar to those so effectively utilized during

---

[103] To quiet fears of military control, Roosevelt named as CCC Director the union leader Robert Fechner whom he had first encountered when both were engaged in determining war labor policies. The real control of the camps, however, lay with the military (Tucker Smith to Jane Addams, March 8, 1933, Swarthmore College Peace Collection, Swarthmore, Pa., Jane Addams MSS, Box 22; 'Unofficial Observer' [John Franklin Carter], *The New Dealers*, New York, 1934, pp. 163–65; Rawick, 'The New Deal and Youth,' chap. v.
[104] Charles W. B. Hurd, 'The Forestry Army at the Front,' *Literary Digest*, CXVI, September 9, 1933, 5–6; Joseph Cream, 'The Genesis of the Civilian Conservation Corps' Master's thesis, Columbia University, 1955, pp. 45 ff.
[105] Reprinted in Oliver and Dudley, *This New America*, p. 133.
[106] *Happy Days*, I, May 20, 1933, 8. Cf. Levette J. Davidson, 'C.C.C. Chatter,' *American Speech*, XV, 1940, 210–11.
[107] *Happy Days*, I, June 3, 1933, 2; June 24, 1933, 3.
[108] *Ibid.*, I, July 1, 1933, 1.

[109] Christian, 'America's Peace Army,' p. 43. Cf. Tulsa, *World*, April 10, 1933, clipping in University of Oklahoma, Norman, Okla., W. A. Pat Murphy MSS.
[110] Ferdinand Silcox, 'Our Adventure in Conservation: The CCC,' *Atlantic Monthly*, CLX, 1937, 714. Moley recalls that when the question of James's influence was raised, Roosevelt conceded there might be a relationship, but he had no conscious awareness of one. Then the President added: 'But look here! I think I'll go ahead with this—the way I did on beer' (Moley, *After Seven Years*, p. 174).
[111] A *Detroit News* cartoon which bore the title, 'The Old Veterans of the Conservation Army Will Have Something Worth Bragging About,' showed an elderly man holding a little boy by the hand and pointing with his cane to a great forest. The caption read: 'In 1933 I planted all of these in the great war against depression' (Hurd, 'The Forestry Army at the Front,' p. 6).
[112] Henry T. Rainey to K. G. Baur, March 13, 1934, Library of Congress, Rainey MSS, Box 1.
[113] *New York Times*, April 29, 1933; Rexford Tugwell, 'Notes from a New Deal Diary,' May 30, 1933; Jerome Frank, COHC, p. 27. An article which appeared after this essay was written amply demonstrates the importance of the war precedent: Gerald D. Nash, 'Experiments in Industrial Mobilizations: WIB and NRA,' *Mid-America*, XLV, 1963, 157–74.

the World War by the War Industries Board.'[114] When the President commissioned Raymond Moley to frame legislation for industrial recovery, Moley asked General Hugh Johnson, who in World War I had functioned as a liaison between the Army and the War Industries Board, to take over for him. 'Nobody can do it better than you,' Moley coaxed. 'You're familiar with the only comparable thing that's ever been done—the work of the War Industries Board.'[115] The recovery bill, drafted by Johnson and others, won Senate approval by only the narrowest of margins; conservatives foresaw that the measure would enhance the power of the state and progressives believed the proposal would encourage cartelization. Franklin Roosevelt was more sanguine. When the President signed the recovery act of June 16, he commented: 'Many good men voted this new charter with misgivings. I do not share these doubts. I had part in the great co-operation of 1917 and 1918 and it is my faith that we can count on our industry once more to join in our general purpose to lift this new threat. . . . '[116]

Before labor would agree to the industrial-recovery program, it insisted on the same degree of government recognition of the right to organize as it had enjoyed in World War I. In December, 1932, shortly after he learned that Frances Perkins would be the new Secretary of Labor, Sidney Hillman sent her a memorandum which urged the government to pursue the kinds of policies the War Labor Board had initiated.[117] In framing the recovery bill, W. Jett Lauck, who had been secretary of the War Labor Board, served as spokesman for John L. Lewis's United Mine Workers. Lauck, who sponsored a plan for 'a national board composed of labor modeled after the War Labor Board,' played a prominent part in shaping the labor provisions of the legislation.[118] When the national industrial-recovery bill emerged from the drafting room, it incorporated the pivotal section 7 (a) which granted labor's demand for recognition of the right of collective bargaining. The essential provisions of 7 (a) noted Edwin

Witte, were 'but restatements' of principles first recognized by the National War Labor Board.[119]

Franklin Roosevelt had not only had a prominent part in framing World War I labor policies, but had, as Gerald Nash has pointed out, 'sketched out the blueprint for the War Labor Policies Board which was modeled on his directive.'[120] To staff the National Labor Board of 1933, the President named men he had first encountered in developing war labor programs. William Leiserson, executive secretary of the board, had been Roosevelt's personal adviser on labor affairs in 1918.[121] In formulating labor policy—from interpreting 7 (a) through the adoption and administration of the Wagner Act—Roosevelt and his lieutenants drew heavily on war precedents. The war agencies had established the basic principles of the New Deal labor program: that workers had the right to unionize, that they must not be discharged for union activity, and that presidential boards could restrain employers from denying such rights. More than this, they had evolved the procedure of plant elections to determine bargaining representatives which was to be the crucial instrumentality employed by Roosevelt's labor boards.[122]

To head the NRA Roosevelt named the fiery General Johnson, who could boast pertinent experience not only with the War Industries Board but in organizing the draft.[123] In mid-July, Johnson launched a national campaign dramatized by the

---

[114] Meyer Jacobstein and H. G. Moulton, 'A Plan for Economic Recovery,' Wagner MSS.

[115] Moley, *After Seven Years*, p. 188.

[116] Roosevelt, *Public Papers*, II, 252.

[117] Matthew Josephson, *Sidney Hillman: Statesman of American Labor*, Garden City, N.Y., 1952, p. 357. Hillman had been a member of the Board of Control and Labor Standards for Army Clothing during the war.

[118] 'Docket—Coal & Stabilization,' April 24, May 6, May 23, 1933, National Recovery Act file, Alderman Library, University of Virginia, Charlottesville, Va., W. Jett Lauck MSS; *Business Week*, May 24, 1933, pp. 3–4.

[119] Edwin E. Witte, 'The Background of the Labor Provisions of the N.I.R.A.,' *University of Chicago Law Review*, I, 1934, 573.

[120] Nash, 'Franklin D. Roosevelt and Labor: The World War I Origins of Early New Deal Policy,' *Labor History*, I, 1960, 49. See, too, Frank Freidel, *Franklin D. Roosevelt: The Apprenticeship*, Boston, 1952, pp. 328–32.

[121] Nash, 'Franklin D. Roosevelt and Labor,' p. 51.

[122] Irving Bernstein, *The New Deal Collective Bargaining Policy*, Berkeley and Los Angeles, 1950, pp. 19–20; 'Address by Milton Handler, General Counsel of National Labor Board, before the Legal Division of the National Industrial Recovery Administration,' n.d., Franklin D. Roosevelt Library, Hyde Park, N.Y., Leon Henderson MSS, Box 6; Wagner to Rep. William Ashbrook, April 24, 1935, Wagner MSS.

[123] 'Now the battle for recovery has shifted from the stage of map work at GHQ to the firing line of action,' wrote Raymond Clapper. Administrators like Peek and Johnson were 'the top sergeants of recovery' (Clapper, 'Top Sergeants of the New Deal,' *Review of Reviews and World's Work*, LXXXVIII, August, 1933, 19).

symbol of the Blue Eagle.[124] 'In war, in the gloom of night attack, soldiers wear a bright badge on their shoulders to be sure that comrades do not fire on comrades,' explained the President. 'On that principle, those who co-operate in this program must know each other at a glance. That is why we have provided a badge of honor for this purpose. . . .'[125]

Cabinet members greeted with skepticism Johnson's proposal for a mass movement to enlist the nation behind the NRA. Homer Cummings pointed out that the country was not at war, and it might be difficult to get everyone to sign a pledge. Johnson replied that he felt it could be put over, for the depression was more real than the war had been to most Americans. 'Almost every individual has either suffered terribly, or knows of friends and relatives who have; so there is waiting here to be appealed to what I regard as the most fertile psychology that you could imagine. . . . I think this has anything that happened during the War backed off the board.'[126]

To enforce the Blue Eagle, Johnson enlisted the housewives of the country. 'It is women in homes— and not soldiers in uniform—who will this time save our country.' he proclaimed. 'They will go over the top to as great a victory as the Argonne. It is zero hour for housewives. Their battle cry is "Buy now under the Blue Eagle!"'[127] By kindling the spirit of the Liberty Loan drives and the draft registration of World War I, Johnson kept alive the intense spirit of the Hundred Days through another season. 'There is a unity in this country,' declared Franklin Roosevelt, 'which I have not seen and you have not seen since April, 1917. . . .'[128]

The Recovery Administration conceived of the depression as, in part, a crisis in character. The New Dealers hoped that businessmen would place the public weal above their private interests, just as the copper magnates had responded to Baruch's appeal in 1917 by supplying metal to the army and navy at less than half the market price. In 1933, businessmen were asked to accept as a patriotic duty the assignment to raise wages and agree to a 'truce' on price-cutting. The recovery drive, it was argued, would succeed only if it aroused the same kind of 'spiritual' fervor that World War I had awakened. Morris Cooke wrote:

Conversations with a good many different kinds of people convince me that there is needed to expedite industrial recovery a talk by the President in which he would read into our 57 varieties of effort an ethical and moral quality and call on us individually and collectively to put our shoulders to the wheel just as if we were at war. . . .
Everywhere I get the impression of our people wanting to be told that the main purpose of the Recovery Administration is not exclusively the rehabilitation of our material wellbeing but a reaffirmation of the spiritual values in life.[129]

To man the New Deal agencies, Roosevelt turned to the veterans of the war mobilization.[130] Top NRA officials included Johnson's chief of staff, John Hancock, who had managed the War Industries Board's naval industrial program; Charles F. Horner, the genius of the Liberty Loan drive; Leo Wolman, who had headed the section on production statistics of the War Industries Board; and Major General Clarence Charles Williams, who had been Chief of Ordnance in charge of the vast war

[124] The idea of an NRA insignia has been suggested by Bernard Baruch in a speech in May. Baruch based the proposal on a War Industries Board notion. (Bernard Baruch, *The Public Years*, New York, 1960, pp. 73, 251). In his speech, Baruch had declared: 'If it is commonly understood that those who are coöperating are soldiers against the enemy within and those who omit to act are on the other side, there will be little hanging back. The insignia of government approval on doorways, letterheads, and invoices will become a necessity in business. This method was a success in 1918.'—Hugh Johnson, *The Blue Eagle from Egg to Earth* (Garden City, N.Y., 1935), p. 251.
[125] Roosevelt, *Public Papers*, II, 301.
[126] Schlesinger, Jr., *The Coming of the New Deal*, p. 113.
[127] Hugh Johnson, *The Blue Eagle from Egg to Earth*, p. 264. Johnson, who had planned and directed the draft registration, used many of the same techniques in administering the NRA (Peek, *Why Quit Our Own*, pp. 122–23; Russell Owen, 'General Johnson Wages a Peace-Time War,' *New York Times Magazine*, July 30, 1933, p. 3; Division of Press Intelligence, 'Memorandum on Editorial Reaction, Week from April 30 through May 6,' May 7, 1935, Louis Howe MSS, Box 85). Ruth McKenney observed of Akron: 'Precisely like the old draft board, a local N.R.A. Compliance Committee was set up, its members the very "best" people in town.'—McKenney, *Industrial Valley*, p. 107.
[128] Roosevelt, *Public Papers*, II, 345.

[129] Cooke to Louis Howe, July 3, 1933, Franklin D. Roosevelt Library, Hyde Park, N.Y., Morris Cooke MSS, Box 51. Russell Leffingwell of the House of Morgan observed later: Just as the war tore us all up by the roots, and made us seek such opportunity as there might be to serve our country in its need, so every man of good-will, every man of imagination and understanding has been struggling these last four and one-half years to find out how the human agony of the deflation could be stopped.'—Leffingwell, 'The Gold Problem and Currency Revaluation,' Academy of Political Science, March 21, 1934, Franklin D. Roosevelt Library, Hyde Park, N.Y., Franklin D. Roosevelt MSS, President's Personal File 866.
[130] Political scientists had been disappointed by Hoover's failure to name social scientists to government agencies. 'During the World War,' wrote Arthur Holcombe, 'economists and sociologists and statisticians were found to be very useful in Washington and were employed in large numbers. They should be used also in times of peace.'—Holcombe, 'Trench Warfare,' *American Political Science Review*, XXV, 1931, 916.

purchasing.[131] Many other New Dealers had had their first taste of government service during the war. The first Administrator for Public Works, Colonel Donald H. Sawyer, had built cantonments; Felix Frankfurter had chaired the War Labor Policies Board; Captain Leon Henderson of Ordnance had served with the War Industries Board; and Senator Joseph Guffey had worked in the War Industries Board on the conservation of oil.[132] For many, the summer of 1933 seemed like old times. 'Washington is a hectic place,' wrote Isador Lubin in August. 'The hotels are filled, and the restaurants remind me very much of war times. One cannot go into the Cosmos Club without meeting half a dozen persons whom he knew during the war.'[133]

The commandants of New Deal agencies thought of themselves as soldiers in a war against depression. The young men who came to Washington said they had 'volunteered in peacetime.'[134] Some even claimed they were conscripts. When Holgar Cahill expressed reluctance to accept a bid to head the new Federal Art Project, an associate advised him he had no alternative. 'An invitation from the Government to a job like that is tantamount to an order. It's like being drafted.'[135] This theme quickly became commonplace. From his 'general headquarters in Washington, D.C.,' reported one writer, 'General' Harry L. Hopkins had organized

the Federal Emergency Relief Administration as 'only one division of the "American Army" in the War on Want.'[136] One of Hopkins' 'noncoms,' a relief worker in northern Michigan observed: 'We were like an army, drafted into service during a war.' She wrote of the FERA Field Director: '... He had been in the front-line trenches with the rest of us when the battle raged at its worst. ... ' When the FERA gave way to the Works Project Administration late in 1935, her staff was broken up. 'At this time,' she commented, 'I lost the other two members of my shock troops. ... '[137]

The processes of New Deal government owed much to the war legacy. The war provided a precedent for the concentration of executive authority, for the responsibility of government for the state of the economy, and for the role of Washington as the arbiter among social groups. It originated the practice of shunting aside the regular line agencies and creating new organizations with dramatic alphabetical titles. When the RFC, the first of the new agencies, was established, one periodical reported: 'R.F.C., of course, is Reconstruction Finance Corporation, and the newspapers have fallen into the war-time habit of using the simple initials instead of the rather cumbersome full name of this anti-hard-times organization.'[138] The war offered a precedent, too, for setting up co-ordinating bodies like the National Emergency Council headed by Frank Walker.[139] Not least in importance, the war experience was used to justify the New Deal's emergency legislation in the courts.[140]

[131] One commentator noted that General Williams, as 'an old army man, could think in terms of the government interest' ('Unofficial Observer' [John Franklin Carter], *The New Dealers*, p. 47). For the high incidence of army officers in New Deal agencies, see John D. Millett, *The Works Progress Administration in New York City*, Chicago, 1938, p. 221.
[132] Joseph Guffey, *Seventy Years on the Red-Fire Wagon* Lebanon, Pa., 1952, p. 46. The New Deal's oil controls as well as the coal agencies Guffey helped establish rested, in part, on the precedent of the wartime Fuel Administration (Carl Brent Swisher, *American Constitutional Development*, p. 661).
[133] Lubin to Louis Brandeis, August 25, 1933, University of Louisville Law Library, Louisville, Ky., Brandeis MSS, G5. Lubin, United States Commissioner of Labor Statistics, had served as Thorstein Veblen's assistant in the Food Administration and later under Wesley Mitchell with the War Industries Board.
[134] Russell Lord, *The Wallaces of Iowa*, Boston, 1947, p. 346.
[135] Holgar Cahill, COHC, p. 340. Roosevelt told Carter Glass it was a 'war duty' to accept the post of Secretary of the Treasury (Daniel Roper to Edward House, January 24, 1933, Sterling Memorial Library, Yale University, New Haven, Conn., House MSS). Note, too, his attitude toward Cermak's assassination in Cordell Hull, *The Memoirs of Cordell Hull*, 2 vols.; New York, 1948, I, 158. Tugwell commented on his appointment as Assistant Secretary of Agriculture: 'F.D.R. marshalled me into service.'—Tugwell, 'Notes from a New Deal Diary,' February 18, 1933. That fall, George Creel pledged his 'continued devotion to NRA as soldier in the ranks' (George Creel to Roosevelt, September 23, 1933, Library of Congress, Creel MSS, Box 4).

[136] William Dow Boutwell, "The War on Want: How It Is Being Fought—and Won!' *School Life*, XIX, 1933, 31.
[137] Louise Armstrong, *We Too Are the People*, Boston, 1938, pp. 435, 465.
[138] *Literary Digest*, CXII, February 13, 1932, 9.
[139] Leon Henderson noted a meeting with Hugh Johnson: 'I asked—"who does your work of tieing into the adm. whole plan." He said "I do—but there isn't much done. There is no plan: not like old War Ind. Bd. We've got to have one soon. Walker runs too easy. The super-cabinet is just a lot of prima donnas sitting around—can't please 'em." '—Henderson MS Diary, February 20, 1934, Henderson MSS.
[140] One writer noted that 'the New Deal legislation was heavily garlanded with "emergency clauses" describing the dire national peril. This was because the Court had decided during the World War that war powers were supreme.'— 'Unofficial Observer' [John Franklin Carter], *The New Dealers*, New York, 1934, p. 394. See, too, Jane Perry Clark, "Emergencies and the Law.' *Political Science Quarterly*, XLIX, 1934, 268–83. Cf. Justice Sutherland's dissent in *Home Building and Loan Association* v. *Blaisdell*, 290 U.S. 471, 1934. In his press conference after the adverse ruling in the Schechter case, Roosevelt protested the Court's failure to recognize an emergency in view of 'those war acts which conferred upon the Executive far greater power over human beings and over property than anything that was done in 1933' (Roosevelt, *Public Papers*, IV, 206).

The war example saw service too as a way to refute opponents of the President's economic policies. When critics objected that the country could not 'afford' New Deal reforms, Roosevelt's supporters responded with the now familiar retort that if the country could spend as it had in war, it could spend in this new emergency, 'When people complain to me of the amount of money that the government has been borrowing,' commented Thomas Lamont of the House of Morgan, 'I always answer it by saying: "Well, if the country was willing to spend thirty billion dollars in a year's time to try to lick the Germans, I don't see why people should complain about spending five or six billion dollars to keep people from starving." '[141] By 1936, when Roosevelt returned to Forbes Field in Pittsburgh, where, four years before, he had promised to slash Hoover's reckless spending, the President concluded that the argument now offered the best reply to critics who accused him of a profligate disregard of campaign promises. 'National defense and the future of America were involved in 1917. National defense and the future of America were also involved in 1933,' Roosevelt asserted. 'Don't you believe that the saving of America has been cheap at that price?'[142]

Roosevelt's argument would have been more compelling if he had spent at anywhere near the rate that both he and his conservative foes implied he had. For a time in the winter of 1933–34, the Administration gave a fillip to the economy when it embarked on lavish spending through the Civil Works Administration, but early in 1934, the President, alarmed by mounting deficits, decreed the death of the CWA. Distressed by Roosevelt's verdict, Senator Robert LaFollette, Jr., of Wisconsin inquired: 'In 1917, Mr. President, what Senator would have dared to rise on the floor of the Senate and suggest that we could not fight the war against Germany and her allies because it would unbalance the Budget?'[143]. *The Nation* voiced a similar protest: 'The country is confronted with a vastly greater crisis than it had to meet in the World War but has not yet extended itself financially as it did at that time.'[144] Progressives warned that unless the President began to spend at a wartime pace the country might take years to pull out of the depression.

The progressive Cassandras proved correct. The New Deal mobilization of 1933–34, from which so much had been expected, brought disappointing economic returns.

The crux of the difficulty lay in the fact that the metaphor of war was, in more than one way, inapt. As a model for economic action, World War I was unsatisfactory for the problems confronting Roosevelt in 1933 were quite unlike those Woodrow Wilson had been called on to meet in 1917. As the Harvard economist Edwin Gay wrote: 'War stimulates the full expansion of productive energy, but the deep depression cripples every economic process and discourages even the most sanguine business leaders.'[145] Some who recalled the war experience hoped that it could provide a prototype for the same kind of impressive increases in output that had been achieved in 1917–18. But the aims of the New Deal mobilization were not the same as those of the war General Johnson even called for 'an armistice on increasing producing capacity.'[146] Frank Freidel has pointed out:

Unlike wartime measures, the new agencies were to reduce output in most areas rather than raise it, and encourage price increases rather than restrain them. Thus, waging a war on the depression was in some ways the reverse of waging one on a foreign foe.[147]

John M. Clark has made a similar point. The war, Clark noted, provided precedents for emergency controls, deficit spending, and expanded powers for the Federal Reserve System, but the problems of war and of depression 'were radically different in fact, they were in some respects opposite to one another.'[148] The question of determining priorities in a war economy, Clark observed, was not at all the same as that of reinvigorating sick industries. Clark concluded:

All the machinery for allocating limited supplies of essential resources among conflicting uses, which played so large a part in the wartime controls, had no application to the depression. Where the actuating motives of private industry fail and the result is partial paralysis, the problem is essentially opposite to that of war.[149]

[141] Schlesinger, Jr., *The Coming of the New Deal*, p. 498.
[142] Roosevelt, *Public Papers*, V, 407, Cf. Lewis Kimmel, *Federal Budget and Fiscal Policy*, pp. 190–92.
[143] *Congressional Record*, 73d Cong., 2d Sess., LXXVIII, February 8, 1934, 2174.
[144] 'Not Back to Hoover, Please!' *Nation*, CXXXVIII, 1934, 346.

[145] Edwin F. Gay, 'The Great Depression,' *Foreign Affairs*, X, 1932, 529.
[146] Johnson, *The Blue Eagle from Egg to Earth*, p. 222.
[147] Freidel, *America in the Twentieth Century*, p. 312.
[148] John M. Clark, *Social Control of Business*, New York, 1939, p. 424. The New Deal theorists were captivated by the idea of 'balance.' They sought to redress the imbalances between supply and demand, just as the war mobilizers had done. But they lacked the ingredients the war mobilizers could count upon: ample purchasing power and massive federal spending.
[149] *Ibid.*, p. 425.

These misgivings were not simply the result of hindsight. In the midst of the Hundred Days, the economist Paul Douglas warned that the country did not face the wartime task of rationing scarce resources but the quite different problem of stimulating production. 'Industry must get some business before it can proceed to ration it out,' Douglas gibed. He was disconcerted by the New Deal's obsession with the menace of overproduction when the critical question was how to increase purchasing power. Douglas noted: 'Certainly those who are arguing from the analogy of the War Industries Board miss the point. That body had behind it the gigantic purchasing power of the government, and with this weapon it was able to instill some order in the industrial system. But unless the government creates such purchasing power in the present emergency, the regulatory body will be operating in a void.'[150]

The war analogy proved mischievous in an even more significant respect. The Tugwells thought of the war as a time when the intellectuals had exercised unprecedented power over the economy, and when the feasibility of a planned society had been brilliantly demonstrated. Yet, although the intellectuals did wield power, agencies like the War Industries Board had, after all, been run chiefly by business executives. If they learned anything from the war, it was not the virtues of collectivism but the potentialities of trade associations, the usefulness of the state in economic warfare with the traders of other nations, and the good-housekeeping practices of eliminating duplication and waste. The immediate consequence of the war was not a New Jerusalem of the planners but the Whiggery of Herbert Hoover as Secretary of Commerce. While the war mobilization did establish meaningful precedents for New Deal reforms, it was hardly the 'war socialism' some theorists thought it to be. Perhaps the outstanding characteristic of the war organization of industry was that it showed how to achieve massive government intervention without making any permanent alteration in the power of corporations.

The confusion over the meaning of the war experience helped conceal the ambiguities of the so-called 'First New Deal.' The architects of the early New Deal appeared to be in fundamental agreement, since they united in rejecting the New Freedom ideal of a competitive society in favor of business-government co-ordination in the 1917 style. In fact,

they differed sharply. Tugwell hoped that the co-ordination authorized by the NRA would enable the Recovery Administration to become an agency for centralized government direction of the economy, a possibility insured in part by the NRA's licensing power. Most of the other 'First New Dealers,' however, meant by business-government co-ordination an economy in which businessmen would make the crucial decisions. As administrator of the NRA, General Johnson gave small scope to the government direction Tugwell had envisaged. He never used the licensing power, but relied instead on negotiation with business and on the force of social pressure. Like Moley and Richberg and the President, Johnson placed his faith not in a planned economy but in voluntary business co-operation with government.[151]

The New Deal administrators shared, too, the conviction of the war bureaucrats that progress would be achieved not through worker or farmer rebellions, but through government programs, conceived and executed by agency officials. A month after the armistice, Wesley Mitchell had voiced the need for 'intelligent experimenting and detailed planning rather than for agitation or class struggle.'[152] The war approach which the New Dealers adopted rejected both mass action and socialist planning, and assumed a community of interest of the managers of business corporations and the directors of government agencies. Roosevelt's lieutenants believed that the great danger to such an experiment lay not in the opposition of the conservatives, who were discredited, but in the menace of antiplutocratic movements. Yet in damping the fires of popular dissent, they also snuffed out support they would need to keep the reform spirit alive.

The New Dealers, distrustful of the policies of group conflict, sought to effect a truce like that of 1917 when class and sectional animosities abated. Perhaps no other approach could have accomplished so much in the spring of 1933, yet it was a tactic which had obvious perils for the cause of reform. By presenting the depression not as the collapse of a system but as a personalized foreign enemy,

[150] Paul H. Douglas, 'The New Deal After Ten Weeks,' *The World Tomorrow*, XVI, 1933, 419.

[151] It was not merely that Johnson had the temperament of a war administrator who turned naturally to the tactics of social coercion, but that he had well-founded doubts about whether the Supreme Court would sanction government edicts (Schlesinger, Jr., *The Coming of the New Deal*, pp. 108–9). Schlesinger also suggests that Johnson decided on this course because Harold Ickes moved so slowly in spending for public works. This seems unlikely. Johnson made this decision almost as soon as he took office, well before the outlines of Ickes' operation had become clear.
[152] Lucy Sprague Mitchell, *Two Lives*, p. 303.

Roosevelt as much as Hoover sought to mend the social fabric. In doing so, Roosevelt, like his predecessor, deflected blame away from business leaders whom many thought responsible for hard times, and diverted attention from the fact that the depression was not the consequence of an assault by a foreign foe but evidence of internal breakdown. Even more important, the New Dealers, in the interest of national solidarity, tried to suppress anti-business expressions of discontent. President Roosevelt warned the AF of L convention in 1933: 'The whole of the country has a common enemy; industry, agriculture, capital, labor are all engaged in fighting it. Just as in 1917 we are seeking to pull in harness; just as in 1917, horses that kick over the traces will have to be put in a corral.'[153] General Johnson left no doubt of the intent of the President's words: 'Labor does not need to strike under the Roosevelt plan. . . . The plain stark truth is that you cannot tolerate strikes. Public opinion . . . will break down and destroy every subversive influence.[154] Far from operating a 'labor government,' as conservatives charged, the New Dealers in 1933 deeply resented strikes as acts of 'aggression' which sabotaged the drive for recovery. Frances Perkins recalls that Johnson believed that 'during the period when NRA was attempting to revive industry no stoppage of work could be tolerated under any circumstances. It was like a stoppage of work in war time. Anything had to be done to prevent that.'[155]

An administrator who spurned direct government sanctions but who was determined to have his way soon found that he was either resorting to bluster or encouraging vigilantism. Such had been the pattern in World War I.[156] On one occasion, the War Industries Board's price-fixing committee had warned a producer to co-operate, or become 'such an object of contempt and scorn in your home town that you will not dare to show your face there.'[157] Ray Lyman Wilbur, chief of the conserva-

tion division of the Food Administration, recalled: 'Indiana I found the best organized state for food conservation that I had yet seen. The people were approaching rapidly the stage where violations of wheatless days, etc., were looked upon as unpatriotic enough to require that inquiries as to the loyalty of the guilty citizen, baker or hotel-keeper be made.'[158]

If the New Dealers never ran to such excesses of vigilantism, they were not beyond employing this kind of social coercion, and they matched the war administrators in the technique of bluster. 'I have no patience with people who follow a course which in war time would class them as slackers,' declared Attorney-General Homer Cummings of the alleged hoarders of gold. 'If I have to make an example of some people, I'll do it cheerfully.'[159] When Frances Perkins hit out at the effort of the steel industry to dodge the intent of section 7 (a) by setting up company unions, she denounced these unions as 'war bridegrooms,' the popular epithet for matrimonial draft-dodging during the war.[160] When the economist Oliver W. M. Sprague resigned in protest at the Administration's gold-buying policy, Hugh Johnson accused him of 'deserting with a shot in the flank of the army in which he had enlisted.'[161] During the Blue Eagle drive, Donald Richberg insisted that in a time of crisis there could be 'no honorable excuse for the slacker who wastes these precious moments with doubting and debate—who palsies the national purpose with legalistic arguments.'[162]

Such statements infuriated the conservatives. Senator Carter Glass of Virginia found particularly galling Richberg's denunciation of NRA opponents as 'slackers who deserved to have white feathers pinned on them by the women of the country.' Glass wrote of Richberg's war record: 'He never heard a percussion cap pop; he did not know the smell of gun powder; he did not even reach a training camp to learn the difference between 'Forward March' and 'Parade Rest.' When asked

[153] *Report of Proceedings of the Fifty-third Annual Convention of the American Federation of Labor*, Washington, D.C., 1933, p. 307. In the summer of 1933, the President had made a 'no strike' appeal. He said of it: 'It is a document on a par with Samuel Gompers' memorable war-time demand to preserve the *status quo* in labor disputes. . . . It is an act of economic statesmanship.'—Roosevelt, *Public Papers*, II, 318.

[154] AF of L, *Proceedings*, 1933, p. 359.

[155] Frances Perkins, COHC, VII, 139–40; Roosevelt, *Public Papers*, II, 302.

[156] In a capitalist society, bluster frequently serves as a reform government's alternative to institutional rearrangements that would give government a direct share in corporation policy-determination. President Kennedy's role in the 1962 steel-price-hike incident is a case in point.

[157] Clarkson, *Industrial America in the World War*, p. 99.

[158] Edgar Eugene Robinson and Paul Carroll Edwards (eds.), *The Memoirs of Ray Lyman Wilbur* (Stanford, Calif., 1960), p. 264.

[159] *Time*, XXI (June 19, 1933), 12. 'Hoarders are at heart cowards,' declared Chandler Hovey, senior partner of Kidder, Peabody. 'The government should declare that to hoard at this time is unpatriotic, destructive and against the public interest.' —Clipping in Holy Cross College Library, Worcester, Mass., David I. Walsh MSS.

[160] 'Unofficial Observer' [John Franklin Cater], *The New Dealers*, p. 178.

[161] Hugh Johnson to Carter Glass, Alderman Library, University of Virginia, Charlottesville, Va., December 4, 1933, Glass MSS, Box 4.

[162] Richberg, *The Rainbow*, Garden City, N.Y., 1936, pp. 288–89.

by a responsible newspaperman to give his war record in justification of his vituperative assault on other people, he could do no better than allege he had helped sell some Liberty bonds.'[163] Glass's resentment was shared by other conservative critics. 'The man who lives well within his income,' protested Lewis Douglas, 'has come to be regarded as unpatriotic and as a slacker in the fight against the depression.'[164]

If the rhetoric of coercion disturbed the conservatives, it troubled some of the New Dealers even more. In the summer of 1933, a group of AAA officials protested:

General Johnson, in picturing the results of his campaign, has frequently used the analogy of the war-time 'gasless Sundays.' Then, General Johnson recalls, if a man drove a car on Sunday, his neighbors pushed the car into the ditch. Popular opinion at that time was so inflamed that it expressed itself by violence.

General Johnson's analogy is profoundly significant and disturbing. If his program is adopted, professional drive organizations will soon reappear in full force. Agitators may take advantage of the possible resulting hysteria to set group against group, such as farmers against wage earners, and thus defeat the real progress toward cooperation already made by the Roosevelt Administration.[165]

Some even thought they detected in Johnson's administration of the NRA the glimmerings of a corporate state.[166] If such was Johnson's purpose—

and the grounds for such a supposition are unsubstantial—the General received no encouragement from the President. Roosevelt moved quickly to squelch signs of militarism. When Harry Woodring, Assistant Secretary of War, wrote early in 1934 that the Army stood prepared to organize the CCC, veterans of World War I, and reliefers into a corps of 'economic storm troops,' the White House reprimanded him.[167] In late 1934, the authoritarian-minded Johnson was let go. That same year, Henry Wallace, seeking to pursue a 'middle course,' wrote: 'There is something wooden and inhuman about the government interfering in a definite, precise way with the details of our private and business lives. It suggests a time of war with generals and captains telling every individual exactly what he must do each day and hour.'[168]

Most of all, the Brandeisian faction of the New Dealers objected to the crisis spirit. Felix Frankfurter wrote Louis Brandeis: 'Much too much of "slacker" talk & old coercions.'[169] For the Brandeisians, the 'enemy' was not 'depression' but 'business.' They welcomed the breakup of the nation in 1934 and 1935 from the national interest into class and group interests. The early New Dealers had emphasized the war spirit of cooperation, co-ordination, and exhortation, because they feared that the bonds that held society together might be snapped. By 1935, it was clear that the crisis had been weathered, and the mood of war seemed inappropriate. Brandeisians felt free to assault business interests, other New Dealers lost faith in their ability to convert businessmen, and business groups increasingly viewed Roosevelt as their enemy. As in wartime, the first enthusiasm as the troops paraded to the front had given way to the realization that the army was not invincible, the casualty lists would be long, and the prospect of early victory was no longer promising.[170] Yet the danger of annihilation had been averted too, and as the sense of urgency lessened, the spirit of national solidarity slackened. 'The enemies who began to emerge in the eyes or the imagination of men,' Paul Conkin has observed of the end of the 'wartime effort' in 1935, 'were not such as could demand the hostility of all Americans, for these enemies were not natural, or providential, or

[163] Carter Glass to Walter Lippmann, August 10, 1933, Glass MSS, Box 4.
[164] Lewis W. Douglas, 'There Is One Way Out,' *Atlantic Monthly*, CLVI (1935), 267. Walter Lippmann was troubled by the frequent use the planners made of the war analogy (Lippmann, *The Good Society*, Boston, 1937, pp. 89–105). Cf. John M. Clark, *Social Control of Business*, pp. 463–64.
[165] 'Memorandum on Proposal for Blanket-Code,' July 18, 1933, in George Peek to Frank Walker, July 18, 1933, Peek MSS (letter not sent). The Washington correspondent of the *New Republic* wrote: 'What administration officials—half-consciously, half-unconsciously—want to do is to create a war psychosis in which any corporation head attempting to defy Mr. Roosevelt and the N.R.A. will be at once identified by the country with Kaiser Bill, Hindenburg, Ludendorff and Grover Bergdoll.'—T.R.B., 'Washington Notes,' *New Republic*, LXXV, 1933, 340.
[166] Criticism of the New Deal as fascist was quite common, and not limited to concern over Johnson's predilections. A radical commentary on Tugwell's *The Industrial Discipline and the Governmental Arts* noted: 'The really ominous word which Mr. Tugwell has spoken in his volume lies in his assumption that government in a capitalist society may be imbued with an essentially social aim that is *inclusive*, and may, therefore, in a grave emergency find it necessary to 'compel or persuade a higher co-operation for a national purpose.' The analysis is *liberal*; the solution is essentially *fascist*.'—J. B. Matthews and R. E. Shallcross, 'Must America Go Fascist?' *Harper's*, CLXIX, June, 1934, 12.

[167] Schlesinger, Jr., *The Coming of the New Deal*, p. 339; H. H. Woodring, 'The American Army Stands Ready,' *Liberty*, January 6, 1934.
[168] Henry Wallace, *New Frontiers*, New York, 1934, p. 21.
[169] Frankfurter to Brandeis, August 2, 1933, Brandeis MSS, G6.
[170] 'The Crisis of the N.R.A.,' *New Republic*, LXXVI, 1933, 349.

foreign, but human and native. A class and gronp consciousness was forming.'[171]

Yet the rhetoric of war persisted, even when such agencies of mobilization as NRA died. In the summer of 1935, Representative Robert L. Doughton of North Carolina observed: 'Of course in every War, if it has a chance at all to be successful, there must be a leader, and this Administration and the Congress have been engaged in a war on hunger, destitute [sic], unemployment, bankruptcy and every evil incident to the economic life of our people.'[172] In his 1936 campaign, Franklin Roosevelt told a Massachusetts crowd that, like Marshal Joffre at the First Battle of the Marne, he bore the blame for victory or defeat in war. 'Three and a half years ago we declared war on the depression,' the President asserted. 'You and I know today that that war is being won.' But he was quick to point out that the war had not yet been won. The country still needed the services of its commander-in-chief.[173] In his Franklin Field address, when he accepted renomination in June, 1936, Roosevelt declared: 'I accept the commission you have tendered me. I join with you. I am enlisted for the duration of the war.'[174] But by then references to war had become purely rhetorical.[175] When, that very year, the Administration explored the possibility of using the war power, and especially the precedent of Wilson's War Labor Policies Board, to justify federal regulation of the hours of labor, it concluded that the idea was not feasible.[176]

Only the New Dealers committed to a planned economy held fast to the earlier vision. As late as the summer of 1939, Rexford Tugwell looked back wistfully toward the war collectivism. Tugwell pleaded for a reorientation of progressive thought away from the traditional emphases on freedom for business, a change that only a crisis like that of 1917 or 1929 would produce. Of the two, Tugwell thought that war offered the best hope, for 1929 had yielded only 'atomistic reforms' while 1917 had resulted in 'national organization on a unitary scheme.' 'How different it was in 1917!' Tugwell wrote. 'It was possible . . . to make immense advances toward industrial unity. . . . That great wartime release of energy was achieved by freeing men's minds. Quantities and qualities could be thought of rather than profits.' No sane person would wish a war in order to bring about a 'purposive national organization,' he observed. 'Yet the fact is that only war has up to now proved to be such a transcending objective that doctrine is willingly sacrificed for efficiency in its service.[177]

If the references to war in the later Roosevelt years were largely rhetorical, the rhetoric was often revealing. In his Franklin Field speech, Roosevelt insisted that the nation was waging 'not alone a war against want and destitution and economic demoralization' but 'a war for the survival of democracy.' 'We are fighting to save a great and precious form of government for ourselves and for the world,' the President declared.[178] With each passing year, the challenge of the Fascist powers was more defiant, and the demands of foreign affairs came to supersede the claims of domestic issues. New Deal agencies increasingly directed their attention to preparing for the eventuality of war with the Axis. In 1938, the TVA boasted it was 'developing the power necessary for the large-scale operation of war industries in this well-protected strategic area.' The furnaces at Muscle Shoals, the Authority reported, were being utilized to turn out phosphorus, a material 'used in war for smoke screens and incendiary shells,' and the TVA's electric furnaces, the agency foresaw, 'might be converted to the electrolytic manufacture of aluminum or of chlorine—used in war gases. . . .'[179]

[171] Conkin, *Tomorrow a New World*, p. 130. Cf. Arthur Schlesinger, Jr., *The Politics of Upheaval*, Boston, 1960, pp. 395–98.
[172] Doughton to Henry Baker, July 15, 1935, University of North Carolina, Chapel Hill, N.C., Doughton MSS, Drawer 7.
[173] Roosevelt, *Public Papers*, V, 522–23.
[174] *Ibid.*, p. 236.
[175] Among countless examples of war rhetoric, see Roosevelt. *Public Papers*, V, 207, 475, and VII, 228, 545; Address of Governor George H. Earle, Wilkes Barre, Pa., March 16, 1935, Speech and News File No. 68, Earle MSS Bryn Mawr, Pa. (privately held); Donald McCoy, *Angry Voices: Left-of Center Politics in the New Deal Era*, Lawrence, Kan., 1938, p. 166.
[176] Victor E. Cappa, 'Two Studies of Certain Constitutional Powers as Possible Bases for Federal Regulation of Employer-Employee Relations,' Office of National Recovery Administration Division of Review, *Work Materials No. 68*, Washington, D.C., March, 1936. Mimeographed. Copy in Leon Henderson MSS, Box 17.

[177] R. G. Tugwell, 'After the New Deal,' *New Republic*, XCIX, 1939, 324. Three years later, Stuart Chase wrote: 'Nothing in the agenda of the New Deal was as radical as the war agenda of 1917 in respect to the government control of economic activity.'—Chase, *The Road We Are Travelling 1914–1942*, New York, 1942, p. 42.
[178] Roosevelt, *Public Papers*, V, 236.
[179] Tennessee Valley Authority, *To Keep the Waters in the Rivers and the Soil on the Land*, pp. 43–44. After the war, Judson King claimed: 'TVA and the Columbia River dams 'saved our lives' in World War II. They made possible production of phosphorus, nitrates, light metals and other war materials, including materials for the atom bomb.'—King, *The Conservation Fight*, pp. 280–81.

Henry Wallace had long believed that the AAA was an 'adjustment' program whose machinery could be used to increase output as well as to limit it. If there were a conflict beyond the ocean, a prospect he dreaded, the United States, he observed in 1934, could, through the Triple A, 'provision a war . . . with far less of that plunging, uninformed and altogether unorganized overplanting which got us into so much trouble during and after the last great war.'[180] A week before the outbreak of the European war in September, 1939, Wallace wrote the President that if war came the government might consider developing plans modeled on the Food Administration with which Wallace had worked in World War I. 'When we set up County Committees in AAA in 1933, I couldn't help thinking what a splendid mechanism we would have, if we ever got into a war, to meet the food problem. . . . Again when we set up the Ever Normal Granary System, I thought how marvelously this mechanism with its reserve supplies would help the country in case of war.'[181]

In 1939, James V. Forrestal tried to persuade New Dealers that the way to put across their program was to sell it as preparedness rather than reform; after all, the TVA had had its start in the Defense Act of 1916.[182] He won few converts—most liberals refused to adopt a stratagem that surrendered the theology of liberalism—but when the war in Europe led to a new emphasis on defense, the New Dealers were quick enough to adapt themselves. A month after war began in Europe, Roosevelt phoned Wallace to call all bureau chiefs and ask what their experience had been in World War I, and how the new emergency would affect their present position.[183] Many soon found themselves running the new defense agencies. Leon Henderson controlled prices, AAA Administrator Chester Davis coordinated agriculture with defense requirements, and Brehon Somervell, who had directed the WPA in New York, took charge of military construction.

The NYA began to train aircraft mechanics; CCC workers developed target ranges and airports for the Army; TVA dams produced the power for aluminium needed in bomber production and the REA turned out the electricity for army camps and naval installations.[184] New Dealers charged with developing defense and war labor policies turned repeatedly to the War Labor Board's precedents.[185] When war came, Schlesinger writes, it 'almost seemed an NRA reunion. The child of the War Industries Board, NRA was the father of the War Production Board. Leon Henderson, Donald Nelson, Sidney Hillman, Averell Harriman, William H. Davis, Isador Lubin, Edward R. Stettinius, Jr.,—all had their training in national mobilization in the breathless days of 1933 and 1934.'[186] Many of

[180] *New York Times*, August 19, 1934.

[181] Wallace to Roosevelt, August 26, 1939, Franklin D. Roosevelt MSS, President's Secretary's File 27. Such observations may suggest that, from the beginning, the New Deal was bent on war, and that the intervention in World War II was a logical culmination of Roosevelt's policies, or that there was a symbiotic relationship between war and the New Deal species of reform. Nothing I have found in my own research would support the conclusion that the New Dealers conspired to involve the nation in war, and very little would suggest an inevitable marriage of New Deal reform with war. Yet the relationship between progressivism and war in the twentieth-century state, it should be added, is a subject which is imperfectly understood and one which deserves more exploration and illumination.

[182] Eliot Janeway, *The Struggle for Survival*, New Haven, 1951, p. 20. Although proud of the achievements of the New Deal, Morris Cooke nonetheless believed that what had been done was still inadequate. 'I am convinced,' he wrote in 1938, 'that we have to arouse something akin to a war psychology if we are really to make this a permanent country.'—Cooke to W. C. Lowdermilk, June 30, 1938, cited in Jean Christie, Morris L. Cooke,' draft of Ph.D. dissertation, Columbia University, 1963.

[183] Harry Slattery, Administrator of the Rural Electrification Administration, reported: 'I told the Secretary that I was special assistant to Secretary Lane during the war period when he was Vice Counsel of the National Defense Council; . . . and that finally I was assigned to handle a plan for granting of land for returning soldiers, and had that especially under me.'—'Memorandum of conference with Secretary Henry Wallace, October 11, 1939,' Duke University, Durham, N.C., Slattery MSS.

[184] Kenneth Holland, and Frank Ernest Hill, *Youth in the CCC*, Washington, D.C., 1942, p. 184; H. S. Person, 'The Rural Electrification Administration in Perspective.' *Agricultural History*, XXIV, 1950, 79–80; Harold Ickes, *Autobiography of a Curmudgeon*, New York, 1943, chap. xv.

[185] Frances Perkins, COHC, VII, 776 ff.; Eliot Janeway, *The Struggle for Survival*, p. 161; Matthew Woll to W. Jett Lauck, December 20, 1940, Lauck MSS, Correspondence.

[186] Schlesinger, Jr., *The Coming of the New Deal*, p. 176. Tugwell wrote later: 'New agencies were multiplying as they had not since 1933; and in a way this period was much like that of the earlier one when the enemy had been the impalpable but terrifying depression. Franklin had, indeed, used the analogy of war at that time.'—Tugwell, *The Democratic Roosevelt*, Garden City, N.Y., 1957, p. 600. 'The New Deal was some preparation for this upheaval,' observed Marquis Childs. 'It was a kind of war.'—Childs, *I Write from Washington*, New York and London, 1942, p. 3. Frances Perkins reflected that the New Deal had, unconsciously, prepared the nation to meet the demand of war (Perkins, *The Roosevelt I Knew*, New York, 1964, pp. 349–51). From the very beginning, however, Roosevelt, who wished to maintain personal control of the mobilization, shied away from proposals to reconstitute a War Industries Board ('Meeting with the Business Advisory Council,' May 23, 1940, Franklin D. Roosevelt MSS, President's Secretary's File 17). But there were numerous observations on how World War I could serve as a useful precedent. See, e.g., Maxcy R. Dickson, 'The Food Administration–Educator,' *Agricultural History*, XVI, 1942, 91–96.

these men, it might be added, had first entered government service in World War I.

Precisely as the Keynesians had forseen, defense and war demands sparked an economic boom. In the summer of 1940, Keynes noted that the United States had failed to achieve recovery, because the volume of investment had been 'hopelessly inadequate.' The 'dreadful experience' of war might teach the United States what it had failed to learn in peacetime. He predicted: 'Your war preparation, so far from requiring a sacrifice, will be the stimulus, which neither the victory nor the defeat of the New Deal could give you, to greater individual consumption and a higher standard of life.' Keynes observed sadly: 'It is, it seems, politically impossible for a capitalistic democracy to organize expenditure on the scale necessary to make the grand experiment which would prove my case—except in war conditions.'[187]

Keynes's remark was to the point. The 'grand experiment' of the New Deal had achieved much. But it had not created, or indeed in any serious sense even attempted to create, a new model for American society. The New Dealers resorted to the analogue of war, because in America the sense of community is weak, the distrust of the state strong. Up to a point, the metaphor of war and the precedent of World War I proved invaluable. They helped provide a feeling of national solidarity which made possible the New Deal's greatest achievement: its success in 'nation-saving,' in mending the social fabric. The heritage of World War I justified the New Deal's claim to represent an overarching national interest to which business and other parochial interests must conform. The war proved that, at a time of crisis, the power of private individuals with money to turn the nation's resources to their own benefit could be limited by the prior claim of providing a 'social minimum.'[188] Since the war mobilization had brought to fruition much of progressivism, it offered a useful example for the New Dealers, and since the wartime control of industry went much further than earlier efforts in recognizing the place of the twentieth-century state, it was especially pertinent for some of the problems the New Deal confronted.

Yet in other respects the war analogue proved either treacherous or inadequate. The very need to employ imagery which was so often inappropriate revealed both an inpoverished tradition of reform and the reluctance of the nation to come to terms with the leviathan state. Only in war or in a crisis likened to war was it possible to put aside inhibiting doctrines, create a sense of national homogeneity, and permit the government to act in the national interest. But once the war ended, or the sense of crisis dissipated, traditional doctrine once again prevailed. The country had yet to find a way to organize collective action save in war or its surrogate. Nor had it faced up to the real problems of the relations of order to liberty which the power of the twentieth-century state creates.

World War II rescued the New Deal from some of its dilemmas and obscured others. In the war years, many of the New Deal programs were set aside— the WPA, Roosevelt said, had earned an 'honorable discharge.'[189] The New Dealers turned their talents to 'manning the production line.' The AAA helped increase farm production instead of restricting crops; the new industrial agencies sought to speed factory output rather than curtail it. Perhaps the greatest irony of the New Deal is the most familiar. Only in war was recovery achieved. Only in war did the country finally rescue that one-third of a nation ill-housed, ill-clad and ill-nourished. Only in war was the 'army of the unemployed' disbanded.

[187] Keynes, 'The United States and the Keynes Plan,' *New Republic*, CIII, 1940, 156–59. Morris Cooke, writing in the same issue that he did not think war orders as such would necessarily end unemployment, added: 'But I do feel that in executing billions in war orders we may learn a technique for deploying American manpower in such a way as to change, radically and permanently, our unemployment outlook.'— Cooke, 'Can We Afford the New Deal?' *New Republic*, CIII, 1940, 165. Even before the United States entered the war, writers were predicting that the defense program would provide a precedent for new government intervention to secure full employment in the postwar era. *Business Week* commented: 'It is inconceivable that, when the defense program ends, . . . the government will stand idly by in the midst of a great unemployment crisis born of nationwide demobilization. . . . The operation of the profit motive will be limited by the dominant requirement of full employment for the people.'— *Business Week*, August 16, 1941, pp. 36–37, cited in Stuart Chase, *The Road We Are Traveling, 1914–1942*, p. 98. See, too, Arthur Feiler, 'Economic Impacts of the War,' *Social Research*, VIII, 1941, 297–309. As World War I provided a precedent for the New Deal planners, so World War II taught lessons in 'full employment' to the liberals of the Truman era.

[188] John M. Clark, *Social Control of Business*, pp. 782–85.
[189] Malcolm Cowley, 'The End of the New Deal', *New Republic*, CVIII, 1943, 729.

Literature and the First World War

Prepared by Merryn Williams for the Course Team

Preliminaries

.1.1   This unit is called *Literature and the First World War*, but in fact, of course, we have time to study only a cross-section of this vast body of writing. The Great War inspired poems and novels from many countries. You will find several of the best and most interesting of these poems in the Course Anthology, and if you would like to read more of them I can recommend *Up the Line to Death*, edited by Brian Gardner. Among the many novels about the war or its effects I will just mention *Death of a Hero* by Richard Aldington and *Rough Justice* by C. E. Montague (England); *A Farewell to Arms*, by Ernest Hemingway (America); *All Quiet on the Western Front*, by Erich Maria Remarque (Germany); *The Good Soldier Schweik*, by Jaroslav Hasek (Czechoslavakia) and *Dr Zhivago* by Boris Pasternak (Russia). In this unit we shall be looking at one French novel, *Under Fire*, by Henri Barbusse, and one English poet, Wilfred Owen. *Under Fire* is a set book, and if you have not already done so, you must read it before starting on this unit. The Owen poems that we shall be studying are all in this unit or in the Anthology, *War and the Creative Arts*.

.1.2   In Section 1 I shall ask you to comment on a few of Owen's major poems, bearing in mind what you already know about the war, and to compare some of them with poems by other writers. There is no need for you to read all the First World War poems in the Anthology, but I think you will find it helpful to read several, because they show you the ways in which articulate Englishmen—most of them actually in the trenches—responded to the war. In Section 2 we shall study *Under Fire*, bearing in mind what we know about the war in France. Remember, too, that many young English writers were deeply affected by this book when it came out in 1917.

.1.3   Owen wrote his poetry and Barbusse wrote *Under Fire* while the war was still going on, and the experience of the trenches was still fresh in their minds. They are both *direct records* of the war, unlike novels written years afterwards, or poems by men who had never been to the front. In Section 3 we shall discuss whether they are similar in other ways as well.

SECTION 1   ENGLISH POETS AND THE WAR

7.2.1   In 1914 Great Britain had not within living memory been involved in a European war. There had been the Boer War, of course, fifteen years earlier, which had dragged on for three years, divided the nation into Jingoes and Pacifists, and killed a large number of young Englishmen. (Thomas Hardy wrote some moving poems about this, which you'll find in the Anthology.) But that was on a much smaller scale. The British public was absolutely unprepared for the *kind* of war which broke out in August 1914. Many people thought that it would be a quick glorious campaign, probably over by Christmas, and, even after it became obvious that this was a *total* war, with casualties hitting nearly every family in the country, people in Britain never really understood how terrible the conditions were at the front. As the war dragged on the soldiers often became very bitter about the 'patriots' who were urging them on from behind.

Rupert Brooke (Imperial War Museum).

Rupert Brooke in naval uniform (from C. Hassall, Rupert Brooke, Faber, 1964).

7.2.2   Among the three-quarters of a million English dead were a long line of writers; Edward Thomas, T. E. Hulme, 'Saki', Rupert Brooke, Julian Grenfell, Charles Sorley, Isaac Rosenberg, E. A. Mackintosh, Patrick Shaw-Stewart, W. N. Hodgson, Wilfred Owen. One reason for the high death toll among educated men was that they usually became infantry officers who had to lead their men over the the top and so were among the first to get killed. Most of these young men came from comfortable homes and had been to public school and university, and several of them had known each other at Oxford or Cambridge before the war. Siegfried Sassoon and Robert Graves, two poets who survived the war, had a very similar background, and they have described the impact of the war on their generation in *Siegfried's Journey* and *Goodbye to All That*. Wilfred Owen, whom Graves knew slightly and Sassoon very well, is mentioned in both these books. Graves describes how his old schoolfellows from Charterhouse joined up almost to a man when the war broke out, and how about a third of them were killed. Afterwards these young men became known as the Lost Generation. Many of them would undoubtedly have had brilliant careers and been among the country's leaders if they had lived.

Wilfred Owen

7.3.1   The classic account of Owen's early life was written by his brother, Harold Owen, in *Journey from Obscurity* which I urge you to read if you can. Wilfred was born in

1893 at Oswestry in Shropshire; both his parents had Welsh blood. His father was a railway official in a responsible position, but he lived in terror of losing his job and the family never had enough money. While the four children, of whom Wilfred was the eldest, were growing up they lived in a dingy part of Birkenhead, and 'developed a pinched and rickety look'.

Wilfred Owen as a student (from Harold Owen, Journey from Obscurity: Wilfred Owen 1893–1918, Oxford University Press, 1963).

17.3.2   In 1910 the family moved to Shrewsbury, and Wilfred went to the technical school there. He was developing into a withdrawn and terribly sensitive boy. His family called him the Wolf because he was so solitary. He seems to have made up his mind while he was still very young that he wanted to be 'a great poet', and he spent as much time as possible reading or writing. His father kept asking him when he was going to get a job; his mother wanted him to go into the Church. To please her he spent a year in a country village in Oxfordshire, where he studied with the vicar and worked very hard trying to help the poor people in the parish. But he was already becoming an agnostic, though the moral teaching of Christianity influenced him deeply all his life.

17.3.3   He desperately wanted to go to university and then do some sort of intellectual work which would leave him plenty of time to write. His brother remembers him gazing longingly at the outside of a newspaper office in Torquay and saying 'with terrible bitterness': 'You know, Harold, if Mother and Father would only help me I might be editor of that newspaper—no, no, not that one, a London paper—one day, but I must have help and I just can't get it.'[1] In the end, though he passed the matriculation exams at London University, his parents could never afford to send him away to study.

17.3.4   When the war broke out he was twenty-one and tutoring in a French family. He took a year to decide what he was going to do, but finally went back to England and applied for a commission in the Artists' Rifles (who were eventually wiped out at

[1] H. Owen, *Journey from Obscurity*, Oxford University Press, 1963, Vol. 1, p. 188.

Wilfred Owen, in Dunsden Vicarage garden, early 1912 (from Harold Owen, Journey from Obscurity: Wilfred Owen 1893–1918, Oxford University Press, 1963).

Passchendaele). He hated army life, but it brought about a startling change in him for he became a good and efficient officer, quietly devoting himself to doing everything he could for the men in his charge. He was sent to France early in 1917 with the Manchester Regiment and immediately plunged into the most frightful conditions. He wrote afterwards: 'I have not been at the front. I have been in front of it. I held an advanced post, that is, a "dug-out", in the middle of No Man's land.'[1] It was the coldest winter for years, and he wrote a month later: 'My platoon had no dug-outs, but had to lie in the snow under the deadly wind. . . . The marvel is that we did not all die of cold.'[1] About this time he wrote his first important poem 'Exposure'. Soon afterwards he was either shell-shocked or had a nervous breakdown, and was sent to Craiglockhart Hospital near Edinburgh. According to Robert Graves 'it had preyed on his mind that he had been unjustly accused of cowardice by his commanding officer'.[2]

17.3.5   A few months later the poet Siegfried Sassoon arrived at the same hospital. He was an exceptionally brave officer who had turned against the war and written to his superiors saying that he refused to go on fighting. He expected to get into serious trouble for this, but the tribunal took the charitable view that he must be slightly mad, and sent him to hospital to get better. Owen, who was a great admirer of his work, shyly introduced himself and showed him his own poems. They became friends and Sassoon encouraged him to write more war poetry, as well as introducing him to several figures in the literary world.

Exercise

17.3.6   Do you think, on the basis of what you have read so far, that Owen was a typical member of the group of young poets who took part in the war? (See 17.2.2)

[1] H. Owen and J. Bell (eds.), *Collected Letters of Wilfred Owen*, Oxford University Press, Vol. 1, 1967, pp. 427, 430.

[2] *Goodbye to All That*, Cassell, 1957, p. 234.

Discussion

I think he was very *un*-typical. We noted that most of these young officers came from upper- or upper middle-class families and had been to public school and Oxbridge. Some of them also had links with the literary establishment (Rupert Brooke had published several poems before the war and was regarded as one of the most promising young writers in England). Owen belonged to the lower middle class, had been to technical school in the provinces and had never got anywhere near having anything published. It is unlikely that he ever would have got to know any other writers for a long time, if he had not met Sassoon.

Siegfried Sassoon, photograph by Beresford, 1915 (Radio Times Hulton Picture Library).

17.3.7   It was more than a year before Owen was fit to go back to France, and during this time he wrote most of his best poems. Sassoon told him to read *Under Fire*, which impressed him deeply. He also collected several photographs of hideously wounded men, and when he heard people talking about the gloriousness of war he used to bring them out and say, 'I think these might interest you.'

17.3.8   A friend tried to get him a job in the War Office, but he decided to go back to the front and take his chance, although he had lost any belief he had ever had in the war. Everyone who knew him at this time speaks of him very highly. One of them wrote:

The sentiment he aroused was one both of tenderness and admiration . . . He left Edinburgh and eventually returned to France, as, knowing what he did and feeling as he did about the War, he was, I suppose, bound to do. He was one of those to whom the miseries of the world are misery and will not let them rest,[1] and he went back to spend his life in doing what he could to palliate them.

(E. Blunden (ed.), *The Poems of Wilfred Owen*, Chatto and Windus, 1965, pp. 133, 135.)

---

[1] This is a quotation from Keats, who was Owen's favourite poet.

7.3.9   He was killed on 4 November 1918, only a week before the Armistice. But he had
left over twenty finished poems, which he had been planning to publish as a protest.
In the (unfinished) preface to the collection he wrote:

> Above all I am not concerned with Poetry. My subject is War, and the pity of War.
> The Poetry is in the pity.

> Yet these elegies are to this generation in no sense consolatory. They may be to the
> next. All a poet can do today is warn. That is why the true Poets must be truthful.

(E. Blunden (ed.), op. cit., pp. 40–1.)

The Background to Owen's Poetry

7.4.1   Just before 1914 English poetry was dominated by a group of poets known as 'the
Georgians', who included such men as Alfred Noyes, John Drinkwater, Lawrence
Binyon and, among the younger writers, Rupert Brooke. Most of this poetry was
pretty, melodious, easy to understand and reluctant to talk about anything
unpleasant (Brooke upset a lot of people when he wrote a poem about being sea-
sick). It was not finally displaced until T. S. Eliot published *The Waste Land* soon
after the war.

7.4.2   There is no room to discuss this poetry in detail, but I want to draw your attention
to two things about it—*its attitude to poetry and poets*, and *its attitude to war and
death*.

7.4.3   Most poets at this time seem to have accepted the theory of *art for art's sake*. The
poet's job was to produce beautiful verses, not to take a social or moral or political
stand. Great poets were often described as if they were not quite human (thus
Matthew Arnold had called Shelley a 'beautiful and ineffectual angel'). There was a
cult of poets who died young, like Shelley, Byron and Keats. Wilfred as a teenager
fully expected to die young too, preferably by starving in a garret!

7.4.4   *Attitudes to war and death* can be studied in a typical poem, Brooke's 'The Soldier',
in *1914*. Turn to it in your Anthology and read it over carefully. What are the main
images in this poem?

_____

Discussion

A foreign field, England, earth, dust, flowers, ways (this probably means country
lanes), air, rivers, suns, heaven.

You will see that they are nearly all *positive* images, giving an impression of peace
and beauty. Even when he is talking about earth and dust he calls them 'rich'. There
is certainly nothing painful or unpleasant about death as it is described in this poem.

If one has a positive attitude to death it is easier to have a positive attitude to war,
and you can see from Brooke's other famous sonnet *Peace* that he did in fact
welcome the war when it came. Brooke's war poetry was very popular, then and
afterwards. The Dean of St Paul's preached a sermon about what a fine poem 'The
Soldier' was, and when Brooke died[1] he became something of a national hero.
Winston Churchill wrote his obituary in *The Times*.

[1] He was not actually killed in the war, but died of blood poisoning on the way to Gallipoli with his
ship.

17.4.5 Poets like Owen and Sassoon were strongly influenced by this style of writing when they were growing up. Robert Graves tells us in *Goodbye to All That* (pp. 154–5) that when he first met Sassoon the latter thought 'that war should not be written about in a realistic way. He showed me some of his own poems. One of them began:

> Return to greet me, colours that were my joy,
> Not in the woeful crimson of men slain . . .

Siegfried had not yet been in the trenches. I told him in my old-soldier manner, that he would soon change his style'.

17.4.6 Owen's early poems—those which have survived—seem mostly to have been bad imitations of Keats. It took the war to turn him into a great poet, but, at the same time, I think this would not have happened so quickly if he had not been practising poetry for years.

Exercise

17.4.7 Read Owen's poem 'Exposure', and then read 'Into Battle', by Julian Grenfell. Grenfell was the eldest son of a peer who joined the Regular Army after leaving Oxford. He died of wounds in 1915, a few weeks after finishing this poem.

Julian Grenfell, 1917
(*Radio Times Hulton Picture Library*).

Make notes on:

(a) What is the biggest difference in the attitudes of the two poets?

(b) The images in Grenfell's poem

(c) Anything that strikes you about Owen's style.

Discussion

(a)   I think the biggest difference is that Grenfell's poem is about *action* and Owen's poem is about *non-action*. 'Into Battle' shows soldiers fighting gloriously; 'Exposure' shows them suffering passively. The key line is, '*But nothing happens*'.

(b)   Grenfell uses images like sun, trees, grass, earth, colour, warmth and light to create the impression that a soldier's dangerous life is the only natural and good one. You remember that Brooke uses very much the same kind of language in 'The Soldier'. (17.4.4)

(c)   Owen's poem does not rhyme in the conventional way but uses unobtrusive half-rhymes (silent/salient; stormy/army). So far as we know he had not tried this before, and it was almost unknown in English poetry. But from then on most of his major poems were written in this style.

7.5.1   The Poetry of Disillusionment

One thing we must be quite clear about is that 'The Soldier' and 'Into Battle' were the kind of war poems that people back in England wanted to read. As we noted, the Dean of St Paul's preached a sermon about Rupert Brooke and Grenfell's poem went straight into *The Times* when he died. But as the war dragged on soldiers at the front became increasingly bitter, not about the Germans but about the people at home who didn't seem to care about what they were suffering:

> Fat civilians wishing they
> 'Could go and fight the Hun'
> Can't you see them thanking God
> That they're over forty-one?

—this is how E. A. Mackintosh described them in his poem 'Recruiting'. Robert Graves called them 'those complacent and perfectly unspeakable people who thought the war ought to go on indefinitely until everyone was killed but themselves'.[1]

7.5.2   Siegfried Sassoon discovered in 1917 that he had a talent for short, biting poems denouncing the authorities. (Before you go on reading, make sure that you know everything by Sassoon in the Anthology.) As we have seen, he had a tremendous personal influence on Owen, to whom he was a sort of hero, but I'm not sure that he influenced Owen's poetry much. Owen did write some satirical poems (like '*Dulce et Decorum Est*') but most of his work is in his own very personal style.

Exercise

7.5.3   Read Sassoon's poem 'They' and then Owen's 'At a Calvary near the Ancre'. What have they got in common? Are there any important differences?

Discussion

Both poems are attacking the clergy who, with few exceptions, not only supported the war but were among the loudest in urging their flocks to fight. But I think there is a great difference in the *way* they do this. Sassoon's bishop is merely a pompous

[1] *Goodbye to All That*, p. 228.

*Robert Graves, from a
pastel by Erik Kennington
(Mansell Collection).*

old ass who doesn't know what he is talking about. He could be a politician or a
newspaper editor just as well as a bishop. But the priests in Owen's poem are
guilty in a deeper sense. They are supposed to be servants of Christ, but what they
are in fact doing is betraying the central Christian teaching of love.

17.5.4   There are several wayside crosses in France. Owen is looking at one of them,
damaged by shells, and it occurs to him that those who claim to be Christ's disciples
are running away from the issues—'hiding apart'. The ordinary soldiers, like
Christ, are bearing the cross. Turn to his poem 'Greater Love' and you will see
that it is about those who 'trail, / Your cross through flame and hail'.

17.5.5   Owen said much the same things in a letter written home in 1917:

> I have comprehended a light which never will
> filter into the dogma of any national church:
> namely that one of Christ's essential commands was:
> Passivity at any price! . . .

164

Christ is literally in No Man's land. There
men often hear His voice: Greater love hath no man
than this, that a man lay down his life—for a friend.
Is it spoken in English only and French?
I do not believe so.
Thus you see how pure Christianity will not fit
in with pure patriotism.

(H. Owen and J. Bell (eds.), *Collected Letters of Wilfred Owen*, Oxford University Press, 1967, p. 461.)

17.5.6   Sassoon's poems (of which 'They' is very typical) are wonderful pieces of black humour, but most of them lack the deep compassion of Owen's. I myself think (though you may not) that this is one reason why Owen was the greater poet of the two. Sassoon himself said of his friend, in *Siegfried's Journey*:

In a young man of twenty-four his selflessness was extraordinary. The clue to his poetic genius was sympathy, not only in his detached outlook upon humanity but in all his actions and responses towards individuals.

(*Siegfried's Journey*, Faber, 1945, p. 61.)

17.5.7   Another friend of his wrote after he was killed:

The bond which drew us together was an intense pity for suffering humanity—a need to alleviate it, wherever possible, and an inability to shirk the sharing of it, even when this seemed useless. This was the keynote of Wilfred's character; indeed it was, simply, Wilfred.

(*Poems of Wilfred Owen*, p. 29.)

Exercise

17.5.8   Bearing in mind what you have read about Owen's 'sympathy', turn back to 17.3.9 and read his Preface. Then read 'Insensibility' and ask yourself:

(a)   Why does he say, first that it is a good thing not to have any feelings about the the war, and then—in the last verse—that 'dullards' are 'cursed'?

(b)   Why has he written a poem which speaks contemptuously about poets (in verse 1)?

Discussion

17.5.9   (a)   Owen is talking about two different groups of people. The first are the ordinary soldiers. They have a right to 'laugh among the dying, unconcerned' because they are risking death themselves all the time. They have been forced and battered into becoming 'insensible'. It is just as well for them that they have lost their power to feel, because they have enough to cope with already.

On the other hand the 'dullards whom no cannon stuns' are people who are *not* fighting and who *choose* to be callous. Owen is thinking of the Jingoes who are 'immune to pity'.

He is certainly not saying that 'insensibility' is a good thing for everybody. It is only desirable for 'the lad whose mind was never trained' and who cannot fully understand what is being done to him. You see that in verse 5 he refers to 'we wise, who with a thought besmirch / Blood over all our soul'. Here he is talking about himself. Unlike the inarticulate men with him, he completely understands what is going on and his job is to 'mourn when many leave these shores'.

(b) In the Preface, Owen had written, 'Above all I am not concerned with poetry. My subject is War, and the pity of War.' In 'Insensibility' he wrote:

> The front line withers,
> But they are troops who fade, not flowers
> For poets' tearful fooling.

Obviously he is not rejecting poetry as such (or he wouldn't have been writing it) but a certain *kind* of poetry, the kind which sentimentalizes the horrors of war. As we have seen, he had grown up on the sort of poetry which describes people as flowers. But he now felt that real poetry could only be written out of real compassion for human suffering. 'The poetry', as he said, 'is in the pity.'

Wilfred Owen with small boy (Imperial War Museum).

Exercise

17.6.1   I want you now to look at 'Miners', Owen's one major poem which is *not* about the war, or at least not obviously:

> There was a whispering in my hearth,
> A sigh of the coal,
> Grown wistful of a former earth
> It might recall.
>
> I listened for a tale of leaves
> And smothered ferns;
> Frond-forests; and the low, sly lives
> Before the fawns.

My fire might show steam-phantoms simmer
From Time's old cauldron,
Before the birds made nests in summer,
Or men had children.

But the coals were murmuring of their mine,
And moans down there
Of boys that slept wry sleep, and men
Writhing for air.

And I saw white bones in the cinder-shard,
Bones without number;
For many hearts with coal are charred,
And few remember.

I thought of some who worked dark pits
Of war, and died
Digging the rock where Death reputes
Peace lies indeed.

Comforted years will sit soft-chaired
In rooms of amber;
The years will stretch their hands, well-cheered
By our lives' ember.

The centuries will burn rich loads
With which we groaned,
Whose warmth shall lull their dreaming lids
While songs are crooned.
But they will not dream of us poor lads
Lost in the ground.

(*The Poems of Wilfred Owen*, pp. 98–9.)

Owen said, apropos of this, in a letter: 'Wrote a poem on the Colliery Disaster, but I got mixed up with the War at the end.'

In what ways does the war get 'mixed up' with the suffering of the miners?

Discussion

17.6.2   You'll probably have noticed that in verse 6, just after he has been describing the dead miners, Owen writes

> I thought of some who worked dark pits
> Of war, and died
> Digging the rock where Death reputes
> Peace lies indeed.

(The last two lines were probably inspired by the slogan, 'The War to End All War'.) Does this seem relevant? Or do you think that Owen is so obsessed with the war that he drags it into the poem without a good reason?

17.6.3   It seems to me that it *is* relevant. Owen could certainly have written a fine poem about the miners without mentioning the war, but I think this particular poem becomes richer when the miners' suffering is related to suffering of a different kind.

17.6.4   In the beginning Owen is looking for pictures in the fire, expecting to see something romantic, like forests and ferns. These are the kind of things he might really have seen there when he was a young poet, before the war changed his whole outlook. But now he remembers that he is only able to day-dream in front of a luxurious fire because men risk their lives to get coal. They are sacrificing themselves for the comfort of other people, who rarely or never think about them. In the same way, thousands are being sacrificed in the war for other people's sake, 'And few remember'—nobody will care very much in a hundred years' time.

17.6.5   'Miners' has links with some of his war poetry. In 'Exposure', Owen says that he and the others are sacrificing themselves because 'we believe not otherwise can kind fires burn'. In 'Strange Meeting', he dreams that he escapes, 'down some profound dull tunnel', into a dark place underground which turns out to be hell. The spirit of the dead German he meets there says, 'Now men will go content with what we spoiled', and this is very reminiscent of the last two verses of 'Miners', which describe people living in the 'comforted years' and never thinking about those who died.

17.6.6   Owen is often called 'a war poet', in a way which implies that he was only able to write about one subject, but I think 'Miners' shows that he was able to write great poetry about other kinds of experience.

Exercise

17.7.1   What do you think is the strongest emotion in Owen's poetry?

Discussion

17.7.2   I think undoubtedly *compassion for human suffering*. If you said 'hatred of war', of course this would be true, but it isn't precise enough. Sassoon also wrote poetry about his hatred of the war, but as we've seen the feelings behind it are quite different. Sassoon's aim was to show up the criminal stupidity of those who were responsible for the war, or had illusions about it. Owen sometimes wrote this kind of poetry too, but his main purpose (see 17.3.9) was to show 'the pity of war'. His poems 'Futility', 'The Send-Off', 'Anthem for Doomed Youth' and 'Greater Love' are all elegies for 'the English dead', and in 'Strange Meeting' and 'Miners' he reaches out to show compassion for other groups; the Germans, and the casualties of peace.

German Offensive, March 1918: British dead in a captured trench April–May 1918 (Imperial War Museum).

Henri Barbusse (Radio Times Hulton Picture Library).

SECTION 2 *UNDER FIRE*

17.8.1 In the Great War France suffered even more heavily than England. A million men were killed (including two distinguished poets, Charles Péguy and Guillaume Apollinaire) and huge stretches of the country were turned into a battlefield. In effect it became like two countries; the 'Front' and the 'Rear'.

17.8.2 Henri Barbusse (1873–1935) was over forty and a well-known writer when the war broke out. He had weak lungs and was being treated in a sanatorium, but he joined up at once and was sent to the trenches in 1915. He fought there as a private for several months but was invalided out at the end of the year. While he was still in hospital he wrote *Under Fire: the Story of a Squad (Le Feu)*. It was based on his experiences in the front line and he dedicated it to his dead comrades. When it came out, in 1916, it caused a sensation and won the Goncourt Prize, which is the highest literary award in France. It was translated into English next year and Siegfried Sassoon read it in hospital: 'I will not describe the effect it was creating in my mind. I need only say that it was a deeply stimulating one. Someone was really revealing the truth about the Front Line.'[1]

17.8.3 Wilfred Owen said that it 'set him alight as no other war book had done'.[2] Later on we shall be looking at some of the links between him and Barbusse. Ever since, it has remained one of the classic accounts of the Great War.

[1] *Sherston's Progress*, Faber, 1936, p. 27.

[2] Siegfried Sassoon, *Siegfried's Journey*, Faber, 1945, p. 60.

17.8.4 I want to discuss in this section what *kind* of novel *Under Fire* is (if it *is* a novel!) and why it had such a tremendous effect on its readers as soon as it came out. Below I have listed six possible descriptions; I want you to put a tick opposite them if you think they are good descriptions and a cross if you think they are not.

17.8.5 1   A realistic novel   ☐

2   A poetic novel   ☐

3   A novel about individuals   ☐

4   An adventure story   ☐

5   A patriotic novel   ☐

6   A novel of social protest   ☐

Discussion

17.8.6 My answers would have been:

1   √

2   √

3   ×

4   ×

5   ×

6   √

17.9.1 I expect you will have agreed with me that *Under Fire* is a very *realistic* novel (we will discuss later on whether a novel can be realistic and poetic at the same time). By the phrase 'a realistic novel' we usually mean 'a novel about life as it really is', and sometimes we also mean 'a book without any sentimental nonsense'. This is certainly how *Under Fire* seemed to Sassoon, who felt that he was at last reading a truthful description of the war after having listened to a good many lies. Apparently Barbusse based it on what had actually happened to him in the trenches, even using the real names of his comrades (on page 128, where he has been describing how a soldier was executed for cowardice, he says he has altered names and places, but it seems he only did this when there were strong reasons). You remember I suggested in 17.8.4 that *Under Fire* might not be a novel at all, as we generally use the word. Most novelists make up a story; Barbusse seems to be giving us a direct description (you might call it journalism, or autobiography, or history) of what happened to him and his friends.

17.9.2 Realistic it obviously is: Barbusse tells us about the everyday details of the soldiers' lives; the mud, the wretched rations, the lice. He tells us about the condition of the corpses which have been left unburied for days, and he spares us none of the dreadful details:

'When you've seen men squashed, cut in two, or divided from top to bottom, blown into showers by an ordinary shell, bellies turned inside out and scattered anyhow, skulls forced bodily into the chest as if with a blow by a club, and in place of the head a bit of neck, oozing currant jam of brains all over the chest and back . . .'
(213)

Australian Officer wading through mud: grid trench, Guedecourt, December 1916 (Imperial War Museum).

7.9.3   He is completely frank, too, about the way the soldiers talk among themselves. In Chapter XIII, 'The Big Words', he describes how one of them asks him:

> 'Tell me . . . if you make the common soldiers talk in your book, are you going to make them talk like they *do* talk, or shall you put it all straight—into pretty talk? . . . You'll never hear two poilus open their heads for a minute without saying and repeating things that the printers wouldn't much like to print.' (167)

Barbusse has told him that he is going to write down the whole truth, 'I shall talk about you, and about the boys, and about our life', swear-words and all. But he fully expects that some people will be shocked.

7.9.4   We have seen that, however shocking, the book was enormously popular, even with the literary establishment who gave it the Goncourt Prize. This was not really so surprising, for this kind of writing was already familiar to the French public. The novelist Émile Zola, whom Barbusse greatly admired, had, in the 1870s, led a group of young writers who aimed at describing life exactly as it was. They were called Naturalists—not Realists, for they went a stage beyond realism. These writers insisted that there were no limits on what could go into a novel. They wanted to break down all the barriers between 'art' and 'life'. They described everyday life in the utmost detail, including everyday language (Zola's novel *L'Assommoir* is written entirely in Parisian working-class slang). Most of them were radicals and hoped vaguely that their novels would help to bring about social changes. They were very unpopular with more conventional writers, particularly as they tended to write in a lurid way about sex (as Barbusse does in Chapter XVII). But when they were accused of being cynical, or obscene, or of degrading the art of novel-writing, the Naturalists retorted that they were only writing down what was *true*. This was by far the most important thing where they were concerned.

17.9.5   So Barbusse had his place in a definite tradition within the French novel—unlike the young English war poets, who had to work out their own tradition. But he was also doing something quite new, because earlier writers had obviously not been able to write about the world's first great war.

17.10.1   I also said that *Under Fire* was a *poetic* novel, and here you may not have agreed with me because—as we have just been saying—it is brutally frank about life in the trenches. But then you would also have to say that '*Dulce et Decorum Est*' is not 'really' poetry, because it talks about a hideous death by gassing, and that several of Sassoon's poems are not poetry either, because they are written in slang. But Owen thought that poetry could be written about the horrors of war, even if it was very different from the poetry on which he had been brought up (see 17.5.9).

17.10.2   What *is* a poetic novel, anyway, and isn't it really a contradiction in terms? How can a novel be written in the same way as poetry? The answer is that most novels are not poetic, but there are a few which are; I think *The Rainbow* is, and *Wuthering Heights*, and *Dr Zhivago*. When we call a novel poetic we usually mean one of two things. First, that it uses language in a way we normally only expect in poetry. Second—and perhaps all great novels are poetic in this sense—that it doesn't just describe an event for its own sake, but gives it a meaning which is much wider.

17.10.3   For example, on p. 242 Barbusse is describing the men waiting to go over the top. He writes:

The end of the day is spreading a sublime but melancholy light on that strong unbroken mass of beings of whom some only will live to see the night. It is raining— there is always rain in my memories of all the tragedies of the great war.

17.10.4   I think this is almost pure poetry. Instead of just describing the men as they appear at that moment, Barbusse reminds us—in the first sentence of the paragraph—that several of them are shortly going to die. The night and rain deepen our sense that he is describing a great tragedy. In fact, it is not just this one tragedy which he is mourning for, but 'all the tragedies of the great war'. He is not simply writing about rain, he is writing about death. The effect would have been quite different if he had said, 'It was raining and we got wet.'

17.10.5   I don't think that *Under Fire* is poetic all the way through, but I do think there are some passages which can't be called anything else. For example, the first chapter, where Barbusse and the other invalids in the Swiss sanatorium have a vision of what the war is going to be like:

They seem to see a great livid plain unrolled, which to their seeing is made of mud and water, while figures appear and fast fix themselves to the surface of it, all blinded and borne down with filth, like the dreadful castaways of shipwrecks. (4)

17.10.6   Of course this is not what they really saw in August 1914, but it *is* a poetic expression of what the whole war meant for Barbusse. Both in this chapter and in the last one, *The Dawn*, he uses a conversation between a group of people to get a message across to his readers. This last chapter is another one that I would call poetic. The narrator says here (and I want you to study his words very carefully)

'War is made up of the flesh and the souls of common soldiers only. It is we who make the plains of dead and the rivers of blood, all of us, and each of us is invisible and silent because of the immensity of our numbers. The emptied towns and the villages destroyed, they are a wilderness of *our* making. Yes, war is all of us, and all of us together.' (334)

10.7   Is this what Barbusse really said at the time? I doubt it very much, but it *is* what he felt, and he is expressing these feelings in the kind of language which seems to suit them best. You will see that Brian Rhys, in his introduction to *Under Fire*, calls it a work of 'poetic realism' (xiii). Barbusse is taking the hideousness of war and transforming it into a kind of grim poetry, rather like Dante's poetry about hell.

11.1   I thought it would be a mistake to call *Under Fire* a *novel about individuals*. None of the individual characters is studied in depth, as they would have been in a novel by Tolstoy or George Eliot or most other great writers. It is the group as a whole which chiefly interests Barbusse. Turn to pages 14–17, where he gives a description of his comrades 'Our ages? We are of all ages. . . . Our races? We are of all races; we come from everywhere. . . . Our callings? A little of all—in the lump.' (14–15) He has no room for more than the briefest sketches of these men individually— most of them only get about one sentence each. But it is not necessary to do more than this, he feels, because the differences between them are not really important:

Yes, we are truly and deeply different from each other. But we are alike all the same. In spite of this diversity of age, of country, of education, of position, of everything possible, in spite of the former gulfs that kept us apart, we are in the main alike. Under the same uncouth outlines we conceal and reveal the same ways and habits, the same nature of men who have reverted to the state primeval . . . Here, too, linked by a·fate from which there is no escape, swept willy-nilly by the vast adventure into one rank, we have no choice but to go as the weeks and months go—alike. The terrible narrowness of the common life binds us close, adapts us, merges us one in the other . . . (17)

11.2   So *Under Fire* is not the story of one or two men but, as Barbusse said, 'the story of a squad'. Indeed it ranges even more widely than this. Look at pages 281–2

Mine crater in a street in ruined La Bassée, 3 October 1918; Owen was killed in the assault on La Bassée (Imperial War Museum).

where the wounded airman describes how he flew over the two praying armies and they seemed exactly alike from where he was. Barbusse's final verdict—he says the same thing twice—is this: 'Two armies fighting each other—that's like one great army committing suicide!' (330, cp. 3)

17.11.3   Fundamentally, he is not thinking in terms of individuals but in terms of all the vast numbers of men who have been caught up in the war—'the fighters present and to come—thirty millions of soldiers'. (2–3)

Exercise

17.11.4   Can you suggest a better description of *Under Fire* than my original one, 'a novel about individuals'? If you can't think of one, re-read pages 14–17 and 334–6.

Discussion

17.11.5   My suggestion is, *a novel about the common people in the Great War*. There isn't a hero in this book, the people are the hero. Barbusse's main purpose in writing *Under Fire* was to protest against ordinary Frenchmen and Germans whose interests were the same being made to kill each other. What he offers, as an alternative, is solidarity between people. He shows this, very movingly I think, in the chapter 'On Leave', where he describes how Eudore and his wife give up their only chance of being alone together rather than turning out his friends into the rain. This is the kind of small incident which Barbusse normally uses to show the unconscious heroism of ordinary people: 'They are not the kind of hero one thinks of, but their sacrifice has greater worth than they who have not seen them will ever be able to understand.' (242)

17.12.1   I also thought it would be a mistake to call *Under Fire* an *adventure story*. There are plenty of war novels and war films which are only interested in the action, but this does not specially interest Barbusse. There is only one chapter in the novel which is about action; Chapter XX when the squad goes over the top. The rest of the time Barbusse writes about the long periods when there is no fighting. There is scarcely anything to do at these times except try to make the best of things and perhaps get hold of some food or cigarettes. For example, it's a red-letter day for the narrator when he gets a fresh egg (Chapter XV).

17.12.2   Most novels have a plot; this has none, but I can hardly think of any other novel which is so closely and realistically concerned with the struggle of ordinary people to keep going. Two English novels which *are* concerned with this are *Robinson Crusoe* and *The Ragged-Trousered Philanthropists*, by Robert Tressell, but neither of them are set in a war.

Exercise

17.13.1   You remember I suggested that *Under Fire* was *not* a patriotic novel but *was* a novel of social protest. Bearing these terms in mind, re-read Chapter XXII, 'Going About'. How does it fit in with the rest of the novel? Has Barbusse said similar things in other chapters?

Discussion

17.13.2   This is the only chapter in the novel which is set in the Rear, not the Front. The soldiers on leave in Paris are at first overwhelmed because everything is so splendid.

Then they see 'a ridiculous tableau' about the war, which upsets them because they know what the war is really like, but they have not enough courage to tell people that it is nonsense. After that they meet a smart lady who compliments them on their courage. Her idea of the war is like this:

'How superb a charge must be, eh? All those masses of men advancing like they do in a holiday procession, and the trumpets playing a rousing air in the fields! And the dear little soldiers that can't be held back, and shouting, *"Vive la France!"* and even laughing as they die!' (298-9)

Again, they haven't the nerve to contradict her; they feel so completely cut off from these people that it is no use trying to make them understand. Barbusse concludes:

The sight of this world has revealed a great truth to us . . . a Difference which becomes evident between human beings, a Difference far deeper than that of nations . . . the clear-cut and truly unpardonable division that there is in a country's inhabitants between those who gain and those who grieve, those who are required to sacrifice all, *all*, to give their numbers and strength and suffering to the last limit, those upon whom the others walk and advance, smile and succeed. (301)

Volpatte echoes this: ' "We're divided into two foreign countries. The Front, over there, where there are too many unhappy, and the Rear, here, where there are too many happy." ' (301)

13.3   You'll probably have remembered the many hostile references to the Rear earlier on in the novel. The soldiers are bitterly resentful of the able-bodied men who are doing safer jobs, and often posing as heroes, while they are really suffering and really risking their lives. In Chapter IX, 'The Anger of Volpatte', there is a long conversation about this, and one man says:

' " . . . there are too many rich and influential people who have shouted, 'Let us save France—begin by saving ourselves!' On the declaration of war, there was a big rush to get out of it, that's what there was, and the strongest succeeded. I noticed myself, in *my* little corner, it was especially those that jawed most about patriotism previously. " ' (125)

13.4   This is the kind of thing I had in mind when I said that *Under Fire* was not a patriotic novel, or at least not in the conventional sense. Barbusse declines to tell people in the Rear the kind of things they expect to hear. He makes it clear that the peasants are making a profit out of the war, and that they dislike the soldiers (Chapter V, 'Sanctuary') and also that the soldiers are delighted when they are wounded and can go home for a bit (Chapter IV, 'Volpatte and Fouillade') ' "The Jingoes—they're vermin" ', he makes a soldier say. (332) In the first chapter he gives a conversation between people from different nations:

' "Austria's act is a crime," says the Austrian.
"France *must* win," says the Englishman.
"I hope Germany will be beaten," says the German.' (2)

Here, it seems, he is trying to show that 'patriotism is not enough' (though all the speakers agree that the Allies are right and Germany and Austria wrong). Even while the war was going on, Barbusse was an internationalist. He argues that the German soldiers are not the real enemy 'only poor dupes' (340). He also pays tribute to Karl Liebknecht, the German Socialist leader who resisted the Kaiser's war policy, almost alone. To Barbusse, he was ' "one figure that has risen above the war and will blaze with the beauty and strength of his courage" '. (256)

14.1   So I think we must call *Under Fire* an *internationalist* rather than a *patriotic* novel; is

Karl Liebknecht (Radio Times Hulton Picture Library).

it also a *novel of social protest*? If you are not sure, look again at Chapter XXII and also at pages 339–40. In this last section Barbusse says that those responsible for the war are 'the sword-wavers, the profiteers, and the intriguers . . . interested parties—financiers, speculators great and small . . . those who admire the exchange of flashing blows, who hail like women the bright colours of uniforms . . . the traditionalists for whom an injustice has legal force because it is perpetuated . . . the parsons.'

17.14.2   If we look at Chapter XXII in the light of what comes before and after I think we shall find it is integral to the structure of the novel. Barbusse shows us a society which is getting fat on the war, and which does not understand what the war is all about (like the woman who is thrilled by the idea of a cavalry charge, and who is among those denounced in the passages I have just quoted). In describing this, he is protesting not only against war but against the corrupt society which makes war possible:

' "After all, why do we make war? We don't know at all why, but we can say *who* we make it for. We shall be forced to see that if every nation every day brings the fresh bodies of fifteen hundred young men to the God of War to be lacerated, it's for the pleasure of a few ringleaders that we could easily count; that if whole nations go to slaughter marshalled in armies in order that the gold-striped caste may write their princely names in history, so that other gilded people of the same rank can contrive more business, and expand in the way of employees and shops— and we shall see, as soon as we open our eyes, that the divisions between mankind are not what we thought, and those one did believe in are not divisions." ' (337)

176

Exercise

14.3 Can you sum up, in one word, what social idea Barbusse preaches in opposition to the war and the society which has produced it?

Discussion

14.4 The idea of *equality*. (If you got this wrong, re-read page 336.) This, he believes, is 'an answer to all'.

SECTION 3   SOME COMPARISONS

15.1 You may remember that Brian Rhys says in his Introduction (p. xiv), 'It is in the poems of Wilfred-Owen that, emotionally, we come nearest to the poetic realism of *Under Fire*.' In this section I want you to test that statement by doing some fairly detailed comparisons between poems by Owen and some passages from Barbusse. To begin with, read Owen's 'Strange Meeting', and then turn to page 322 of *Under Fire* and read the first six paragraphs, from 'Quite near . . .' to, 'Hell is water'. Do you think these two pieces have anything in common? Note down anything that strikes you.

Discussion

15.2 I noticed, first of all, that both writers are talking about hell. In 'Strange Meeting' hell is a place where soldiers go after they are killed. Barbusse says that there is more than one kind of hell, which they undergo while they are still alive, but anyway, they have now reached the worst one.

15.3 In both places, people are resting from the battle. In Owen's hell there are several 'encumbered sleepers', and at first he isn't sure if they are really asleep or dead. The poem ends with one ghost saying to the other ghost, 'Let us sleep now. . . .' In the waterlogged landscape of the Barbusse extract, several figures are lying motionless —'Are they dead—or asleep? We do not know; in any case, they rest.'

15.4 The whole point of both pieces is that the common soldiers *from both sides* are there together. Barbusse makes the point that he doesn't know if these sleepers are German or French. They all look the same, 'as much alike as if they were naked . . . clad in exactly the same uniform of misery and filth.' The climax of Owen's poem is when the narrator realizes that he is talking to the ghost of the German he killed.

16.1 The language of these two pieces is so similar that I think Owen must have got part of his inspiration for 'Strange Meeting' from reading Barbusse. But I'm not suggesting that Owen got most of the ideas for his poetry from the pages of *Under Fire*. If the two writers have a good deal in common, and I think they have, it is not so much because one of them had a direct influence on the other as because they had gone through very much the same kind of experience, and came to have the same kind of feelings about this experience, even though one of them was writing poetry and the other prose.

16.2 I won't ask you to compare any more specific passages. Instead I want you to re-

read three poems by Owen, and see if the feelings and ideas which he is expressing in them remind you of any feelings or ideas in *Under Fire*. The poems are:

1   'Strange Meeting' again. In the last exercise we were looking only at the *language* of the poem. In this exercise I want you to describe the *message* which Owen is trying to get across.

2   '*Dulce et Decorum Est*'

3   'Exposure'

Discussion

17.16.3   1   Owen is saying in 'Strange Meeting' that the common enemy is not Germany, but war. He is also terrified that there may be another war in the future:

> Now men will go content with what we spoiled.
> Or, discontent, boil bloody, and be spilled
> They will be swift with swiftness of the tigress,
> None will break ranks, though nations trek from progress.

This is very much the same as what Barbusse is saying, particularly in his last chapter 'The Dawn':

> ' "To-day militarism is called Germany."
> "But what will it be called tomorrow?" . . .
> "It isn't those others we've got to get at—it's war."
> "Can't you see that we've got to finish with war? If we've got to begin again some day, all that's been done is no good." ' (331,333)

17.16.4   2   The title '*Dulce et Decorum Est*' comes from the Latin tag, 'Dulce et decorum est pro patria mori'—'It is a sweet and honourable thing to die for the motherland.' Owen dedicated the first draft to a Miss Jessie Pope who had been writing patriotic jingles for the papers. The message of the poem, in the last verse, is that if people in England could see what the war was really like they wouldn't talk sentimental rubbish about it. An angrier and more sarcastic poem than most of Owen's, it says very much the same things that Barbusse said in the chapter 'Going About', and elsewhere. Consider this passage:

> ' "D'you remember the woman in the town where we went about a bit not so very long ago? She talked some drivel about attacks, and said, How beautiful they must be to see!
>
> . . . Beautiful? Oh, hell! It's just as if an ox were to say, What a fine sight it must be, all those droves of cattle driven forward to the slaughter-house! . . . Beautiful! Oh, hell!" ' (325–6)

17.16.5   3   You remember that when we were comparing 'Exposure' with Grenfell's 'Into Battle' we noticed that Owen's poem—unlike much conventional war writing—is about passive suffering. I think that *Under Fire* is also about this (see the discussion in 17.12.1 about why it is not an adventure novel). Owen's poem also reminds me very strongly of Barbusse's description in Chapter II of waking up in the trenches in 'the poignant misery of dawn'.

Conclusion

17.17.1   These are only a few examples—perhaps you can think of some others—of the ways in which Owen and Barbusse are essentially saying the same things. I hope you have found it rewarding to look at the impact of the Great War on these two very different men. Different as they were, and belonging to literary traditions which had virtually nothing in common, they each dedicated themselves to the same purpose of telling the truth about the war. In doing this, they arrived at a new kind of literature, deeply compassionate and at the same time deeply impersonal. I've already suggested (17.11.5) that *Under Fire* is a novel about the people, not about individuals, and I think that Owen's poetry, too, is concerned, not with himself or other individuals, but with a whole generation 'who die as cattle'. Perhaps they couldn't have written in any other way, after what they had seen, for the slaughter in the First World War was so tremendous that it could only be understood in terms of a disaster convulsing the whole world:

Each country whose frontiers are consumed by carnage is seen tearing from its heart ever more warriors. . . . One's eyes follow the flow of these living tributaries to the River of Death. To north and south and west afar there are battles on every side. Turn where you will, there is war in every corner of that vastness.

(*Under Fire*, p. 28)

This is how Barbusse saw the war as a whole, and Owen saw it like this in his poem 'The End':

> After the blast of lightning from the East,
> The flourish of loud clouds, the Chariot Throne;
> After the drums of Time have rolled and ceased,
> And by the bronze west long retreat is blown,
>
> Shall life renew these bodies? Of a truth
> All death will He annul, all tears assuage?—
> Fill the void veins of Life again with youth,
> And wash, with an immortal water, Age?
>
> When I do ask white Age he saith not so:
> 'My head hangs weighed with snow.'
> And when I hearken to the Earth, she saith:
> 'My fiery heart shrinks, aching. It is death.
> Mine ancient scars shall not be glorified,
> Nor my titanic tears, the sea, be dried."

References

Barbusse, H. *Under Fire*, Everyman's Library, Dent (SET BOOK).

Blunden, E. (ed.) *The Poems of Wilfred Owen*, Chatto and Windus, 1965.

Ferguson, J. (ed.) *War and the Creative Arts*, Macmillan/The Open University Press (COURSE ANTHOLOGY).

Gardner, B. (ed.) *Up the Line to Death*, Methuen, 1964.

Graves, R. *Goodbye to All That*, Cassell, revised edition, 1957; paperback edition, Penguin Books, 1969.

Owen, H. *Journey from Obscurity*, 3 vols., Oxford University Press, 1963–5.

Owen, H. and Bell, J. (eds.) *Collected Letters of Wilfred Owen*, Oxford University Press, 1964.

Sassoon, S. *Sherston's Progress*, Faber, 1936.

Sassoon, S. *Siegfried's Journey*, Faber, 1945.

Acknowledgements

Grateful acknowledgement is made to the following for material used in this unit:

TEXT

E. P. Dutton & Co., Inc. and J. M. Dent & Sons Ltd., Everyman's Library Series for extracts from the book *Under Fire* by Henri Barbusse. Trans. by W. Fitzwater Wray. Copyright 1917 by E. P. Dutton & Co. Inc. Renewal 1947 by J. M. Dent & Sons, Ltd. Published by E. P. Dutton & Co. Inc. and J. M. Dent and Sons, Ltd. and used with their permission; The Estate of the late Harold Owen and Chatto & Windus for *The Poems of Wilfred Owen*, ed. Edmund Blunden.

ILLUSTRATIONS

Faber & Faber Ltd.; Imperial War Museum; Mansell Collection; Oxford University Press; Radio Times Hulton Picture Library.